Railway Stations
From the Air

Railway Stations
From the Air

Aerofilms

Ian Allan
PUBLISHING

List of locations

First published 2003

ISBN 0 7110 2980 6

Published by Ian Allan Publishing

an imprint of Ian Allan Publishing Ltd, Hersham, Surrey KT12 4RG.

Printed by Ian Allan Printing Ltd, Hersham, Surrey KT12 4RG.

Code: 0307/A2

Introduction

Within the huge archive that forms the collection of Aerofilms there are countless views of many of the great public and ecclesiastical buildings of the United Kingdom. There are also numerous photographs that record the ordinary — of work, education and transport. Of the latter, a considerable number feature railway stations and infrastructure, providing the historian and the modeller with a fascinating insight not only into the railway itself but also the whole environment surrounding it.

Researching this collection is an endless source of fascination, as one finds oneself delving in one direction in the hope of finding a specific location, only to be thwarted by the fact that the aerial camera that recorded the local castle failed to turn 180 degrees and photograph the branch terminus that served the town, then following a train through other localities in the same region to emerge with an absolute gem.

Although there have been two recent books featuring photographs from the Aerofilms' collection — *Britain's Railways from the Air: Then & Now* and *From the Air: Britain's Railways Then & Now* — so a conscious decision was made to exclude any photographs reproduced in those two earlier volumes. Whilst odd locations, such as St Ives in Cornwall, may have been featured before, the actual aerial photograph has not.

The basic parameter has been to try and select a range of locations, throughout Britain, that might form the basis of attractive model railway layouts. Thus there is an undoubted bias towards branch line termini and smaller country stations, although more important junctions have not been excluded. The choice of locations has, in part, inevitably, been based around what is available within the collection — oh, for that time machine! — but also a desire to provide locations from the far southwest of England through to the far north of Scotland.

Alongside each of the aerial photographs, which have been enlarged to the maximum extent feasible within the format of the book, there is additional information in the form of Ordnance Survey mapping as well as ground level shots of the infrastructure to enable the proper context to be determined.

One of the strengths of railway modelling is the ability to create a landscape in miniature; reference material, however, to the whole environment in which the railway operated is often difficult to come by. The beauty of aerial photography is that it can provide this unique focus.

Acknowledgements

The compilation of a book of this nature is inevitably a team effort but we would like to thank, in particular, Elaine Amos and her colleagues at Simmons Aerofilms, Brian Lewis for his assistance in sourcing the ground-level photographs and some of the maps, Paul and Shirley Smith for providing help in tracking down the maps and Tony Rawlings of the Map Room at Cambridge University Library for providing most of the maps. All Ordnance Survey maps are Crown Copyright Reserved. Dates of maps are noted where confirmed.

Aerofilms

Aerofilms was founded in 1919 and has specialised in the acquisition of aerial photography within the United Kingdom throughout its history. The company has a record of being innovative in the uses and applications of aerial photography.

Photographs looking at the environment in perspective are called oblique aerial photographs. These are taken with Hasselblad cameras by professional photographers experienced in the difficult conditions encountered in aerial work.

Photographs taken straight down at the landscape are termed vertical aerial photographs. These photographs are obtained using Leica survey cameras, the products from which are normally used in the making of maps.

Aerofilms has a unique library of oblique and vertical photographs in excess of one and a half million in number covering the United Kingdom. This library of photographs dates from 1919 to the present day and is being continually updated.

Oblique and vertical photography can be taken to customers' specification by Aerofilms' professional photographers.

To discover more of the wealth of past or present photographs held in the library at Aerofilms or to commission new aerial photographs, please contact:

Aerofilms Limited
33-34 Station Close
Potters Bar
Herts
EN6 1TL

Telephone: 01707 648390
Fax: 01707 648399

Alloa

By the date that the aerial photograph was taken, looking southwards, passenger services over the ex-North British Railway routes to Alloa had already ceased but the impressive station was still intact and the lines were still operational for freight traffic. The first railway to serve Alloa was that from Oakley, to the east, on the route to Dunfermline which was opened on 28 August 1850. This was followed on 3 June 1851 by the opening of the branch to Tillicoultry, the first stage of the Dollar line, and by the completion of the line to Stirling on 1 July 1852. A second route from Alloa to Dunfermline was opened from Alloa to Kincardine on 18 December 1893. This last named line was the first to lose its passenger services, these being withdrawn on 7 July 1930. Passenger services from Alloa to Kinross via Tillicoultry were withdrawn on 15 June 1964 and the final passenger services through Alloa, from Stirling to Dunfermline via Oakley followed on 7 October 1968. However, the network of lines remained important for freight traffic to and from the Fife coalfield and to the power station at Longannet. The Devon Valley line to Dollar was to be closed completely on 25 June 1973 whilst the line from Alloa to Oakley was to follow on 6 October 1979. This left the line through Longannet; this was to be closed between Alloa East Junction and Longannet on 6 April 1981. Today, the line from Stirling is open to the west of Alloa although there are proposals for the reopening of the line between Stirling and Dunfermline to passenger services.

8 June 1972 (A242226)

By 28 August 1973 Alloa had lost its passenger services, but the station was still intact if increasingly careworn. However, it remained important on the freight network. This view was taken from the cab of an MGR coal train from Barony to Longannet power station; the train was hauled by two Class 20s, Nos 8326 and 8327. *Derek Cross*

[1922]

The scene at Alloa on 17 June 1949 with ex-NBR No 62426 *Cuddie Headrigg* heading the 4.30pm service from Perth to Kinross Junction and Alloa alongside ex-NBR 4-4-2T No 7453, still retaining its LNER number, on the 6.8pm train to Stirling. *SLS Collection*

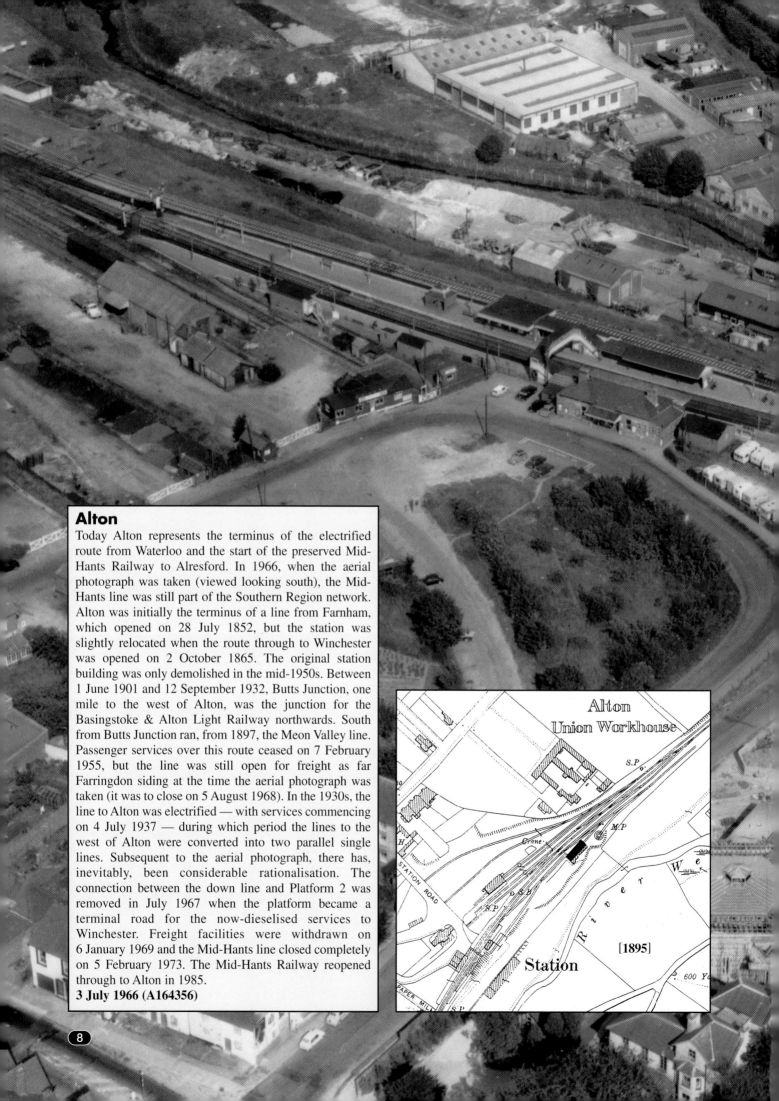

Alton

Today Alton represents the terminus of the electrified route from Waterloo and the start of the preserved Mid-Hants Railway to Alresford. In 1966, when the aerial photograph was taken (viewed looking south), the Mid-Hants line was still part of the Southern Region network. Alton was initially the terminus of a line from Farnham, which opened on 28 July 1852, but the station was slightly relocated when the route through to Winchester was opened on 2 October 1865. The original station building was only demolished in the mid-1950s. Between 1 June 1901 and 12 September 1932, Butts Junction, one mile to the west of Alton, was the junction for the Basingstoke & Alton Light Railway northwards. South from Butts Junction ran, from 1897, the Meon Valley line. Passenger services over this route ceased on 7 February 1955, but the line was still open for freight as far Farringdon siding at the time the aerial photograph was taken (it was to close on 5 August 1968). In the 1930s, the line to Alton was electrified — with services commencing on 4 July 1937 — during which period the lines to the west of Alton were converted into two parallel single lines. Subsequent to the aerial photograph, there has, inevitably, been considerable rationalisation. The connection between the down line and Platform 2 was removed in July 1967 when the platform became a terminal road for the now-dieselised services to Winchester. Freight facilities were withdrawn on 6 January 1969 and the Mid-Hants line closed completely on 5 February 1973. The Mid-Hants Railway reopened through to Alton in 1985.

3 July 1966 (A164356)

Viewed looking east on 15 October 1947, this photograph
shows the site of the locomotive shed, the Fareham motor-
set in the siding (with, out of sight, a Class M7 0-4-4T at the
head of the rake), an EMU approaching and, obscured by the
nearer of the two freight trains, ex-LSWR 0-6-0 No 716 at the
head of a second freight. *SLS Collection*

Taken two decades later, this view, looking eastwards from the island platform,
shows to good effect the SR signage and main station buildings. Visible through the
footbridge is the signalbox. *J. Scrace*

Andover Junction

Pictured looking eastwards, the ex-London & South Western main line can be seen stretching off in the distance towards Basingstoke, whilst the branch towards Andover Town and Fullerton heads to the south. Andover was the junction for the Midland & South Western Junction Railway route to Swindon and Cheltenham, the actual junction being sited slightly to the west of this view. The first route to serve the town was a single-track line from Basingstoke; this was opened on 3 July 1854, from which date the main station building was completed, and was extended to Salisbury on 1 May 1857. The line between Andover Junction and Andover Town was opened on 6 March 1865; the route was doubled in 1885 at which date it was slightly realigned. The M&SWJR route from Red Post Junction (to the west of Andover) to Grafton opened on 1 May 1882; it was to pass to the Great Western Railway in 1923. Passenger services over the M&SWJR ceased on 1 September 1961, at which date the line north of Ludgershall to Savernake closed completely. The line between Andover Junction and Ludgershall remains operational, providing a link for Ministry of Defence traffic. Passenger traffic between Andover Junction and Romsey ceased on 7 September 1964, at which time the line south of Andover Town closed completely. The line to Andover Town was to close completely on 18 September 1967.
10 July 1924 (C17445)

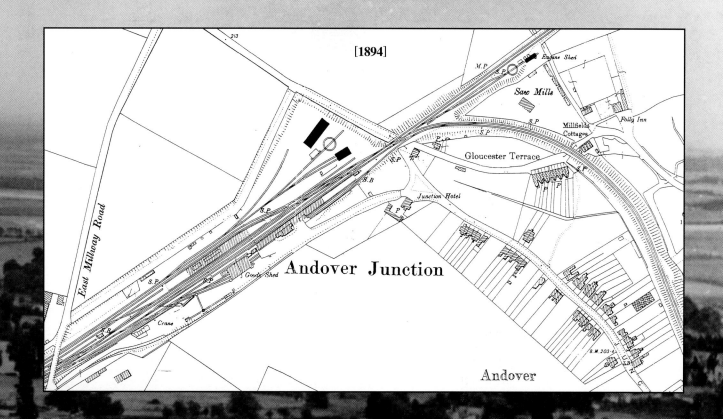

[1894]

East Millway Road

Andover Junction

Andover

Engine Shed

Saw Mills

Folly Inn

Millfields Cottages

Gloucester Terrace

Junction Hotel

Goods Shed

Crane

By the early 1980s, rationalisation had seen the complexity of the track at Andover Junction significantly reduced. However, the station buildings and other facilities remain largely unchanged as Class 204 DEMU No 1403 awaits departure with the 10.10 service from Salisbury to Reading. *Brian Morrison*

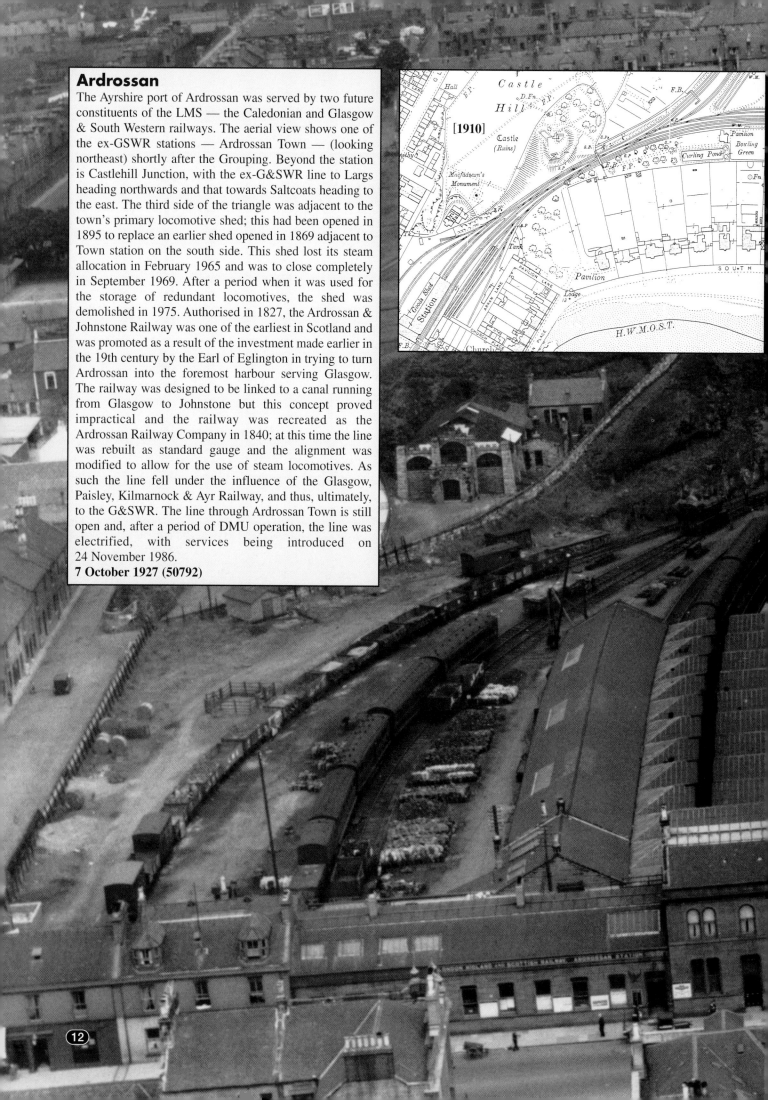

Ardrossan

The Ayrshire port of Ardrossan was served by two future constituents of the LMS — the Caledonian and Glasgow & South Western railways. The aerial view shows one of the ex-GSWR stations — Ardrossan Town — (looking northeast) shortly after the Grouping. Beyond the station is Castlehill Junction, with the ex-G&SWR line to Largs heading northwards and that towards Saltcoats heading to the east. The third side of the triangle was adjacent to the town's primary locomotive shed; this had been opened in 1895 to replace an earlier shed opened in 1869 adjacent to Town station on the south side. This shed lost its steam allocation in February 1965 and was to close completely in September 1969. After a period when it was used for the storage of redundant locomotives, the shed was demolished in 1975. Authorised in 1827, the Ardrossan & Johnstone Railway was one of the earliest in Scotland and was promoted as a result of the investment made earlier in the 19th century by the Earl of Eglington in trying to turn Ardrossan into the foremost harbour serving Glasgow. The railway was designed to be linked to a canal running from Glasgow to Johnstone but this concept proved impractical and the railway was recreated as the Ardrossan Railway Company in 1840; at this time the line was rebuilt as standard gauge and the alignment was modified to allow for the use of steam locomotives. As such the line fell under the influence of the Glasgow, Paisley, Kilmarnock & Ayr Railway, and thus, ultimately, to the G&SWR. The line through Ardrossan Town is still open and, after a period of DMU operation, the line was electrified, with services being introduced on 24 November 1986.

7 October 1927 (50792)

[1910]

13

On 2 May 1956 '14xx' class 0-4-2T No 1470 waits under the overall roof at Ashburton station with a one-coach departure for Totnes. *SLS Collection*

Ashburton

Promoted by the Buckfastleigh, Totnes & South Devon Railway, the 9.5-mile long branch from Totnes to Ashburton was authorised by two acts, in 1864 and 1865, and was opened on 1 May 1872. Originally constructed as a broad-gauge route, the line was converted to standard gauge on 21/22 May 1892. Initially the route was operated by the South Devon Railway, with the Great Western Railway taking over in 1876. Ownership of the line passed to the GWR on 28 August 1897. Ashburton was provided with a small locomotive shed, which housed the branch loco. Apart from passenger traffic, another regular source of income for the route was represented by cattle traffic, with four cattle fairs held annually in the town. Such was the extent of cattle traffic that improvements to the facilities for handling them continued into the 1920s. Another regular source of traffic was coal for the local gasworks. Locomotive types seen regularly over the branch included '14xx' 0-4-2Ts, '517' class 0-4-2Ts, '44xx' 2-6-2Ts and '45xx' 2-6-2Ts. From the early 1930s onwards, most passenger trains were formed of auto-trailers, with the locomotives at Totnes end. The branch lost its passenger services on 3 November 1958 and was to close completely on 7 September 1962. This was, however, not to be the end of the story as the line was preserved by the Dart Valley Railway and, initially, services on the preserved line continued through to Ashburton. Construction of the new A38, however, severed the formation between Buckfastleigh and Ashburton, and the latter lost its passenger services for the second time on 4 October 1971.

29 April 1963 (A110749)

On 2 July 1957, a second Class 14xx 0-4-2T, No 1427, is seen at Ashburton with a two-coach train prior to returning to Totnes. *R. C. Riley*

[1904]

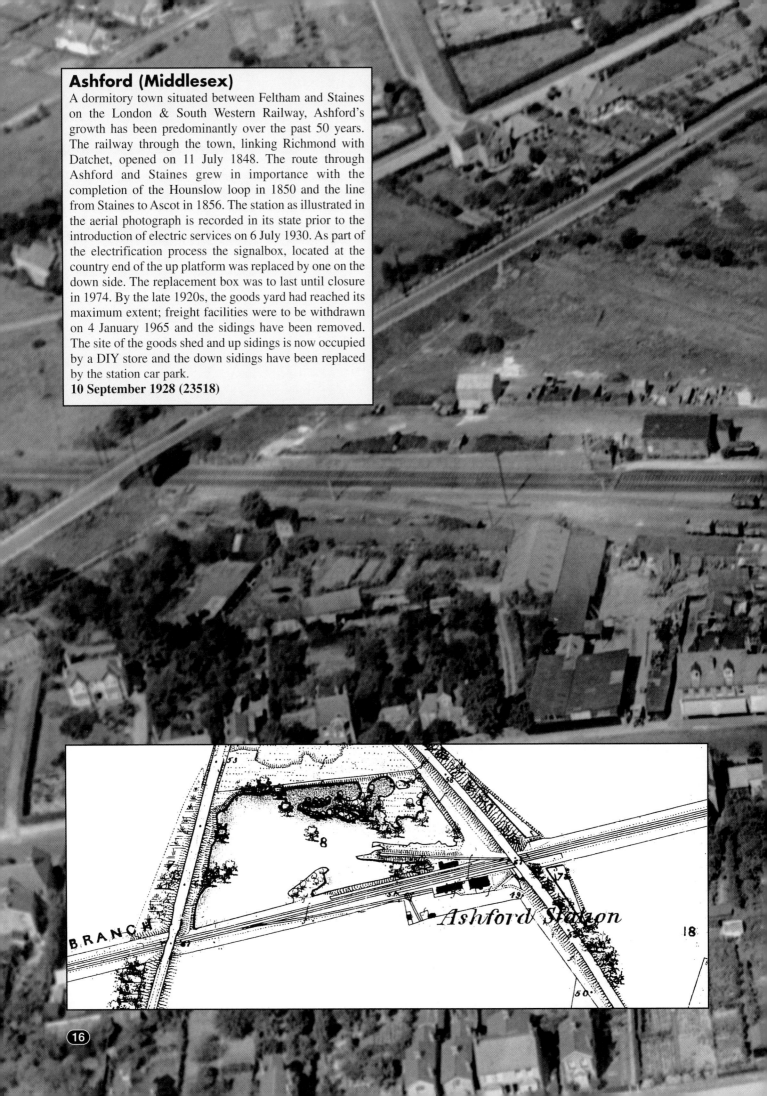

Ashford (Middlesex)

A dormitory town situated between Feltham and Staines on the London & South Western Railway, Ashford's growth has been predominantly over the past 50 years. The railway through the town, linking Richmond with Datchet, opened on 11 July 1848. The route through Ashford and Staines grew in importance with the completion of the Hounslow loop in 1850 and the line from Staines to Ascot in 1856. The station as illustrated in the aerial photograph is recorded in its state prior to the introduction of electric services on 6 July 1930. As part of the electrification process the signalbox, located at the country end of the up platform was replaced by one on the down side. The replacement box was to last until closure in 1974. By the late 1920s, the goods yard had reached its maximum extent; freight facilities were to be withdrawn on 4 January 1965 and the sidings have been removed. The site of the goods shed and up sidings is now occupied by a DIY store and the down sidings have been replaced by the station car park.

10 September 1928 (23518)

BRANCH

Ashford Station

It's 12 July 1951 and a rake of '2-NOL' EMUs, headed by No 1867, passes through Ashford with an up working towards Waterloo. *D. Sutton/Ian Allan Library*

Twenty-three years later, on 28 August 1974, Class 73 No 73129 heads the 11.50 service from Fratton to Clapham Junction through the station. By this date the goods yard on the down side had been cleared and the down sidings had been replaced by a car park. The buildings on the up platform would survive until replacement in the early 1990s. *J. Scrace*

Viewed looking towards Carlisle, No 42581 is caught at the station with the 4.20pm service from Carlisle to Whitehaven (Bransty). Note the water tower on the down line and the column on the up. *SLS Collection*

Aspatria

Aspatria is one of the most important intermediate stations on the Cumbrian Coast line between Carlisle and Barrow and was also the junction for the alternative Maryport & Carlisle line via Mealsgate. The Maryport & Carlisle Railway was authorised by an Act of 12 July 1837 to construct a railway between those two points, although construction was a somewhat drawn out affair. Aspatria was first reached on 12 April 1841 with the opening of the 1.25-mile long extension northwards from Bullgill. The line opened from Aspatria to Low Row on 2 December 1844 and the route was only completed throughout on 10 February 1845. The Bolton loop, via Mealsgate, was opened — effectively as two branch lines served from either end — on 2 April 1866 and passenger services from Aspatria to Mealsgate commenced on 26 December 1866. The loop ceased to be a through route when it was closed completely north of Mealsgate on 1 August 1921 and passenger services between Aspatria and Mealsgate ceased on 22 September 1930. The line from Aspatria to Mealsgate was to close completely on 1 December 1952 although, as is evident in the aerial photograph taken almost two decades later, the track was still in situ for many years and is here being used to store redundant wagons. Also visible in the aerial photograph is the signalbox and redundant goods shed; Aspatria lost its general freight facilities on 30 January 1967.
21 August 1972 (A244185)

The northern end of Aspatria station showing clearly the junction of the line towards Mealsgate and signalbox. *SLS Collection*

Located on the ex-Great Eastern main line between Ely and Norwich, Attleborough was one of the most important intermediate stations on the route. The Norwich & Brandon Railway was incorporated in 1844, but was to become part of the Norfolk Railway when it merged with the Yarmouth & Norwich on 30 June 1845. The line was opened on 30 July 1845, forming a connection with the Eastern Counties Railway, which opened from Newport (in Cambridgeshire) to Brandon on the same day. Amongst industries served by Attleborough was a cider works, established by the end of the 19th century, and, as elsewhere, in East Anglia freight traffic was to be expanded considerably during World War 2, when the yard was increased. Attleborough was to lose its freight facilities on 12 September 1966, but the line is still used by passenger services. Also still extant is the signalbox serving the station, which was built by the GER in 1883.
22 July 1932 (39234)

Aviemore

With evidence of the significant investment in the town for the winter sports business forming a backdrop, the sizeable junction station at Aviemore can be seen in the foreground. The first railway to reach Aviemore was the original Highland Railway main line from the north, which opened from Forres via Boat of Garten on 3 August 1863. The route southwards from Aviemore to Pitlochry opened on 9 September 1863, thereby completing the line between Perth and Inverness. For 30 years, the route via Boat of Garten was the main line, until the opening of the route via Carr Bridge saw it relegated. By the date of the aerial photograph, the original route to Forres had already seen its passenger services withdrawn, on 18 October 1965, and had in fact closed completely between Aviemore and Boat of Garten (on 4 November 1968). The track, however, from Aviemore is still *in situ* and was destined to remain so as the route to Boat of Garten was reopened by the Strathspey Railway in 1978. Initially, Strathspey services operated into a separate station, but more recently the preserved railway has run into the main line station. Slightly to the north of the area shown in the aerial photograph, Aviemore possessed an engine shed, which is still extant and is today occupied by the preservation society.
12 June 1969 (A194534)

Viewed looking northwards, Class 40 No 40001 heads an up freight through Aviemore station on 31 May 1977.
Brian Morrison

Six years later, on 9 June 1983, the station at Aviemore is still largely unchanged as Class 47 No 47419 heads northbound with the 13.22 service from Edinburgh to Inverness. The platform occupied by the train of track panels on the left is now used by the services of the preserved Strathspey Railway to Broomhill. *Paul A. Biggs*

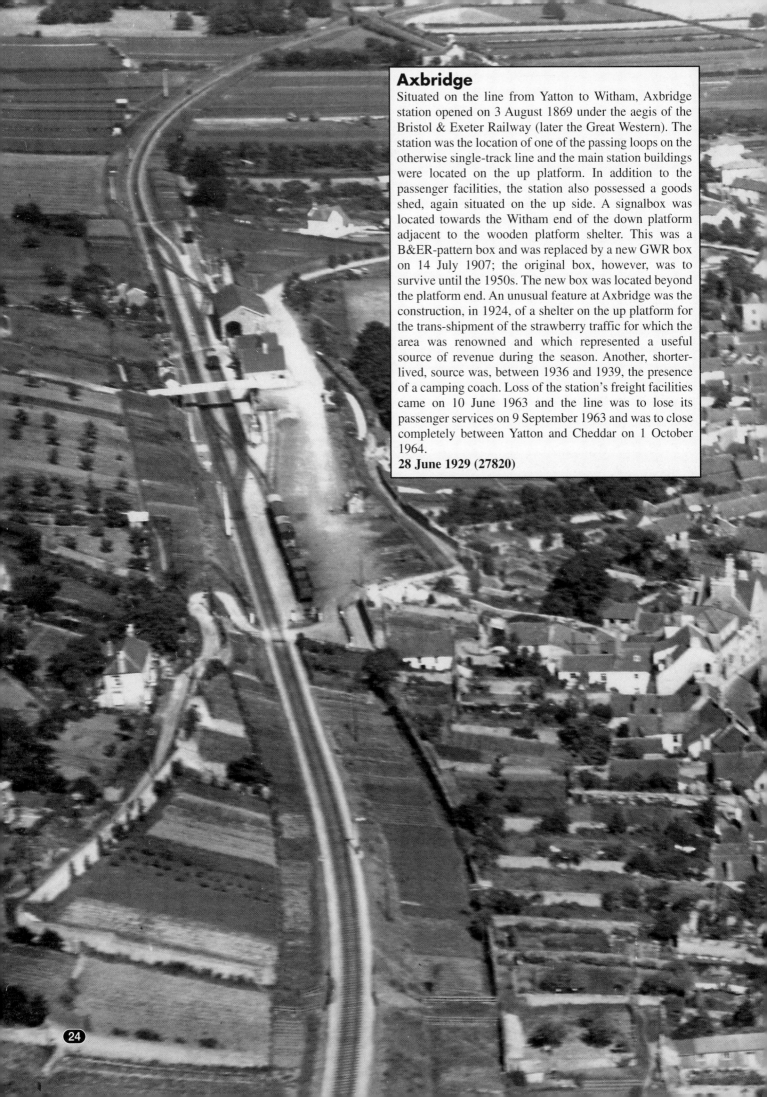

Axbridge

Situated on the line from Yatton to Witham, Axbridge station opened on 3 August 1869 under the aegis of the Bristol & Exeter Railway (later the Great Western). The station was the location of one of the passing loops on the otherwise single-track line and the main station buildings were located on the up platform. In addition to the passenger facilities, the station also possessed a goods shed, again situated on the up side. A signalbox was located towards the Witham end of the down platform adjacent to the wooden platform shelter. This was a B&ER-pattern box and was replaced by a new GWR box on 14 July 1907; the original box, however, was to survive until the 1950s. The new box was located beyond the platform end. An unusual feature at Axbridge was the construction, in 1924, of a shelter on the up platform for the trans-shipment of the strawberry traffic for which the area was renowned and which represented a useful source of revenue during the season. Another, shorter-lived, source was, between 1936 and 1939, the presence of a camping coach. Loss of the station's freight facilities came on 10 June 1963 and the line was to lose its passenger services on 9 September 1963 and was to close completely between Yatton and Cheddar on 1 October 1964.

28 June 1929 (27820)

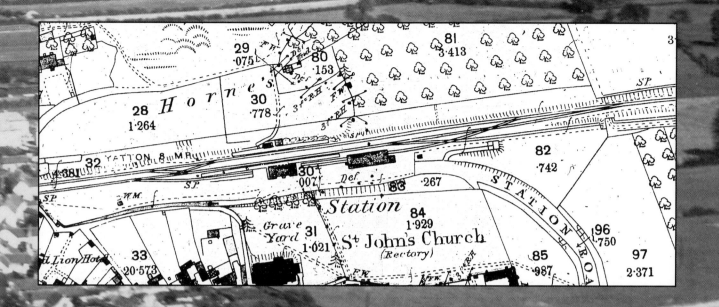

On 2 July 1960 a Yatton-Wells (Cheddar Valley) local service enters Axbridge station hauled by Ivatt Class 2MT 2-6-2T No 41240. *R. E. Toop*

Aylesbury

Viewed towards the south, the main line towards Marylebone heads southwards, whilst the route towards Princes Risborough heads southwestwards. The line through the station was controlled by a Joint Committee formed of two other committees — the Met & GC Joint (which controlled the line south to Amersham and north to Verney Junction) and the GW & GC Joint (which controlled the line to Princes Risborough). Of the lines shown here — there was also an ex-LNWR route serving the town — the Princes Risborough-Aylesbury line opened on 1 October 1963; this was followed on 23 September by the route to Verney Junction. This route was originally worked by the Great Western, but operation was eventually handled by the Metropolitan, whose line from Amersham was opened on 1 September 1892. The importance of the route was further increased with the completion of the Great Central's London Extension in 1898/9. At the date of the aerial photograph, Metropolitan services still operated to Aylesbury, but these were to cease north of Amersham on 9 September 1961. Adjacent to the station, on the down side, can be seen the small two-road engine shed built by the GWR in 1893 to replace an earlier structure. At one stage a turntable had been provided, but this had been removed by the date of the aerial photograph. The shed was to be closed on 16 June 1962.

9 May 1954 (R20439)

On 23 August 1950 ex-LNER Class N5 0-6-2T No 69259 is pictured arriving at Aylesbury at 2.30pm with a service from Princes Risborough. *E. C. Griffith*

[1898]

By the date of this photograph, 9 August 1969, passenger services through Bardney were approaching their final year and there is already evidence from the platform in the foreground of partial demolition. Pictured are the crews of the 15.22 Firsby-Lincoln service (on the left) and 16.00 Lincoln-Tumby Woodside (on the right) having a chat on the large island platform. *John A. M. Vaughan*

Bardney

Located on the ex-Great Northern line from Boston to Lincoln, Bardney was the junction for the line across to Louth. The Boston-Lincoln line opened on 17 October 1848. The branch between Bardney and Louth was originally promoted by the Louth & Lincoln Railway in the mid-1860s, but it was not until 1 December 1876 that the single-track was opened. For much of its existence, Bardney was simply a country junction, with no more than four return workings per day over the route to Louth connecting with the main line services between Boston and Lincoln. This was to change, however, in the 1920s when, encouraged to diversify, British agriculture started to produce vast quantities of sugar beet. Factories, such as that visible in this 1930 aerial view of Bardney, were constructed on behalf of the British Sugar Corporation; these factories required considerable quantities of coal during the processing period and were, therefore, located close to the railway network. Similar factories were built at Peterborough and Bury St Edmunds, for example. The line to Louth was to lose its passenger services on 5 November 1951 and to close completely between Bardney and Wragby on 1 February 1960. Passenger services through Bardney ceased on 5 October 1970, at which time the line south of the station closed completely. General freight facilities were withdrawn on 3 May 1965 and the line survived after October 1970 to serve the sugar factory; this traffic ceased in August 1983.
29 April 1930 (31747)

Barnham Junction

Railway Inn

Station

30

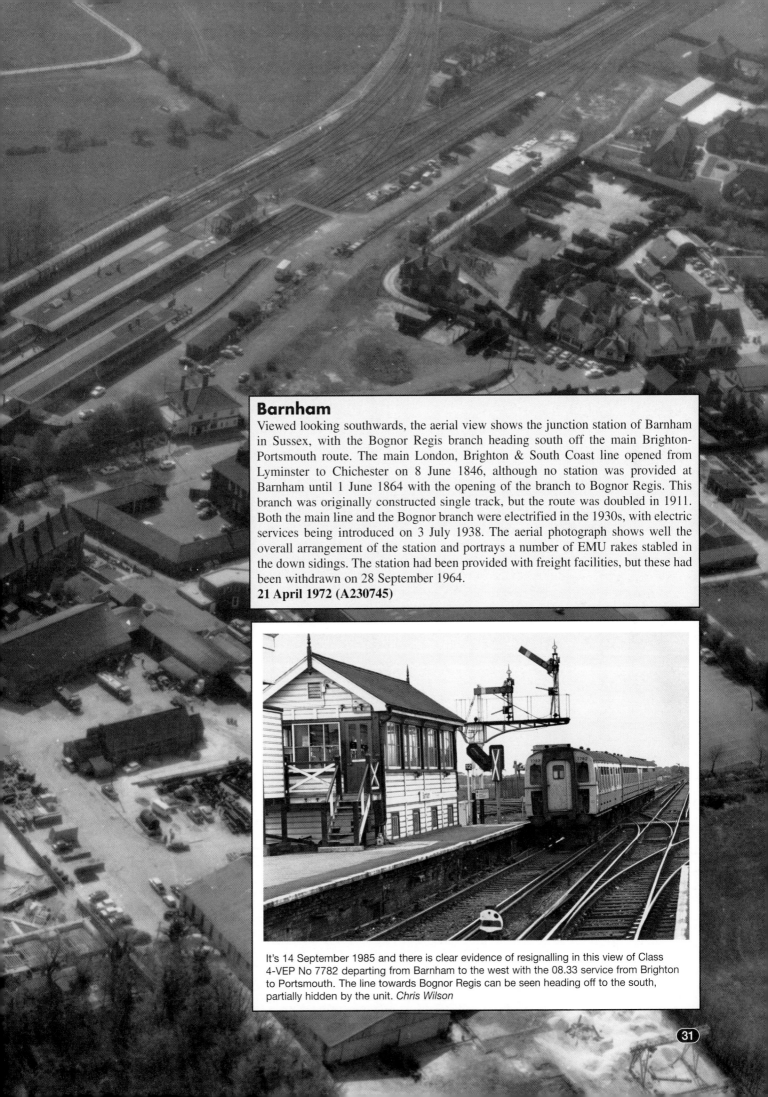

Barnham

Viewed looking southwards, the aerial view shows the junction station of Barnham in Sussex, with the Bognor Regis branch heading south off the main Brighton-Portsmouth route. The main London, Brighton & South Coast line opened from Lyminster to Chichester on 8 June 1846, although no station was provided at Barnham until 1 June 1864 with the opening of the branch to Bognor Regis. This branch was originally constructed single track, but the route was doubled in 1911. Both the main line and the Bognor branch were electrified in the 1930s, with electric services being introduced on 3 July 1938. The aerial photograph shows well the overall arrangement of the station and portrays a number of EMU rakes stabled in the down sidings. The station had been provided with freight facilities, but these had been withdrawn on 28 September 1964.

21 April 1972 (A230745)

It's 14 September 1985 and there is clear evidence of resignalling in this view of Class 4-VEP No 7782 departing from Barnham to the west with the 08.33 service from Brighton to Portsmouth. The line towards Bognor Regis can be seen heading off to the south, partially hidden by the unit. *Chris Wilson*

Battle

In 1066, when William the Conqueror invaded England, he defeated the Anglo-Saxon king, Harold, at the Battle of Hastings and, in gratitude, he founded a monastery near to the site at Battle, in Sussex. The abbey was dissolved by Henry VIII but its remains are in the care of English Heritage with a girls' school occupying much of the site. The town that grew up around the abbey, however, still thrives and is served by the EMUs on the Hastings-Tonbridge line. The line between Tunbridge Wells and Bopeep Junction at Hastings was opened in three stages by the South Eastern Railway: from Tunbridge Wells to Robertsbridge on 1 September 1851; Robertsbridge to Battle on 1 January 1852; and from Battle to Hastings on 1 February 1852. Three tunnels along the route were constructed with restricted loading gauge, which required specially-constructed narrow-bodied DEMUs when the line was dieselised in 1957. As befitted a station serving such a well-known location, the SER provided a well-appointed station, in this case designed in a Gothic style by William Tress. The station building can be seen clearly in the aerial photograph, as can the other facilities. Note the tender locomotive shunting the goods yard on the extreme left. Freight facilities were withdrawn from Battle on 26 February 1966.

24 April 1929 (26220)

When the line through Battle was under construction, the SER ensured that the town was provided with a well-designed station in the then popular Gothic style. Taken on 6 September 1969, this view of the station exterior shows to good effect the Gothic detailing of William Tress's design. *J. Scrace*

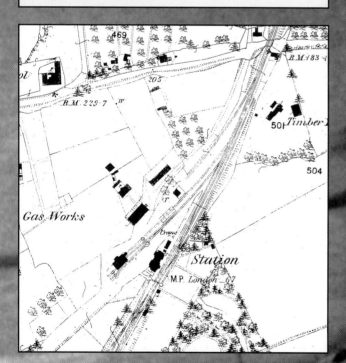

Taken on the same occasion as the previous view, this shot of the station at Battle illustrates the staggered platforms, footbridge and main station buildings on the up platform. At this date the line was still diesel operated; it would be more than a decade before the SR's third-rail electrification brought EMUs to the route. *J. Scrace*

The Bembridge branch was primarily the haunt of 2-4-0Ts until it was upgraded to accommodate Class O2 0-4-4Ts. One of the Beyer-Peacock 2-4-0Ts is pictured at Bembridge with three ex-Golden Valley coaches. *Ian Allan Library*

Bembridge

Bembridge, on the Isle of Wight, was the terminus of the 2.75-mile long branch from Brading. The line was a development of a short spur built to serve Brading Wharf. The line was authorised as part of the Brading Harbour Improvement & Railway Co's act of 1874 and was opened on 27 May 1882. At Bembridge connection was made to a ferry service to Langston, but this was to prove shortlived, being withdrawn in 1888. The line was worked from the outset by the Isle of Wight Railway, which was to take over the bankrupt concern in 1898. Early rolling stock for the line included Manning Wardle 0-6-0T *Bembridge* and ex-Golden Valley six-wheel coaches. After this locomotive was requisitioned (and never returned) during World War 1, the line was operated by 2-4-0Ts for a period. Latterly, it was operated by 'O2s' following an upgrade. As shown in the aerial photograph, Bembridge was, like Ventnor, provided with a turntable rather than runround spur and points. At Bembridge, however, this facility was retained until closure, having been replaced to accommodate the 'O2s'. Passenger services between Brading and Bembridge were withdrawn on 21 September 1953, at which time the line closed completely.

6 August 1938 (R4644)

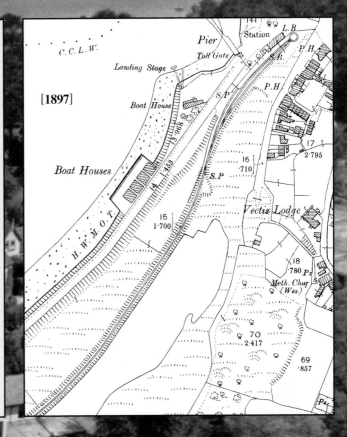

[1897]

The exterior of Bembridge station recorded in April 1953, shortly before the line closed. *SLS Collection*

Blair Atholl

It is surprising to note how extensive were the railway facilities at a station like Blair Atholl, situated on the ex-Highland Railway main line between Perth and Inverness, in the early 1930s. Apart from the station building, there were also sidings, engine shed with turntable, signalbox and good shed. Close examination of the photograph would suggest at least three locomotives clearly visible — one in the station and two by the shed — and it may well be that there are at least two others. The section of line between Pitlochry and Aviemore, via Blair Atholl, opened on 9 September 1863. The engine shed illustrated was a two-road structure built originally in 1868 to replace an older, wooden-built, shed that had opened with the line. The 1868 shed was originally provided with a 42ft turntable but this was later replaced by one of 55ft diameter. As illustrated here, the shed had been modified to provide two through roads and would be further modified shortly after Nationalisation. The shed closed in the early 1960s and was demolished in the late 1990s. Freight facilities were withdrawn from the station on 7 November 1966.

22 September 1932 (40530)

On 13 June 1949, ex-CR Pickersgill Class 3P 4-4-0 No 54467, still without its BR numberplate, heads southwards through Blair Atholl with an up service from Inveness. *H. N. A. Shelton*

In August 1965 preserved ex-HR 'Jones Goods' 4-6-0 No 103 is pictured taking water at Blair Atholl as it heads towards Inverness. *Andrew Muckley*

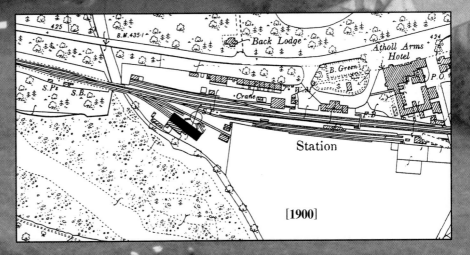

[1900]

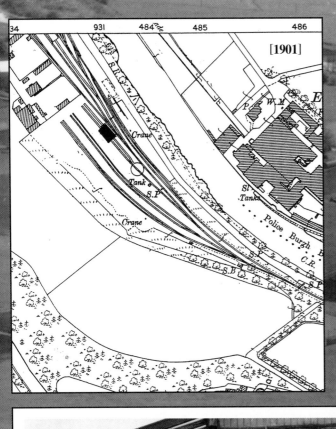

[1901]

Blairgowrie
One of a number of branches built to exploit the agricultural wealth of Strathmore off the line from Stanley Junction through Forfar to Kinnaber Junction, the five-mile long Blairgowrie line, which was single track throughout, joined the main line at Coupar Angus. The branch opened in 1855 and was to survive until 10 January 1955 (passenger traffic) and 6 December 1965 (freight). The station was provided with an overall roof constructed of wood.
21 May 1963 (A112898)

McIntosh-designed ex-CR 0-4-4T No 55194 stands at the head of a two-coach train at Blairgowrie station. The angle that the photographer has taken allows for good detail of the platform canopy and supports. *SLS Collection*

On 1 September 1952 ex-CR 0-4-4T No 55226 heads the 6.20pm service from Blairgowrie to Dundee West out of the station. *N. R. Knight*

Blenheim & Woodstock

Opened (as 'Woodstock') on 19 May 1890, Blenheim & Woodstock was the terminus of the short — 3.5-mile long — branch from Kidlington. Promoted by the Woodstock Railway and authorised on 25 September 1886, the line was operated by the Great Western Railway from the outset and the original company was taken over by the GWR on 1 July 1897. For many years the line was associated with 0-4-2T No 1473 *Fair Rosamund*, but the line also played host to a number of other yellow and unrestricted GWR types, including '14xx' class 0-4-2Ts and 0-6-0PTs; given the gradients on the line, weight restrictions applied, with a maximum of 120 and 150 tons respectively. For a short period before closure, the line also saw ex-GWR diesel railcar No 2 in operation. The formal announcement of closure came in early 1954, with services ceasing on 27 February of that year. Track lifting over the branch was completed in January 1958. The branch terminus was originally provided with station building, goods shed, small engine shed and signalbox. However, the signalling was abolished in 1926 and, with the introduction of auto-train working, the signalbox also became redundant. It was replaced by the provision of two small ground frames, Blenheim West and East. The aerial photograph shows the station site in 1929; the signalbox, signalling, engine shed and the latter's associated siding had, by this date, already been removed. **20 May 1929 (26925)**

Pictured on 24 August 1939, a week or so before the outbreak of World War 2, GWR 0-4-2T No 1159 stands at Blenheim station with auto-trailer No 187. *SLS Collection*

Although the garden is well tended, judging from the carefully pruned shrubs in the background, the state of the track in the foreground is perhaps more indicative of the position of the Blenheim branch, when this view of a one-coach auto-train at the station was taken in circa 1950. *SLS Collection*

Bodmin

The station illustrated here is the ex-London & South Western Railway terminus Bodmin North. This station had opened on 1 November 1895 and was to survive until passenger services were withdrawn on 30 January 1967 (freight facilities had been withdrawn earlier, on 29 November 1965). The original promoter of the line to Bodmin was the Bodmin & Wadebridge Railway, which opened its branch to Bodmin, off the Wenford Bridge line, on 4 July 1834. The B&WR route passed to the LSWR in 1846, albeit illegally and was not to be connected to the remainder of the LSWR network until completion of the route from Halwill Junction to Wadebridge. The B&WR passenger station was closed on 1 November 1886 in connection with the upgrading of the line and the construction of the new station, which opened on 1 November 1895. Passenger services were limited with in August 1939 six arrivals and five departures Mondays-Fridays (the latter being at 7.27am, 9am, 11.28am, 2.5pm and 5.36pm); there was no service on Sundays. Services were regularly formed of a single coach and, on 15 June 1964, in an effort to make the service more viable, a four-wheel railbus was introduced to the line providing a link from a new platform at Boscarne Junction to Bodmin North (although a three-coach school service was also run).

1 June 1961 (A90917)

Viewed looking towards the buffer stops at Bodmin, this view is of particular interest in that it shows one of the LSWR's railmotors standing in the platform. *Ian Allan Library*

Taken in 1937, this view from the buffer stops shows the station looking westwards shows, in the distance, the tower of Bodmin gaol. *Ian Allan Library*

Taken looking westwards, this view of Bradford-on-Avon station is dated 23 April 1921.
As such it provides an excellent reference to the facilities provided to passengers at this
station in the period immediately prior to the creation of the 'Big Four' in 1923.
SLS Collection

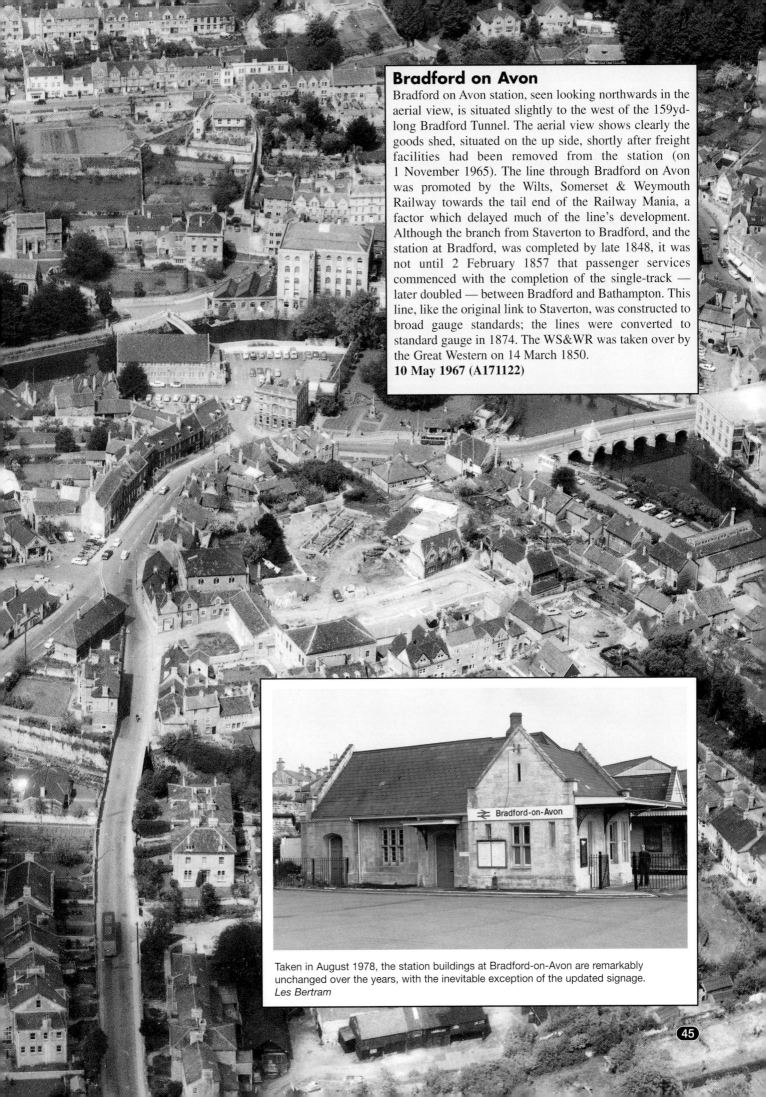

Bradford on Avon

Bradford on Avon station, seen looking northwards in the aerial view, is situated slightly to the west of the 159yd-long Bradford Tunnel. The aerial view shows clearly the goods shed, situated on the up side, shortly after freight facilities had been removed from the station (on 1 November 1965). The line through Bradford on Avon was promoted by the Wilts, Somerset & Weymouth Railway towards the tail end of the Railway Mania, a factor which delayed much of the line's development. Although the branch from Staverton to Bradford, and the station at Bradford, was completed by late 1848, it was not until 2 February 1857 that passenger services commenced with the completion of the single-track — later doubled — between Bradford and Bathampton. This line, like the original link to Staverton, was constructed to broad gauge standards; the lines were converted to standard gauge in 1874. The WS&WR was taken over by the Great Western on 14 March 1850.

10 May 1967 (A171122)

Taken in August 1978, the station buildings at Bradford-on-Avon are remarkably unchanged over the years, with the inevitable exception of the updated signage.
Les Bertram

Brechin

Although there were proposals as early as 1819 for the construction of a line from the important agricultural centre of Brechin, in Angus, to Montrose, it would be three decades before Brechin was actually rail-served, with the opening of the Aberdeen Railway line from Dubton on February 1848. The importance of Brechin as a rail centre grew with the opening of the line to Forfar, on 7 January 1895, and the branch to Edzell, which opened on 1 June 1896. The aerial photograph shows the extensive facilities offered at Brechin shortly after the passenger services to Edzell were withdrawn (on 27 April 1931). The station was largely the result of the rebuilding and expansion of railway facilities in the town by the Caledonian Railway in the 1890s. Apart from the terminus, the railway facilities also included a large goods shed, extensive sidings and an engine shed with 50ft turntable. The engine shed illustrated here replaced the 1848 Aberdeen Railway structure in 1894. It was closed by BR on 2 August 1952 and used briefly as a wagon repair shop before demolition. Brechin was to lose its passenger services with the withdrawal of trains from both the route to Bridge of Dun and that to Forfar on 4 August 1952. The line from Brechin to Careston (on the Forfar line) closed completely on 17 March 1958, to be followed on 7 September 1964 by the complete closure of the line to Edzell. Brechin continued to be served by freight services until these were withdrawn on 4 May 1981. In later years, the traffic was almost exclusively coal, fertiliser, seed potatoes and lime, much of it on behalf of Carnegie Crop Services. After closure, the section from Bridge of Dun to Brechin was preserved and is today operated by the Caledonian Railway (Brechin) Ltd.

26 September 1932 (40479)

More than a decade after the end of the 'Big Four', Brechin still proudly shows its allegiance to the LMS in this September 1960 view of the station's exterior. By this date, Brechin was no longer on the passenger network, but the station buildings were (and remain) intact. *Ian Allan Library*

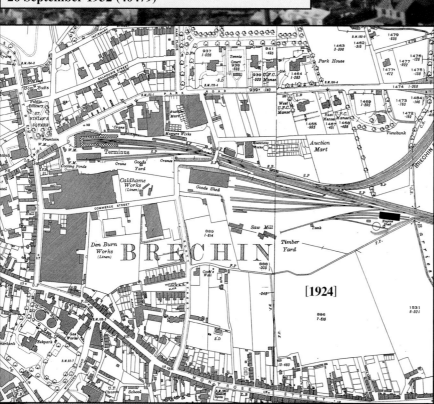

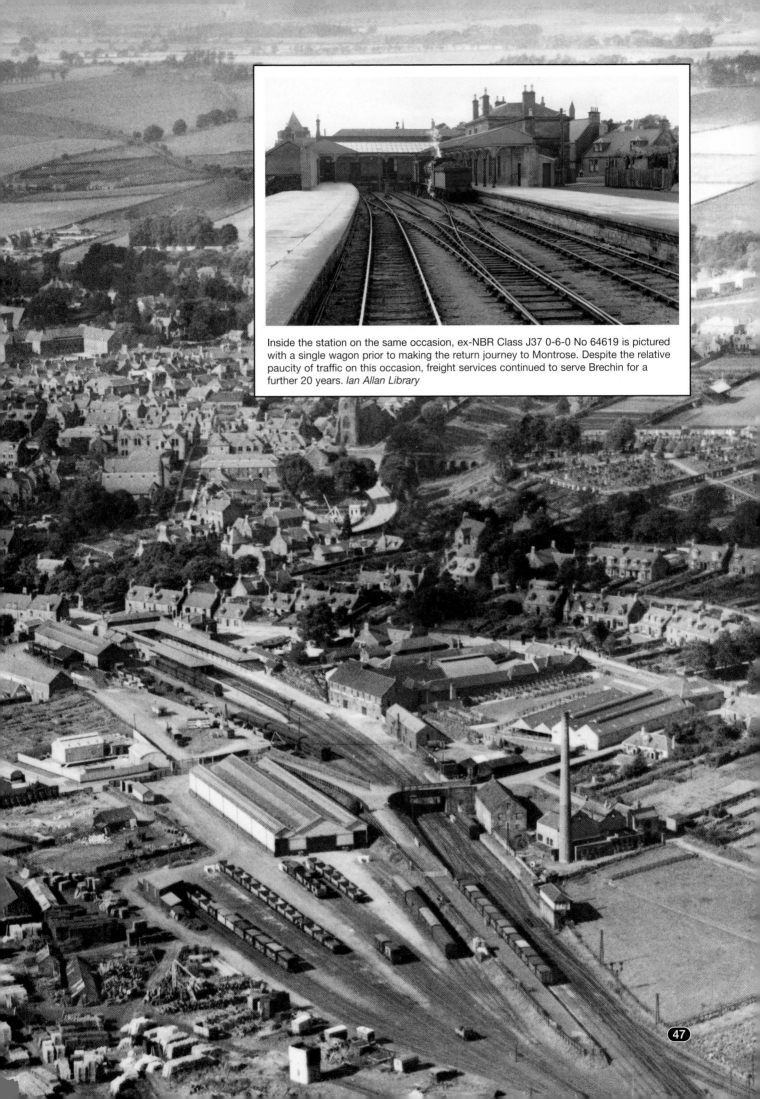

Inside the station on the same occasion, ex-NBR Class J37 0-6-0 No 64619 is pictured with a single wagon prior to making the return journey to Montrose. Despite the relative paucity of traffic on this occasion, freight services continued to serve Brechin for a further 20 years. *Ian Allan Library*

Brixham

Opened by the Torbay & Brixham Railway to passenger traffic on 28 February 1868 and to freight on the following 1 May, the Brixham branch was just over two miles in length and joined the Newton Abbot-Kingswear line at Churston. The primary driving force for the construction of the line, which was absorbed into the Great Western Railway in 1883, was fish traffic, as Brixham was one of the most important fishing harbours in south Devon and, throughout the line's existence, fish traffic remained important. The date of the aerial photograph is 1928, shortly before the closure of the engine shed (on 22 July 1929). The track remained as a siding after the closure of the shed, with the only alteration being effected in December 1931 when the point leading to it was transferred to the down line. The former engine shed siding was lifted in September 1959. Passenger services to Brixham were withdrawn on 13 May 1963 and freight facilities also ceased to be provided from the same day.

August 1928 (23784)

[1938]

A view along the platform at Brixham in 1921, towards the buffer stops.
Ian Allan Library

Over 30 years later, in August 1953, Class 14xx 0-4-2T No 1466 stands at Brixham with a service to Churston. Note that, despite the passage of time, the 'GENTLEMEN' sign is still unchanged, although the enamel sign has been replaced by one saying 'Brixham' and the light fitting has also been changed. *Ian Allan Library*

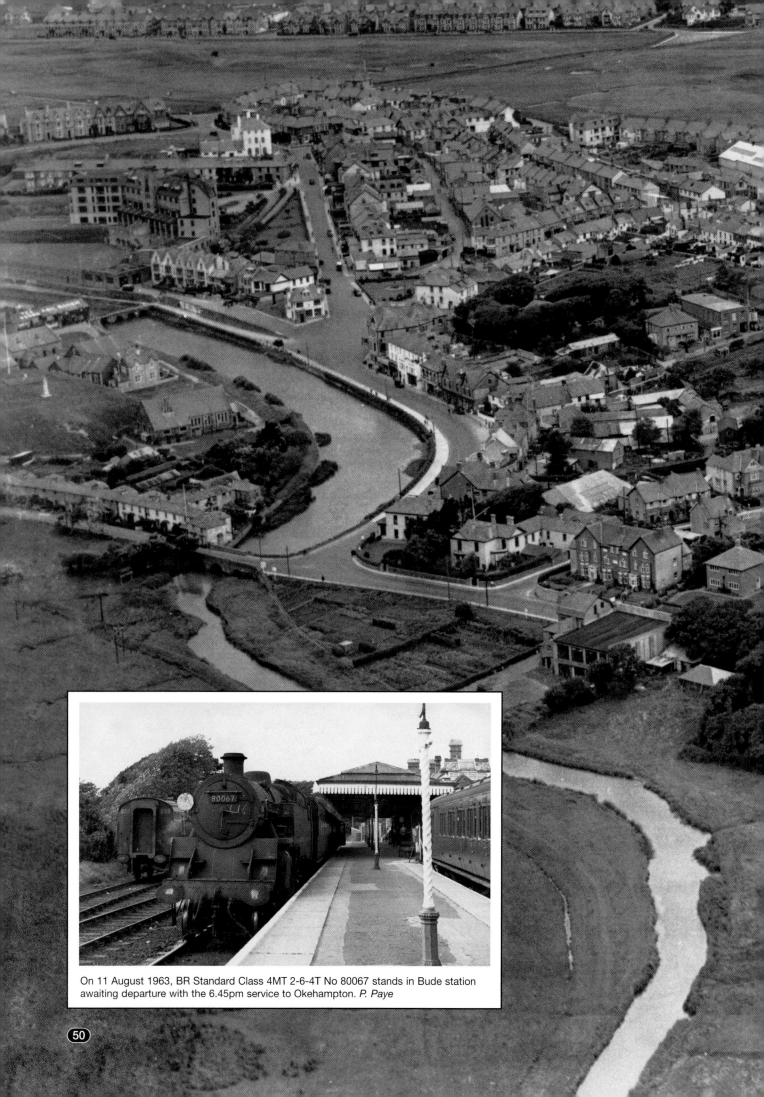

On 11 August 1963, BR Standard Class 4MT 2-6-4T No 80067 stands in Bude station awaiting departure with the 6.45pm service to Okehampton. *P. Paye*

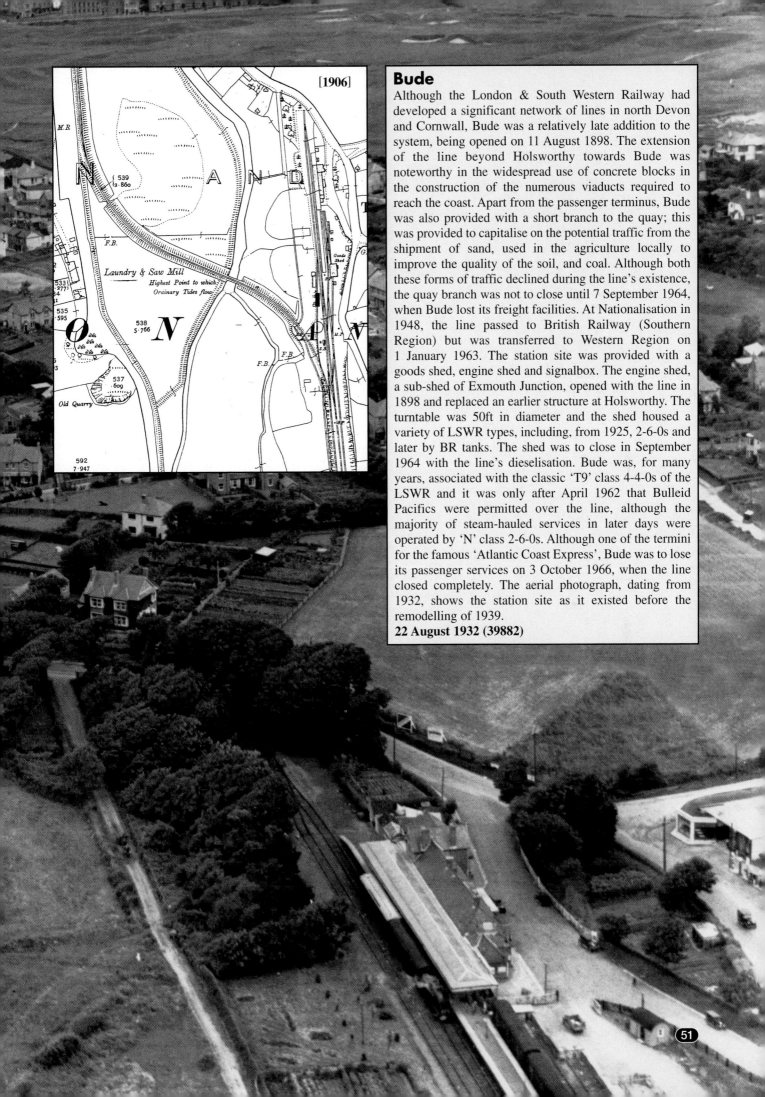

[1906]

Bude

Although the London & South Western Railway had developed a significant network of lines in north Devon and Cornwall, Bude was a relatively late addition to the system, being opened on 11 August 1898. The extension of the line beyond Holsworthy towards Bude was noteworthy in the widespread use of concrete blocks in the construction of the numerous viaducts required to reach the coast. Apart from the passenger terminus, Bude was also provided with a short branch to the quay; this was provided to capitalise on the potential traffic from the shipment of sand, used in the agriculture locally to improve the quality of the soil, and coal. Although both these forms of traffic declined during the line's existence, the quay branch was not to close until 7 September 1964, when Bude lost its freight facilities. At Nationalisation in 1948, the line passed to British Railway (Southern Region) but was transferred to Western Region on 1 January 1963. The station site was provided with a goods shed, engine shed and signalbox. The engine shed, a sub-shed of Exmouth Junction, opened with the line in 1898 and replaced an earlier structure at Holsworthy. The turntable was 50ft in diameter and the shed housed a variety of LSWR types, including, from 1925, 2-6-0s and later by BR tanks. The shed was to close in September 1964 with the line's dieselisation. Bude was, for many years, associated with the classic 'T9' class 4-4-0s of the LSWR and it was only after April 1962 that Bulleid Pacifics were permitted over the line, although the majority of steam-hauled services in later days were operated by 'N' class 2-6-0s. Although one of the termini for the famous 'Atlantic Coast Express', Bude was to lose its passenger services on 3 October 1966, when the line closed completely. The aerial photograph, dating from 1932, shows the station site as it existed before the remodelling of 1939.

22 August 1932 (39882)

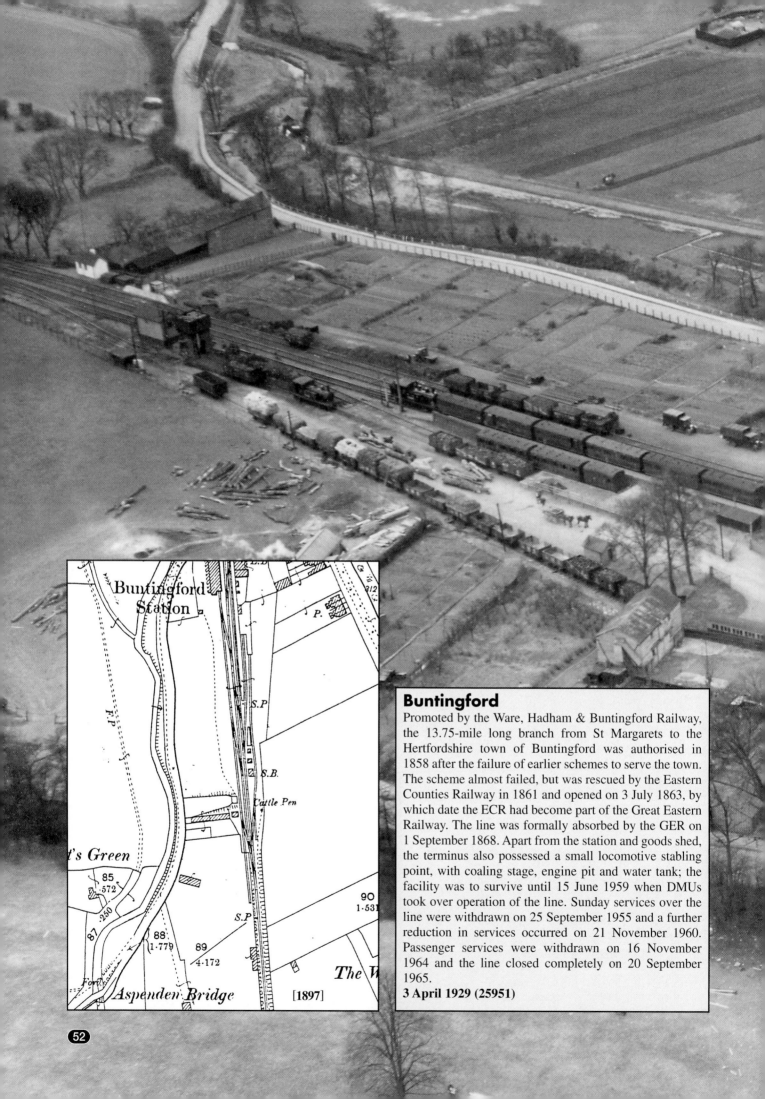

Buntingford

Promoted by the Ware, Hadham & Buntingford Railway, the 13.75-mile long branch from St Margarets to the Hertfordshire town of Buntingford was authorised in 1858 after the failure of earlier schemes to serve the town. The scheme almost failed, but was rescued by the Eastern Counties Railway in 1861 and opened on 3 July 1863, by which date the ECR had become part of the Great Eastern Railway. The line was formally absorbed by the GER on 1 September 1868. Apart from the station and goods shed, the terminus also possessed a small locomotive stabling point, with coaling stage, engine pit and water tank; the facility was to survive until 15 June 1959 when DMUs took over operation of the line. Sunday services over the line were withdrawn on 25 September 1955 and a further reduction in services occurred on 21 November 1960. Passenger services were withdrawn on 16 November 1964 and the line closed completely on 20 September 1965.

3 April 1929 (25951)

Viewed looking towards the buffer stops, this view shows to good effect the relationship between the main station buildings and goods shed. *A. M. Lawrence*

Pictured towards St Margarets, an unidentified Class N7 0-6-2T stands behind the coaling stage and water tower at Buntingford. *A. M. Lawrence*

Burwell

Located between Barnwell Junction and Fordham Junction, on the branch to Mildenhall, Burwell was an important intermediate station on the single-track line. The Great Eastern Railway route from Cambridge to Mildenhall was authorised by an act of 18 July 1871 and was opened between Barnwell Junction and Fordham Junction on 2 June 1884. The extension to Mildenhall opened on the following 1 April. Although services over the route were relatively sparse, with passenger services between Cambridge and Mildenhall totalling four per day in 1949 (with one of the Mildenhall-Cambridge services returning via Newmarket rather than Burwell), the route through Burwell was a useful diversionary line when the main Cambridge-Ely route was blocked. In July 1958 two of the German-built railbuses were allocated to the service, but these proved unreliable and were replaced by two-car DMUs during the last years of the passenger service. In October 1961 it was proposed that passenger services be withdrawn, and these succumbed with the last train running on 16 June 1962. The aerial photograph records the scene shortly after the cessation of passenger services when the route remained opened for freight throughout. The large factory behind the station building belonged to Corrugated Fittings and when it opened in 1957, a special train was operated to Burwell. The section of line between Burwell and Barnwell Junction closed completely on 13 July 1964 and the final closure of the section between Burwell and Fordham came on 19 April 1965. The station was demolished in October 1967 to allow for expansion of the factory.

6 June 1963 (A115339)

On 24 July 1955 an RCTS-sponsored special can be seen passing through Burwell station. 'The Fensman' commenced at Liverpool Street and was scheduled to operate over a number of lines in the Cambridge area. Although a 'Britannia' handled the journey over the London-Cambridge main line, the various workings in rural Cambridgeshire were handled, as here, by ex-GER Class J17 0-6-0 No 65562.
SLS Collection

Viewed towards the end of its life, Burwell station provides a sad image in this picture. Although there is evidence of decay — note the missing letters on the nameboard — the view does, however, give a reasonably good impression of the facilities afforded by this country station. *SLS Collection*

Calne

Promoted by the Calne Railway, but operated (and later absorbed) by the Great Western Railway, the 5.25-mile long Calne branch opened from Chippenham to freight traffic on 29 October 1863 and to passenger services on the following 3 November. The station as illustrated in the aerial photograph had received a number of modifications over the previous 15 years. During World War 1 the loading bank and additional sidings had been built whilst, in 1927/8, a private siding to serve the pork pie factory of S. M. O. C. & T. Harris had been added. The next alterations postdate the aerial photograph; these were, in 1942, the extension of the passenger platform towards the signalbox and the construction of new wooden booking office and waiting room, after which the original booking office, as illustrated in the aerial photograph was converted into a parcels office. Although the line was relatively busy through to the late 1950s, the process of rationalisation started in the early 1960s. Sunday passenger services were withdrawn on 5 March 1962 and freight facilities ceased on 2 November 1964. Final closure came with the withdrawal of passenger services on 20 September 1966.

14 September 1929 (29301)

[1899]

On 4 October 1948 '14xx' class 0-4-2T No 1453 arrives at Calne with the 1.1pm service from Chippenham. The coaching stock is formed of Nos 80 and 75. In the distance, steam can be seen rising from 0-6-0PT No 9720, which is heading a short freight train. *SLS Collection*

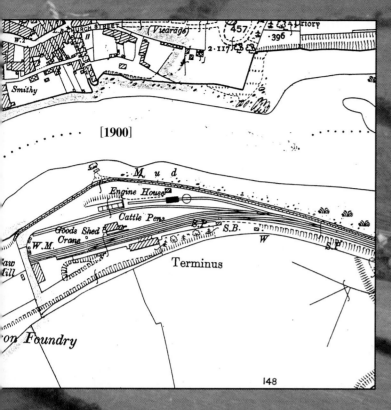

[1900]

Cardigan

This was the terminus for the 27-mile long branch from Cardigan Junction, on the Carmarthen-Fishguard line. The section of line between Cardigan and Crymmych Arms was opened under the auspices of the Whitland & Cardigan Railway on 1 September 1886 (although there had been earlier proposals to serve the town). The W&CR was bought by the Great Western Railway in 1890; the GWR had agreed in 1883 to work the line from opening. Although the station served a significant area of West Wales, the actual provision at the terminus was relatively limited, with a single platform with station buildings, goods shed, signalbox and small engine shed with turntable. The locomotive shed was opened by the W&CR in 1886 and was to survive until 16 September 1962. During the early 1950s Class 45xx 2-6-2Ts were the usual locomotives for both passenger and freight workings. By the date of the aerial photograph, the railway was in terminal decline. Passenger services had been withdrawn on 10 September 1962 and public goods traffic had been withdrawn on 27 May 1963. Final closure of the line came on 6 September 1965.

24 June 1964 (A133932)

Designed by Hawksworth, the first of the '16xx' class of 0-6-0PT was delivered after Nationalisation. A total of 70 of the type were ultimately constructed. No 1648 is pictured at the head of a one-coach train at Cardigan. *SLS Collection*

Caterham

The almost irresistible rise of the dormitory town in southeast England is perhaps well exemplified by Caterham, which developed rapidly from the mid-19th century once the branch towards Purley was opened. Promoted by the Caterham Railway (which had been incorporated in 1854), the line was completed by 21 September 1855. However, due to a dispute between the Caterham Railway and both the London, Brighton & South Coast and South Eastern railways, the line did not actually open until 4 August 1856, with normal services commencing the following day. Initially, the Caterham railway operated its own services, but in July 1859 it went bankrupt and was taken over by the SER. The route was originally constructed single-track, but was doubled in 1897 and the station illustrated here was the result of a SER replacement in 1900, when the original station closed. The line was electrified by the Southern Railway during the 1920s, with services commencing on 25 March 1928. At the time of the aerial photograph, Caterham was still provided with freight facilities; these were, however, to be withdrawn on 28 September 1964.

23 October 1952 (A47572)

[1895]

Pictured in 1914, looking towards the buffer stops, this view illustrates the facilities provided at Caterham, including the small goods yard, at the outbreak of World War 1. *Ian Allan Library*

A second pre-Grouping era shot shows an SECR 0-4-4T marshalling a rake of six-wheel coaches. A second rake of coaches is visible in the distance. Also clearly shown is the signalbox and signalling arrangements at the platform end. *Ian Allan Library*

Widgett's Lane

1092
.885

106

1094
.580

1095 1.145

1098
2.527

1100
.634

1099
1.269

1101
1.682

M.P

S.P

S.P

Goods
Shed

Cattle Pens

Station

1086ª
.424

1091
2.799

1090
.621

1087
.198

1086
1.452

1085
322

1097
.949

1102
1.824

1088
.528

1089
.478

1096

1104ª
.944

1103
232

G.P

1079
1.863

1094ª

1083
.833

1104
2.316

[1903]

62

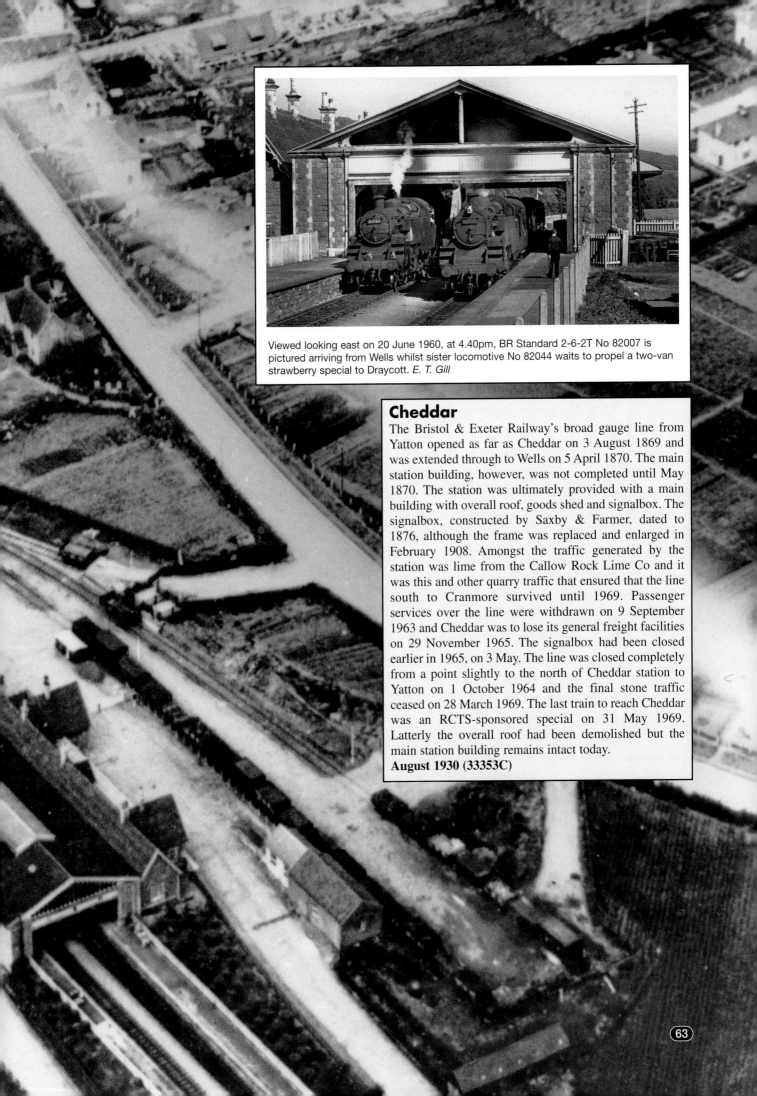

Viewed looking east on 20 June 1960, at 4.40pm, BR Standard 2-6-2T No 82007 is pictured arriving from Wells whilst sister locomotive No 82044 waits to propel a two-van strawberry special to Draycott. *E. T. Gill*

Cheddar

The Bristol & Exeter Railway's broad gauge line from Yatton opened as far as Cheddar on 3 August 1869 and was extended through to Wells on 5 April 1870. The main station building, however, was not completed until May 1870. The station was ultimately provided with a main building with overall roof, goods shed and signalbox. The signalbox, constructed by Saxby & Farmer, dated to 1876, although the frame was replaced and enlarged in February 1908. Amongst the traffic generated by the station was lime from the Callow Rock Lime Co and it was this and other quarry traffic that ensured that the line south to Cranmore survived until 1969. Passenger services over the line were withdrawn on 9 September 1963 and Cheddar was to lose its general freight facilities on 29 November 1965. The signalbox had been closed earlier in 1965, on 3 May. The line was closed completely from a point slightly to the north of Cheddar station to Yatton on 1 October 1964 and the final stone traffic ceased on 28 March 1969. The last train to reach Cheddar was an RCTS-sponsored special on 31 May 1969. Latterly the overall roof had been demolished but the main station building remains intact today.

August 1930 (33353C)

Clare

One of the intermediate stations on the Stour Valley line from Long Melford to Cambridge, Clare was originally the target of a proposal in 1847 for the extension of the Colchester, Stour Valley, Sudbury & Halstead Railway's line to Sudbury, which was opened in 1849. Although these original proposals came to nothing, the scheme was revived in the 1860s and, on 9 August 1865, the route from Long Melford to Haverhill via Clare was opened. The station was provided with two platforms and served as a passing loop with block post; the station also possessed a good shed and sidings. As with other ex-Great Eastern lines, the route passed to the LNER in 1923 and to British Railways (Eastern Region) in 1948. During the 1950s, efforts were made to encourage increased passenger traffic, with dieselisation. However, despite these efforts, traffic remained insufficient to justify the retention of the line, and the full route from Shelford to Marks Tey was slated for closure in the Beeching report. Although services between Sudbury and Marks Tey were reprieved, passenger services from Shelford to Sudbury via Clare were withdrawn on 6 March 1967. By this date freight services over the line had already been withdrawn; Clare lost its freight facilities on 12 September 1965.

26 April 1953 (A48835)

Seen on 30 August 1965, a Derby-built DMU forms the 10.55 service from Cambridge to Sudbury departing from Clare station. *G. R. Mortimer*

In April 1958, Class B1 4-6-0 No 61281 awaits departure from Cleethorpes station. Although the platforms seem deserted at this stage, it won't be long before the summer crowds descend upon this Lincolnshire resort. *Ian Allan Library*

On 24 May 1980, the 12.45 service from Manchester Piccadilly arrives at Cleethorpes formed of a Class 124 DMU, with car No E51958 leading. *Brian Morrison*

Cleethorpes

A seaside resort on the Lincolnshire coast, Cleethorpes owes much of its development to the promotion of the town by the Manchester, Sheffield & Lincolnshire Railway, which invested heavily in developing facilities for the holidaymaker in the 20 years after 1880. Although promoted earlier, the extension from Grimsby to Cleethorpes was delayed due to opposition from landowners. The line was authorised in 1861 and opened, as a single line, on 6 April 1863. The route was doubled in 1874 and the popularity of the town as a holiday destination grew considerably, with many tens of thousands also making day trips to the sea. Such was the scale of the traffic that the station was rebuilt from a single platform to six terminal roads. As illustrated in the aerial photograph the station predates the modernisation of the early 1960s. Clearly visible are the proximity of the station to the seafront, the large signalbox (on the extreme right of the photograph) and locomotives and carriages awaiting their next duty.

25 May 1953 (R18630)

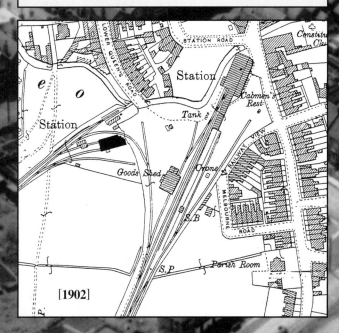

Clevedon

The three-mile Bristol & Exeter Railway branch from Yatton to Clevedon was authorised on 31 July 1845 and opened on 28 July 1847. Initially worked by the Great Western Railway, the B&ER took over operation on 1 May 1849. The B&ER and GWR amalgamated in 1876. The branch was initially constructed to the broad gauge but was to be converted to standard gauge on 28 September 1879.

Although the line was provided with an intensive service, operated by the late 1950s, on the principle of one engine in steam, freight services were withdrawn on 10 June 1963 and the passenger service ceased on 3 October 1966.

The station was provided with a slightly unusual platform roof, with an overall roof at the extreme end of the track with a canopy running down the platform. Although a small signalbox was provided, by the date of the main photograph this had been reduced to no more than a lever-frame, with the signalling provided — a platform starter, advance starter and fixed distant — having been removed in the 1920s. There was a second line at Cleveden, shown in the map and connected to the GWR station: the Weston, Cleveden & Portishead, which existed from 1897 until 1940.

5 April 1961 (A86956)

[1902]

It's the mid-1930s and a GWR auto-train awaits departure with a service to Yatton. This photograph portrays well the supports of the platform canopy and the arrangement of seating and posters under it. *SLS Collection*

By the mid-1960s and towards the end of the branch's life, facilities at Clevedon were reduced to that illustrated in this view of single-car diesel unit No 55032 departing with a service to Yatton in July 1966. *Andrew Muckley*

The 1899 map inset shows:

Linne Dhubh
Highest Point to which Ordinary Spring Tides flow
Well
Recreation Room
Free Ch.
Falls of Lora Hotel
Standing Stone (Site of)
Cattle Pens
Station
W.M.
School
M u

[1899]

70

Taken looking eastwards, this view shows Connel Ferry station as it was on 19 June 1956, with footbridge, water column, station buildings and, on the left-hand platform, the starter signal for the Ballachulish branch. *M. A. Arnold*

Connel Ferry

Situated on the line to Oban, Connel Ferry was once the junction from the branch to Ballachulish. The Callander & Oban Railway opened its route from Dalmally to Oban on 30 June 1880. Although the C&OR was operated by the Caledonian Railway, when it came to the promotion of the branch northwards, the C&O originally contemplated operation by its own stock, although this never occurred. The line to Ballachulish was authorised in 1897, theoretically to connect with a North British line from Fort William (which was never, in fact, constructed), and was opened on 24 August 1903. One of the major engineering features of the branch was the bridge at Connel Ferry, visible on the extreme right of this photograph. The line to Ballachulish was to close completely on 28 March 1966 and, subsequently, the railway bridge was modified to take road transport. As can be seen in the aerial photograph, although Connel Ferry was (and still is) an operational passenger station, its facilities have been reduced to a single track with the removal of the passing loop. Limited freight facilities, as evinced by the two tank wagons, remained, however.

13 September 1972 (A246286)

Also in June 1956, two 'Black 5s', Nos 44721 and 45153, are seen arriving with a passenger train from Oban to Glasgow. In the adjacent platform can be seen ex-CR Class 2P 0-4-4T No 55215 awaiting departure with a service to Ballachulish. Note, adjacent to the Ballachulish train, two men with a small roller engaged in repairing the platform. *Ian Allan Library*

Corfe Castle

The branch line through Corfe Castle to Swanage was opened by the Swanage Railway on 20 May 1885 and passed to the London & South Western Railway the following year. Control passed to the Southern Railway in 1923 and to British Railways (Southern Region) in 1948. Although there were industries around Corfe Castle, linked by tramways to a point slightly north of the station, it was the boom in seaside holidays, particularly fostered from the 1930s by the Southern Railway, that led to the significant growth in passenger traffic over the line. Overshadowed by the castle, Corfe Castle was the only intermediate station on the line from Wareham. It was provided with a stone-built station building, small goods shed and signalbox. Freight facilities were withdrawn from Corfe Castle on 20 September 1965. With the closure of the signalbox at Swanage on 6 June 1967 along with the introduction of DEMUs on the branch, the section south of Corfe Castle was operated on the one engine in steam principle. Through carriages to Waterloo were withdrawn from 3 October 1969 and the branch was to close completely with the withdrawal of passenger services on 3 January 1972. After closure, the track was lifted south of Furzebrook, although the establishment of a preservation scheme at Swanage held out hope that services would be reintroduced at some stage. The official reopening of the line through Corfe Castle to Norden occurred in February 1996 and, in 2002, following the completion of the connection at Furzebrook, the first train from the national network in 30 years operated to Swanage.

4 May 1963 (A49047)

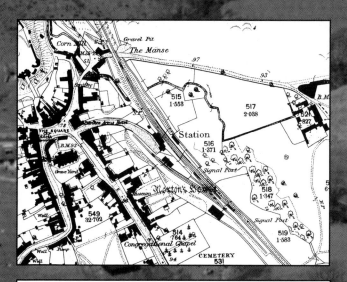

Ex-LSWR Class M7 0-4-4T No 30107 is seen at Corfe Castle in this 1963 view propelling the down service towards Swanage. *SLS Collection*

Taken at the same time as the previous photograph, this view taken looking northwards shows to good effect the station as it existed in the early 1960s. Dominated by the castle in the background, this scene can be easily recreated today courtesy of the now preserved Swanage Railway. *SLS Collection*

73

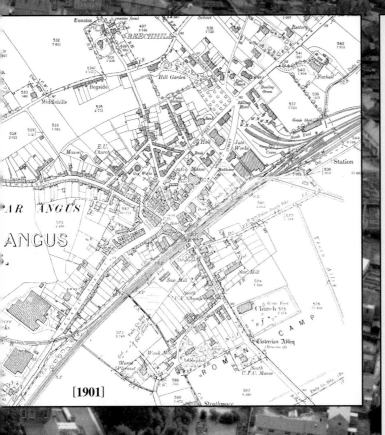

[1901]

Coupar Angus

Strathmore, the area of rich agricultural land between Perth and the North Sea coast and north of the Sidlaw Hills, formed an obvious and prosperous alignment for the development of the main line from central Scotland towards Aberdeen. Although Dundee was the region's main centre, it was separated from the rich hinterland by the Sidlaw Hills and, although it was the destination of the early Dundee & Newtyle Railway, the main axis for development in the region was east-west, through towns such as Coupar Angus and Forfar. Viewed looking westwards, the aerial photograph shows the ex-Caledonian main line heading westwards with, in the middle distance, the junction for the branch to Blairgowrie. The branch opened in 1855 and was to survive until 10 January 1955 (passenger traffic) and 6 December 1965 (freight). The first railway to Coupar was an extension of the Dundee & Newtyle line that opened in February 1837 under the auspices of the Newtyle & Coupar Angus Railway, although its construction was poor. The line from the west opened on 20 August 1848 under the aegis of the Scottish Midland Junction Railway, a concern that also took over and upgraded the original N&CAR line. For many years the route through Coupar represented the main line between Glasgow and Aberdeen and was also to feature in the 'Railway Races to North' in the late 19th century when the North British and Caledonian railways competed, along with their English partners, to provide the fastest services between London and Aberdeen. However, rationalisation in the 1960s saw passenger services withdrawn between Stanley Junction and Kinnaber Junction, via Coupar Angus, on 4 September 1967. The line, now singled, was retained between Stanley Junction and Forfar for freight until 5 June 1982, when freight facilities were withdrawn from Coupar as well.
27 June 1963 (A115923)

On 31 May 1966, towards the end of Scottish Region steam, 'Black 5' No 44997 shunts the yard at Coupar Angus after arriving with a freight from Perth. *C. W. R. Bowman*

Shortly after Nationalisation comes this view of ex-GWR '14xx' 0-4-2T No 1421 at Cowbridge station with its single coach. Although post 1948, the signage remains vintage GWR. *SLS Collection*

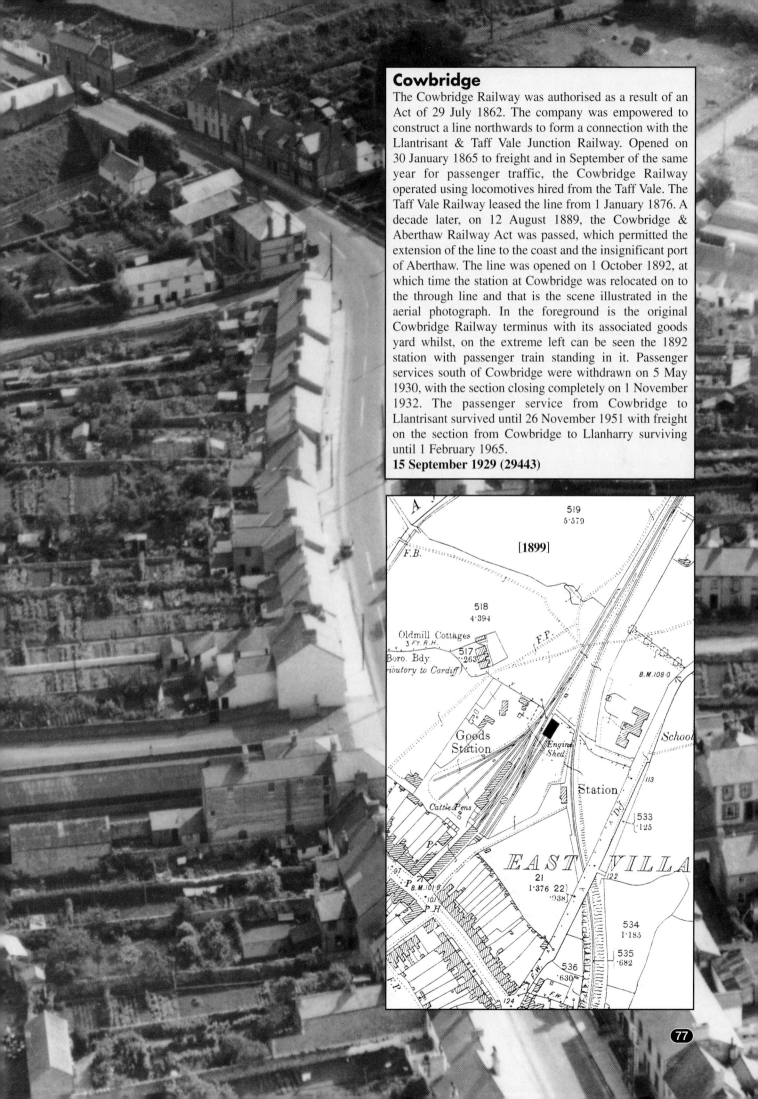

Cowbridge

The Cowbridge Railway was authorised as a result of an Act of 29 July 1862. The company was empowered to construct a line northwards to form a connection with the Llantrisant & Taff Vale Junction Railway. Opened on 30 January 1865 to freight and in September of the same year for passenger traffic, the Cowbridge Railway operated using locomotives hired from the Taff Vale. The Taff Vale Railway leased the line from 1 January 1876. A decade later, on 12 August 1889, the Cowbridge & Aberthaw Railway Act was passed, which permitted the extension of the line to the coast and the insignificant port of Aberthaw. The line was opened on 1 October 1892, at which time the station at Cowbridge was relocated on to the through line and that is the scene illustrated in the aerial photograph. In the foreground is the original Cowbridge Railway terminus with its associated goods yard whilst, on the extreme left can be seen the 1892 station with passenger train standing in it. Passenger services south of Cowbridge were withdrawn on 5 May 1930, with the section closing completely on 1 November 1932. The passenger service from Cowbridge to Llantrisant survived until 26 November 1951 with freight on the section from Cowbridge to Llanharry surviving until 1 February 1965.
15 September 1929 (29443)

Cowes

Cowes station was located a short distance from the ferry pier that provided a connection to Southampton. The station, as clearly shown in the aerial view, was provided with curved platforms and small goods yard. The footbridge was provided to maintain a public right of way rather than for passenger use. Under it was a crossover, the only means of facilitating a locomotive release; this often resulted, therefore, in the unofficial practice of gravity shunting to enable the locomotive to run round its train. The Cowes & Newport Railway was the first line to be authorised (on 8 August 1859) to serve the Isle of Wight; it was opened on 16 June 1862 to passenger traffic. The line was amalgamated into the Isle of Wight Central Railway on 1 July 1887, before passing to the Southern Railway at Grouping. Passenger services to Cowes were withdrawn on 21 February 1966 and freight on the following 16 May. Today, the whole station site has been redeveloped.

14 July 1959 (A77251)

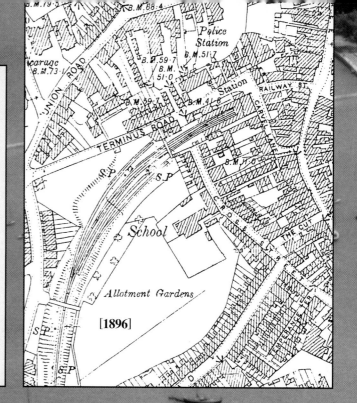

[1896]

Class O2 0-4-4T No W28 *Ashey* is pictured on arrival at Cowes station on Saturday 19 February 1966. *Graham S. Cocks*

A panoramic view of 'O2' No W31 *Chale* departing from Cowes shows to good effect the country end of Cowes station and signalbox. *P. J. Sharpe*

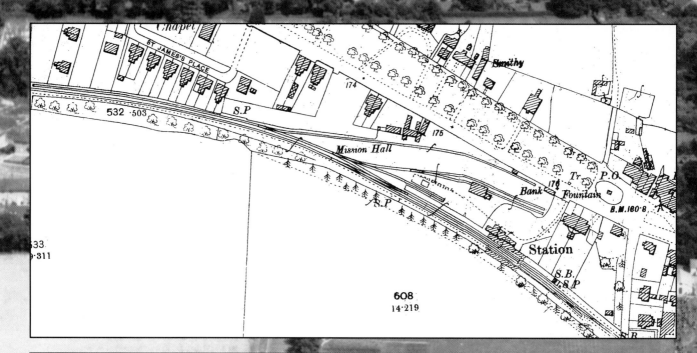

Heading northwards on the 3.9pm service from Horsham to Guildford, Ivatt Class 2 2-6-2T No 41230 pauses at Cranleigh on 5 April 1963. *Neil Caplan*

On 10 October 1964 the 9.8am service from Guildford to Baynards stands at Cranleigh headed by 'Q1' class 0-6-0 No 33012. *W. G. Sumner*

Cranleigh

One of the intermediate stations on the line between Guildford and Christ's Hospital, Cranleigh was provided with passenger and freight facilities as evinced in this aerial view taken in the early 1950s. The line through Cranleigh was promoted by the Horsham & Guildford Direct Railway, which was incorporated in the 1860s for the construction of the 15.5-mile long line. The company was sold to the London, Brighton & South Coast Railway in 1864, prior to the line's opening on 2 October 1865. Freight facilities were withdrawn from Cranleigh on 10 September 1962 and the line was to lose its passenger services on 14 June 1965 at which time it was closed completely.

15 July 1953 (A50730)

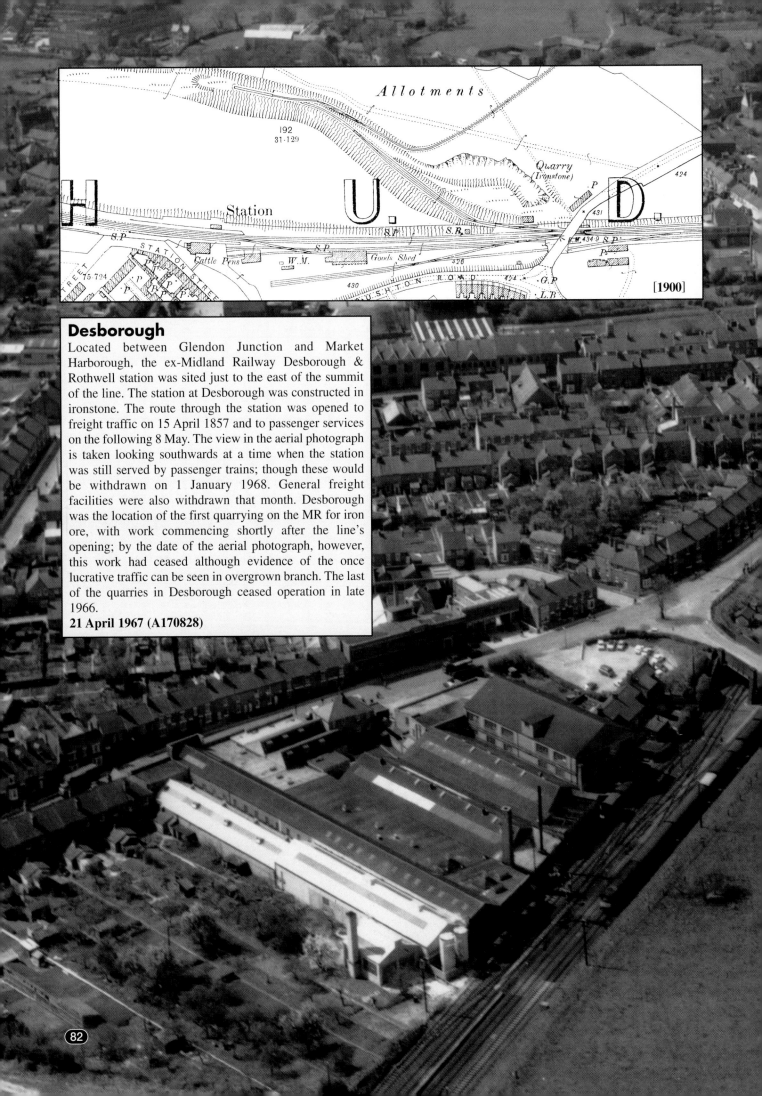

[1900]

Desborough

Located between Glendon Junction and Market Harborough, the ex-Midland Railway Desborough & Rothwell station was sited just to the east of the summit of the line. The station at Desborough was constructed in ironstone. The route through the station was opened to freight traffic on 15 April 1857 and to passenger services on the following 8 May. The view in the aerial photograph is taken looking southwards at a time when the station was still served by passenger trains; though these would be withdrawn on 1 January 1968. General freight facilities were also withdrawn that month. Desborough was the location of the first quarrying on the MR for iron ore, with work commencing shortly after the line's opening; by the date of the aerial photograph, however, this work had ceased although evidence of the once lucrative traffic can be seen in overgrown branch. The last of the quarries in Desborough ceased operation in late 1966.

21 April 1967 (A170828)

On 21 April 1965 Class 8F 2-8-0 No 48609 climbs towards Desborough station with a down iron ore train. *P. F. Fleming*

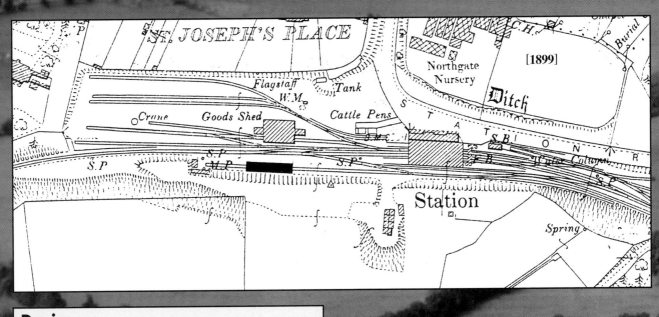

St. Joseph's Place ... *Flagstaff* ... *Tank* ... *W.M.* ... *Northgate Nursery* ... *Ditch* ... *[1899]* ... *Crane* ... *Goods Shed* ... *Cattle Pens* ... *S.P.* ... *M.P.* ... *S.P.* ... *Station* ... *Spring*

Devizes

Bypassed by the original Great Western Railway main line and thwarted during the Railway Mania of the 1840s, it was not until 1 July 1857 that Devizes joined the railway network with the opening of the branch from Holt Junction (on the Chippenham-Westbury line). The line was extended from Devizes to Patney & Chirton (on the Westbury-Reading line) on 11 November 1862. The route was constructed as a single track with loops. Devizes, with a population at the time of some 5,000, was the major intermediate station on the line. The total length of the route, from Holt Junction to Patney & Chirton was about eight miles and the line was originally constructed as broad gauge, being converted to standard gauge over the weekend of 28 June 1874. The station building originally possessed an overall roof, although this was replaced with the platform canopies and footbridge as illustrated in the aerial photograph at some time between 1892 and 1920. Other facilities included a goods shed, signal box and shed. With the opening of the Berks & Hants route as a main line from Patney to Westbury in 1900, the line via Devizes reverted to a branch having been a secondary main line since 1862. Freight facilities were withdrawn from Devizes on 2 November 1964 and passenger services ceased on 18 April 1966, at which time the line closed completely.

27 August 1962 (A104643)

By 2 April 1966, when this photograph was taken, passenger services on the line through Devizes were about to be withdrawn and there is already evidence of rationalisation, with the boarded up signalbox. Here a three-car DMU awaits departure with the 09.46 service from Trowbridge to Patney & Chirton. *O. H. Prosser*

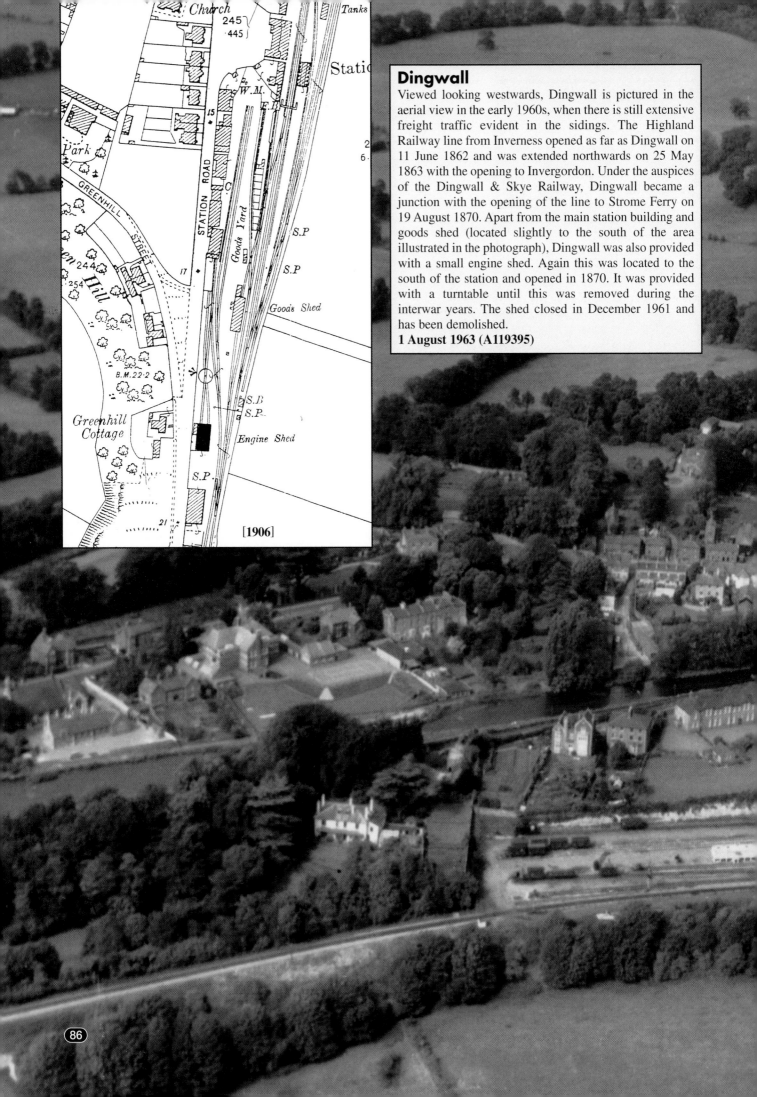

Dingwall

Viewed looking westwards, Dingwall is pictured in the aerial view in the early 1960s, when there is still extensive freight traffic evident in the sidings. The Highland Railway line from Inverness opened as far as Dingwall on 11 June 1862 and was extended northwards on 25 May 1863 with the opening to Invergordon. Under the auspices of the Dingwall & Skye Railway, Dingwall became a junction with the opening of the line to Strome Ferry on 19 August 1870. Apart from the main station building and goods shed (located slightly to the south of the area illustrated in the photograph), Dingwall was also provided with a small engine shed. Again this was located to the south of the station and opened in 1870. It was provided with a turntable until this was removed during the interwar years. The shed closed in December 1961 and has been demolished.

1 August 1963 (A119395)

[1906]

In July 1955 'Black 5' No 44788 heads south through Dingwall station with an early morning service from Wick. *Ian Allan Library*

On 8 June 1983 Class 37 No 37085 arrives at Dingwall with the 11.40 service for Wick and Thurso. *Nigel Hunt*

[1926]

Eye

Authorised on 5 July 1865, the Mellis & Eye Railway opened on 2 April 1867. Worked from the start by the Great Eastern Railway, the line passed to the LNER in 1923 and to British Railways (Eastern Region) in 1948. Whilst efforts were made to effect cost savings, these were inadequate and passenger services were withdrawn from 2 February 1931. Freight, however, continued for a further 30 years, with much of the traffic reflecting the agricultural bias of the local economy. Final closure came on 13 July 1964.

26 August 1953 (A51610)

This view of Eye, taken in the early 1920s, shows a two-coach train standing in the platform with a guards van beyond. The collection of enamel signs is impressive as is the number of milk churns. *SLS Collection*

By the time that this view of the station building was taken in 1950, Eye had been freight-only for almost 20 years. The station building remained intact although there had been some modifications. Freight trains would continue to serve this terminus for a further 14 years. *Ian Allan Library*

Faringdon

The short — 3.5 mile — branch from Uffington to Faringdon opened on 1 June 1864. The line was promoted locally in order to try and exploit the rich agricultural area surrounding. Originally built for broad-gauge services, it was converted to standard gauge in 1878 and was taken over by the Great Western Railway eight years later. The station was provided with an engine shed, goods shed and signalbox as well as a small ground frame. By the date of the aerial photograph, the line had already lost its passenger services, which had been withdrawn on 31 December 1951. The line was to be closed completely on 1 July 1963.

18 August 1955 (R25375)

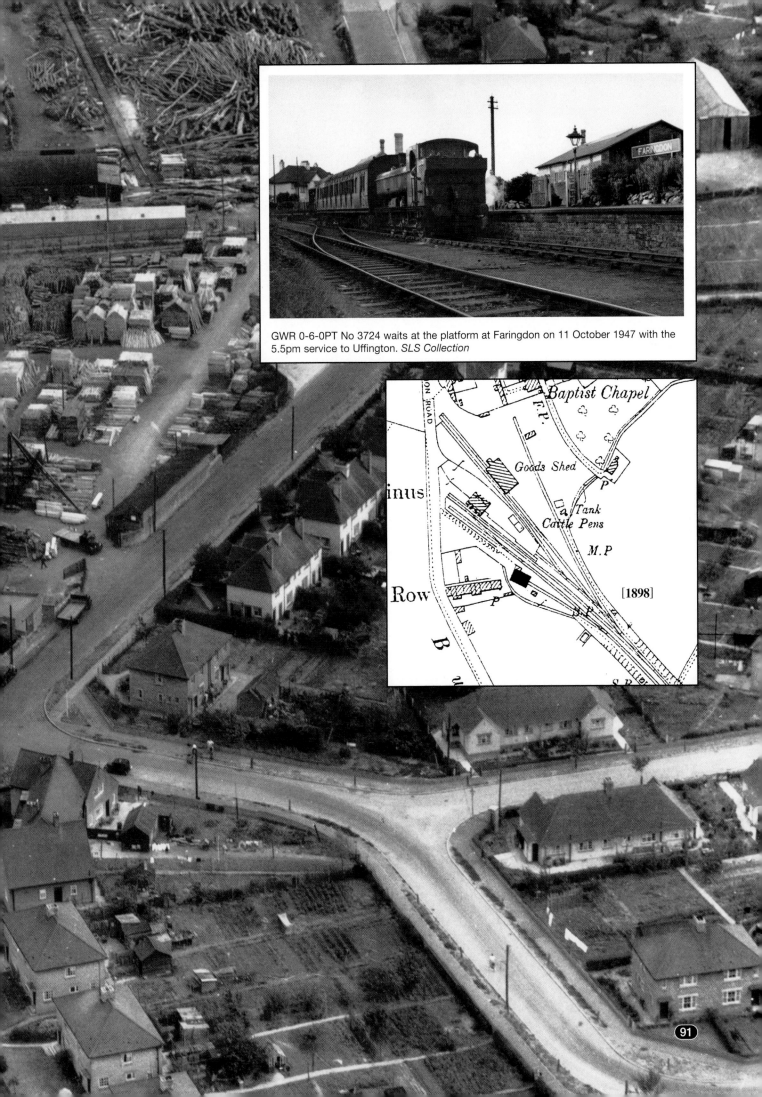

GWR 0-6-0PT No 3724 waits at the platform at Faringdon on 11 October 1947 with the 5.5pm service to Uffington. *SLS Collection*

Baptist Chapel

F.P.

Goods Shed

Tank

Cattle Pens

M.P

[1898]

inus

Row

P

P

91

Frome

The Wilts, Somerset & Weymouth Railway, which was absorbed by the Great Western on 14 March 1850, was authorised in 1845 to construct a line from Thingley Junction to Weymouth. It opened from Thingley to Westbury on 5 September 1848, but it was not until 7 October 1850 that a single track was opened from Westbury to Frome. The branch to Radstock was opened on 14 November 1854 to freight (passenger traffic did not commence until 1875) and, on 1 September 1856, a single track was opened between Frome and Yeovil. The lines were originally broad gauge but were subsequently converted to standard; Westbury-Frome was doubled in 1874 and thence to Yeovil seven years later. The aerial photograph shows Frome station in the late 1920s; this predates the opening of the cut-off route, in early 1933, which resulted in the replacement of the existing South and Middle boxes by a new South box located at the north end of the down platform. As is shown in the photographs, Frome was provided with an overall roof; this was designed by J. R. Hannaford, one of Brunel's assistants, which is now one of the last surviving ex-GWR train sheds still in railway use. Apart from a goods shed, Frome was also provided with a small PW Department and engine shed which was opened in 1854 and rebuilt in 1890; it was to survive until closure by BR in September 1963.

21 June 1929 (27741)

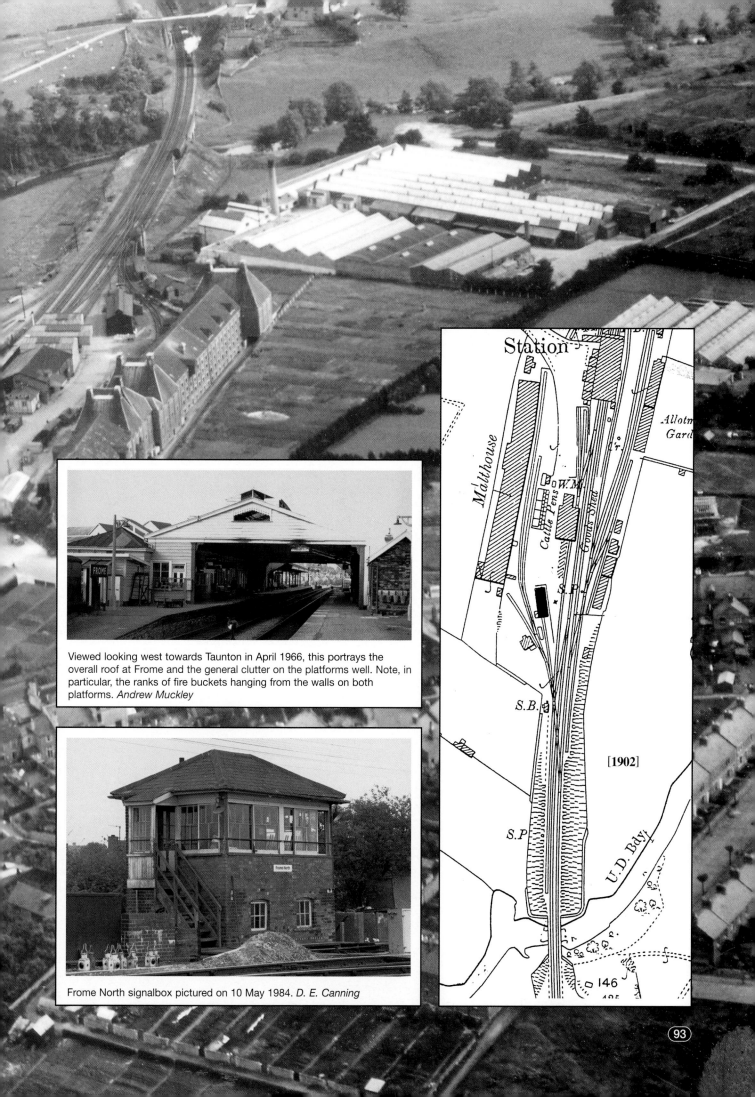

Viewed looking west towards Taunton in April 1966, this portrays the overall roof at Frome and the general clutter on the platforms well. Note, in particular, the ranks of fire buckets hanging from the walls on both platforms. *Andrew Muckley*

Frome North signalbox pictured on 10 May 1984. *D. E. Canning*

Station

Malthouse

Cattle Pens

W.M.

Goods Shed

Allotm Gard

S.P.

S.B.

[1902]

S.P.

U.D. Bdy

146

By the date that this photograph was taken looking northwards, on 9 June 1968, Galashiels station on the Waverley route was earmarked for closure in January 1969. Through the footbridge can just be determined the signalbox at the north end of the station. *Andrew Muckley*

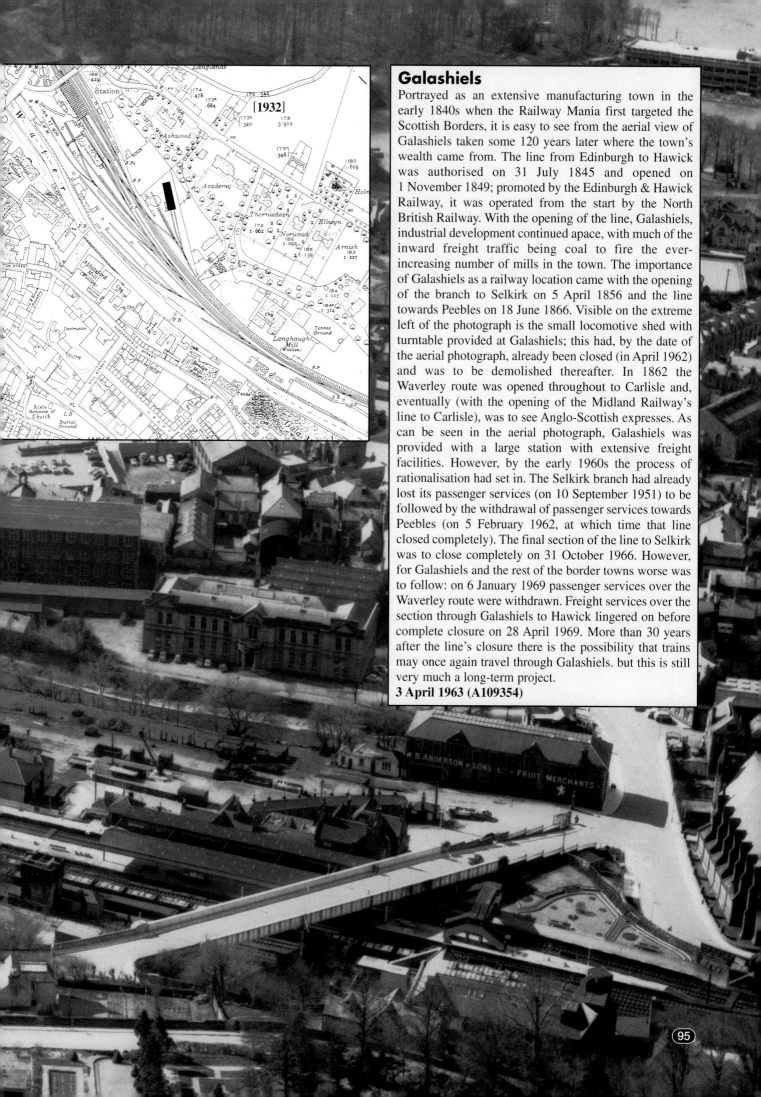

Galashiels

Portrayed as an extensive manufacturing town in the early 1840s when the Railway Mania first targeted the Scottish Borders, it is easy to see from the aerial view of Galashiels taken some 120 years later where the town's wealth came from. The line from Edinburgh to Hawick was authorised on 31 July 1845 and opened on 1 November 1849; promoted by the Edinburgh & Hawick Railway, it was operated from the start by the North British Railway. With the opening of the line, Galashiels, industrial development continued apace, with much of the inward freight traffic being coal to fire the ever-increasing number of mills in the town. The importance of Galashiels as a railway location came with the opening of the branch to Selkirk on 5 April 1856 and the line towards Peebles on 18 June 1866. Visible on the extreme left of the photograph is the small locomotive shed with turntable provided at Galashiels; this had, by the date of the aerial photograph, already been closed (in April 1962) and was to be demolished thereafter. In 1862 the Waverley route was opened throughout to Carlisle and, eventually (with the opening of the Midland Railway's line to Carlisle), was to see Anglo-Scottish expresses. As can be seen in the aerial photograph, Galashiels was provided with a large station with extensive freight facilities. However, by the early 1960s the process of rationalisation had set in. The Selkirk branch had already lost its passenger services (on 10 September 1951) to be followed by the withdrawal of passenger services towards Peebles (on 5 February 1962, at which time that line closed completely). The final section of the line to Selkirk was to close completely on 31 October 1966. However, for Galashiels and the rest of the border towns worse was to follow: on 6 January 1969 passenger services over the Waverley route were withdrawn. Freight services over the section through Galashiels to Hawick lingered on before complete closure on 28 April 1969. More than 30 years after the line's closure there is the possibility that trains may once again travel through Galashiels. but this is still very much a long-term project.

3 April 1963 (A109354)

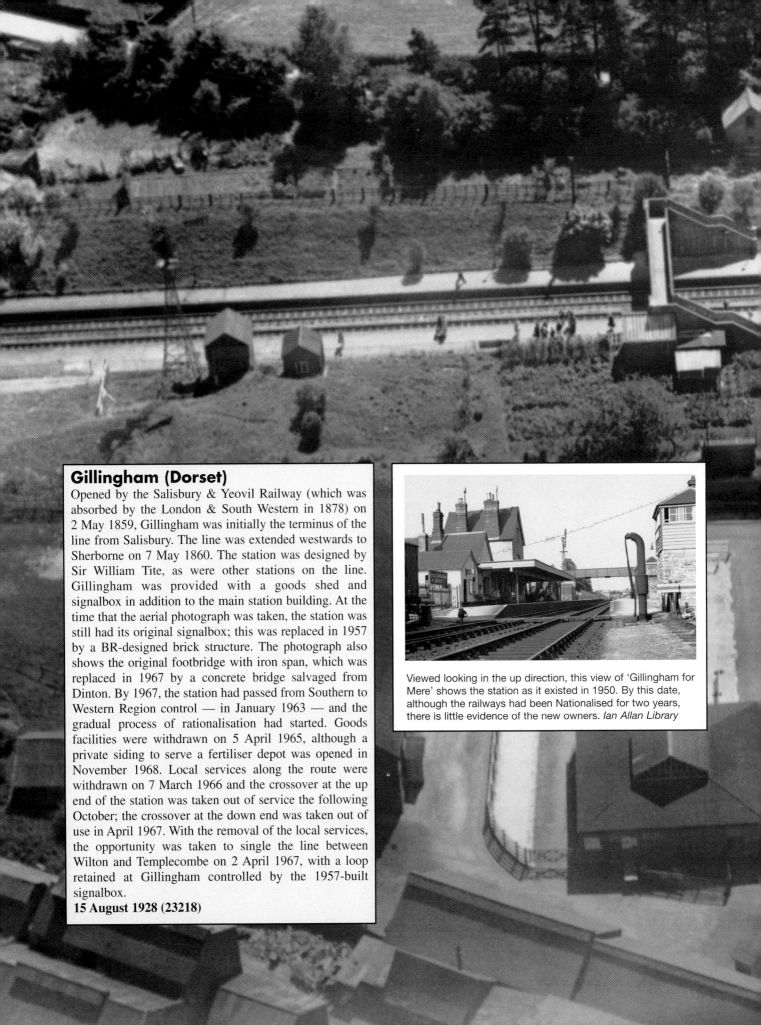

Gillingham (Dorset)

Opened by the Salisbury & Yeovil Railway (which was absorbed by the London & South Western in 1878) on 2 May 1859, Gillingham was initially the terminus of the line from Salisbury. The line was extended westwards to Sherborne on 7 May 1860. The station was designed by Sir William Tite, as were other stations on the line. Gillingham was provided with a goods shed and signalbox in addition to the main station building. At the time that the aerial photograph was taken, the station was still had its original signalbox; this was replaced in 1957 by a BR-designed brick structure. The photograph also shows the original footbridge with iron span, which was replaced in 1967 by a concrete bridge salvaged from Dinton. By 1967, the station had passed from Southern to Western Region control — in January 1963 — and the gradual process of rationalisation had started. Goods facilities were withdrawn on 5 April 1965, although a private siding to serve a fertiliser depot was opened in November 1968. Local services along the route were withdrawn on 7 March 1966 and the crossover at the up end of the station was taken out of service the following October; the crossover at the down end was taken out of use in April 1967. With the removal of the local services, the opportunity was taken to single the line between Wilton and Templecombe on 2 April 1967, with a loop retained at Gillingham controlled by the 1957-built signalbox.

15 August 1928 (23218)

Viewed looking in the up direction, this view of 'Gillingham for Mere' shows the station as it existed in 1950. By this date, although the railways had been Nationalised for two years, there is little evidence of the new owners. *Ian Allan Library*

It is May 1967 and a three-car DMU waits at the station with a up service towards Salisbury. *SLS Collection*

Glenfarg

Located to the south of Perth, Glenfarg was one of the intermediate stations on the former North British main line between Perth and Edinburgh via Kinross. The aerial view shows the neat station, with small goods shed, looking westwards. At this point, and through the steeply-sided valley of the River Farg, the railway ran parallel to the main A90(T), which can be seen — remarkably devoid of traffic — behind the station building. The impetus for the construction of the line through Glenfarg came with the opening on 4 March 1890 of the Forth Bridge, and the potential for improved links with Perth that the bridge offered. However, construction delays in Glenfarg, to the north of the station (where two tunnels needed to be constructed), resulted in the new main line not being opened until two months later, on 4 May 1890. Although the line was to be closed completely with the withdrawal of through passenger services between Edinburgh and Perth and of freight services between Bridge of Earn and Milnathort, Glenfarg had in fact closed slightly after the date of the aerial photograph: passenger facilities were withdrawn on 15 June 1964 and freight on 21 June 1965.

9 October 1963 (A122362)

[1895]

459

S.P

Und.

S.B

Smithy
465

S.P

357
.538

P.

P.

P.

C.R.

P.

354
1.642

6.396

471

P.

302
.331

301

W.M.

300
.148

S.P
490

Und.

B.M. 476.3
303
.750

475

297 15.761

.328

S.P

P.

Police Sta.
299

Sta

ary

99

In the late 1980s, the Italianate station building at Gobowen underwent major refurbishment. Work is in progress when this photograph was taken on 14 September 1988. *Steve Turner*

Gobowen

Viewed looking northeastwards, the junction station at Gobowen is situated on the ex-Great Western line from Shrewsbury to Chester and provides the junction for the ex-GWR line towards Oswestry. The Shrewsbury & Chester Railway was opened on 12 October 1848 and Gobowen station was one of the intermediate stations opened at that time; the station, which survives today, was constructed in an Italianate style. The branch to Oswestry opened on 23 December 1848. As can be seen in the aerial view, Gobowen was provided with two signalboxes and freight facilities; the latter were withdrawn on 2 November 1964. Passenger services between Gobowen and Oswestry were withdrawn on 7 November 1966, although the line remained open for traffic to and from the quarry at Blodwell until the late 1980s when it was mothballed. The track remains in situ and is the subject of a preservation scheme based at Oswestry.

27 June 1956 (R27217)

Viewed looking southwards, with the line to Oswestry heading off to the west in the distance, Class 25 No 25199 heads into the station with a rake of empty ballast wagons. The locomotive was about to run round the wagons before taking the Oswestry branch towards Blodwell Junction. *M. H. Hughes*

[1900]

BR Standard Class 2MT No 78020 stands at Godmanchester with a westbound service towards Huntingdon. The view shows to good effect the staggered platform and footbridge arrangement. *SLS Collection*

Godmanchester

Situated slightly to the east of Huntingdon and on the River Great Ouse, Godmanchester station was in fact significantly closer to Huntingdon than it was to the settlement it purported to serve. The line from St Ives to Godmanchester, which was known as 'Huntingdon' until 1 July 1882, opened under the aegis of the Ely & Huntingdon Railway on 17 August 1847, which became part of the East Anglian Railways in the same year. The line was extended to meet up with the new Great Northern main line at Huntingdon on 29 October 1851, but the connection was little used, but the line westwards was to be linked up to an extension of the Midland Railway route from Kettering, which opened on 21 February 1866, by which date the EAR had been incorporated into the Great Eastern Railway. From 1 May 1883 the old Ely & Huntingdon line was transferred to form part of the Great Northern & Great Eastern Joint line and thus passed to the LNER in 1923 and the British Railways (Eastern Region) in 1948. In 1947 there were seven services per day (Mondays to Saturdays) between St Ives and Huntingdon East (three being designated LMS) and eight from Huntingdon eastwards (seven on Saturdays; again three being designated LMS). By the date of the aerial photograph, passenger services between St Ives and Huntingdon East had been withdrawn (on 15 June 1959) and the line had been closed completely east of Godmanchester at the same time. Freight continued to serve Godmanchester, as evinced by the coal wagons in the photograph, from the west until complete closure came on 4 June 1962.

20 October 1959 (A79328)

[1900]

Boat House

Sicing Bridge

DOCK

Mill House

Corn
Mill

Pier

B.M.44·8

Boat House

Inn

Boat Slip

P.H.

Boat House

Cattle Pen

S.B.

S.P.

P

Goods Shed

S.P.

S.P

W.M.

Godmanchester
Station

ROMAN ROAD

STREET

W   e   s   t   s   i

L   i   a   b   l   e

493
5·192

103

Hadleigh station seen on 29 March 1937, viewed looking towards the buffer stops.
SLS Collection

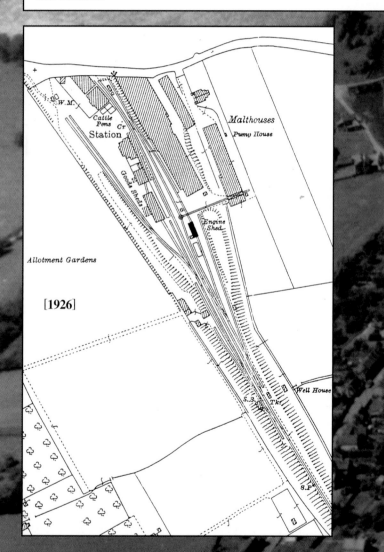

W.M.

Cattle Pens

Station

Cr

Malthouses

Pump House

Goods Shed

Engine Shed

Allotment Gardens

[1926]

Well House

S.B. Tkt

S.P.

The exterior of the station taken towards the end of its operational life showing well the architectural style of the building and the extent that the site was overshadowed by the adjacent factory. *SLS Collection*

Hadleigh

Promoted by the Eastern Union & Hadleigh Junction Railway, the seven-mile long line received its Royal Assent on 18 June 1846, being opened throughout from the junction at Bentley on 21 August 1847 to freight traffic and to passenger services on the following 2 September. The line was operated by the Eastern Union (later the Great Eastern Railway) from opening, being formally absorbed by the EUR in 1848, and passing to the LNER in 1923 and to British Railways (Eastern Region) in 1948. The line was another to lose its passenger services during the early 1930s, with the last passenger train operating on Saturday 27 February 1932. Passenger traffic was transferred to a replacement bus service. Freight traffic was, however, still carried and two workings per day were still timetabled in the mid-1950s serving the branch. Freight services continued serving the town's malting and other businesses until complete closure on 15 April 1965, by which date freight duties had been dieselised, with Brush Type 2 No D5699 hauling the last working.
26 July 1956 (R27577)

Halifax North Bridge

Although Halifax is still served by trains on the Calder Valley route between Bradford and Manchester, there was a second passenger station serving the town centre — North Bridge. This station was situated on the Halifax & Ovenden Junction Railway. This route was authorised by an act of 30 June 1864, with work commencing almost immediately, However, shortage of funds led work to be suspended in 1867 and this was not resumed until after 1870 when the line was vested in the Lancashire & Yorkshire and Great Northern railways. Further delays meant that the line did not open to North Bridge (for freight) until 17 August 1874 and thence to Holmfield on the following 1 September. Passenger services over the route commenced in mid-December 1879, with the commencement of GNR services over the route from Holmfield to Bradford via Queensbury. GNR services were later extended from Queensbury to Keighley. North Bridge station was opened for passenger services from 25 March 1880. From Holmfield, there was also the H&OJR line to St Pauls, which opened in 1890. North Bridge possessed both passenger and freight facilities, but the major source of traffic for the latter came from the private siding that served the Crossley carpet factory at Dean Clough. Passenger services over the Queensbury triangle routes ceased on 23 May 1955 (although those from St Pauls to Holmfield had ceased in 1917). The line beyond Holmfield to Queensbury closed completely on 28 May 1956. Freight continued through North Bridge to St Pauls until 27 June 1960. North Bridge, however, retained freight facilities, served from the Halifax-Bradford line over the viaduct, until 1 April 1974. The impressive viaduct linking the two stations was demolished in the early 1980s.

24 September 1931 (36893)

A view along the single platform looking towards the signalbox and level crossing. The extensive goods facilities provided at this location were sited behind the photographer. *SLS Collection*

HALSTEAD

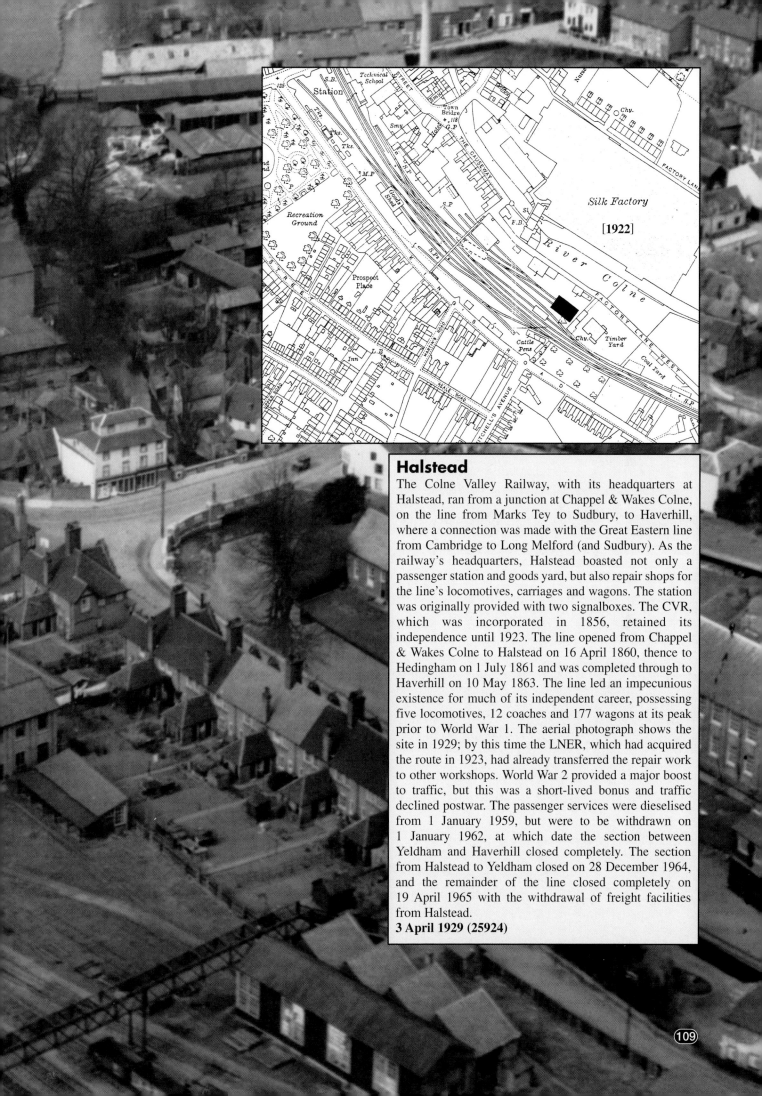

[1922]

Silk Factory

Halstead

The Colne Valley Railway, with its headquarters at Halstead, ran from a junction at Chappel & Wakes Colne, on the line from Marks Tey to Sudbury, to Haverhill, where a connection was made with the Great Eastern line from Cambridge to Long Melford (and Sudbury). As the railway's headquarters, Halstead boasted not only a passenger station and goods yard, but also repair shops for the line's locomotives, carriages and wagons. The station was originally provided with two signalboxes. The CVR, which was incorporated in 1856, retained its independence until 1923. The line opened from Chappel & Wakes Colne to Halstead on 16 April 1860, thence to Hedingham on 1 July 1861 and was completed through to Haverhill on 10 May 1863. The line led an impecunious existence for much of its independent career, possessing five locomotives, 12 coaches and 177 wagons at its peak prior to World War 1. The aerial photograph shows the site in 1929; by this time the LNER, which had acquired the route in 1923, had already transferred the repair work to other workshops. World War 2 provided a major boost to traffic, but this was a short-lived bonus and traffic declined postwar. The passenger services were dieselised from 1 January 1959, but were to be withdrawn on 1 January 1962, at which date the section between Yeldham and Haverhill closed completely. The section from Halstead to Yeldham closed on 28 December 1964, and the remainder of the line closed completely on 19 April 1965 with the withdrawal of freight facilities from Halstead.

3 April 1929 (25924)

Haltwhistle

Viewed looking northeastwards, this aerial photograph shows the station of Haltwhistle in Northumberland, situated on the line between Newcastle and Carlisle and the location of the junction for the branch to Alston. The main line was authorised as the Newcastle & Carlisle Railway by an Act of 22 May 1829 and the section through Haltwhistle, from Greenhead to Haydon Bridge, was the final section of the through route to be completed, being opened on 18 June 1838. The line to Alston was originally authorised in 1846 but these plans were amended three years later and it was not until 17 November 1852 that the branch was opened. The North Eastern Railway took over the N&CR in 1862. One of the factors in the construction of both the main line and the Alston branch was the coal industry and evidence of the extensive sidings provided at Haltwhistle for this traffic can be clearly seen in the aerial photograph. Also clearly visible are the three platform faces of the station, signalbox at the eastern end of the station and goods shed. Although the Alston branch served a town regularly cut off by bad weather during the winter, the construction of a supposedly all-weather road in the early 1970s brought about the branch's closure; passenger services were withdrawn on 3 May 1976, freight services having been withdrawn earlier. Haltwhistle continues to provide facilities for the DMU services between Newcastle and Carlisle.

7 October 1962 (A107673)

On 19 February 1972 two DMUs are seen at Haltwhistle: heading eastbound is a service from Carlisle to Newcastle, whilst a two-car unit awaits departure with a branch line train to Alston. *Derek Cross*

Four years later and the Alston branch is approaching its finale. On 23 April 1976 the 16.30 service from Newcastle to Carlisle heads westbound whilst the 17.46 departure to Alston. With the semaphore signalling, manual signalbox and water column, the scene could have been taken decades earlier; only the presence of the DMUs and the track rationalisation show that it is a more modern view. *L. A. Nixon*

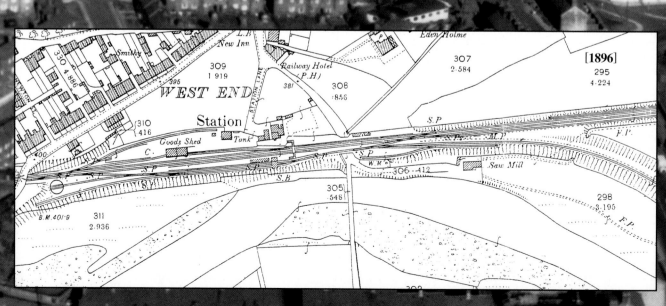

111

A view taken looking southwards showing the station after its wartime reconstruction. Notice the second platform and wartime signalbox. *SLS Collection*

Hampstead Norris

Located between Didcot and Newbury on the Didcot, Newbury & Southampton line, Hampstead Norris opened on 13 April 1882. The line, as built, was constructed as a single track and, as illustrated in the aerial photograph, Hampstead Norris was provided with a single platform and a small goods shed. However, the formation was constructed with sufficient space for the provision of double track, if required, and during World War 2, with the DN&S providing a major route between the Midlands and South Coast, this work was undertaken. The station was modified in May 1943 with the line being doubled and a second, down, platform being constructed. The new platform was constructed of reinforced concrete; a small waiting shelter was added subsequently. The wartime work also included the replacement of the original signalbox. As a result of the work involved in doubling the line, the station was temporarily closed between August 1942 and March 1943. Although the DN&SR had proved itself invaluable during the war, postwar traffic declined and passenger services through Hampstead Norris ceased on 10 September 1962. Freight facilities were withdrawn on 10 August 1964 when the line between Didcot and Newbury closed completely.

14 September 1929 (29277)

On 1 April 1961, ex-GWR 2-6-2T No 6156 is pictured at Hampstead Norris with the 5.40pm (SO) service from Newbury to Didcot. *R. F. Roberts/SLS Collection*

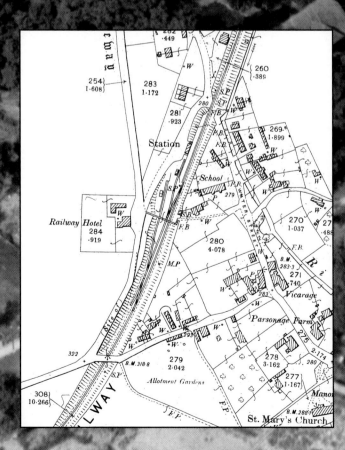

Havant

Viewed looking northeastwards, Havant station is seen in the aerial view in the late 1920s before the station was considerably rebuilt by the Southern Region. A four-coach train, plus a van, can be seen in the up platform although the bay for services to Hayling Island is unoccupied. Whilst Havant was a London, Brighton & South Coast station, the London & South Western Railway had running powers in order to access Portsmouth from the line through Guildford; the exercise of running powers did, however, on occasion lead to friction between the two railways. The first line to reach Havant was the LBSCR from Chichester, a route which opened on 15 March 1847 and from Havant to Portsmouth on 14 June 1847; the station seen in the aerial photograph is the second station built to serve the town, opening in 1863, on a slightly different site. The LSWR route from Guildford, authorised in 1853, was opened on 28 December 1858. The last addition to the local railway network was the Hayling Island branch. This was incorporated as the Hayling Railway Co in 1860 and opened on 17 July 1867. The LBSCR took over operation of the 4.5-mile long branch on 1 January 1872. The main lines through Havant were electrified during the 1930s: Portsmouth-Guildford on 29 May 1937 and Havant-Chichester on 3 July 1938. The Hayling Island branch, however, remained steam-operated, regular locomotives being the diminutive Stroudley 'Terrier' class 0-6-0Ts. Passenger and freight services were withdrawn from the Hayling Island branch on 4 November 1963 and freight facilities were withdrawn from Havant on 6 January 1969.

1 September 1928 (23038)

On 26 July 1958 a 12-car set, headed by '4-Cor' No 3116 passes eastbound through Havant with a service from Portsmouth to Waterloo. *Colin Boocock*

Hawick station was built partially on a viaduct over the River Teviot as is clearly shown in this view of ex-LNER Class V2 2-6-2 No 60976 heading southbound with a service for Carlisle. Also clearly visible in the distance, poking out above the footbridge, is the unusual Hawick South signalbox. *P. Sunderland*

Viewed looking northwards, this illustrates well another aspect of the station at Hawick: the sharp curve through the platforms. Again visible above (and now below) the footbridge, is Hawick South box. The curve of the station was the result of the realignment of the line through the town when the existing route from Edinburgh to Hawick was extended southwards in the 1860s. *Andrew Muckley*

[1897]

Hawick

The line from Edinburgh to Hawick was authorised on 31 July 1845 and opened on 1 November 1849; promoted by the Edinburgh & Hawick Railway, it was operated from the start by the North British Railway. The Border Union (North British Railway) Act of 21 July 1859 authorised the NBR's building of the line south of Hawick and resulted in the construction of the viaduct through the town and of a replacement passenger station. On 1 July 1862 the Waverley route was opened throughout to Carlisle and, eventually (with the opening of the Midland Railway's line to Carlisle), the route was to see Anglo-Scottish expresses. In addition to the other facilities, Hawick was provided with a small engine shed which was opened on 1 November 1849 and modified by Scottish Region four years after the date of the aerial photograph. The shed was to close on 3 January 1966. On 6 January 1969 passenger services over the Waverley route were withdrawn, but freight services over the section to Hawick survived until complete closure on 28 April 1969. More than 30 years after the line's closure there is the possibility that trains may once again travel over part of the route although this is still very much a long-term project and is compounded in Hawick by the demolition of the viaduct through the town.

30 August 1951 (A139322)

Hay

Now perhaps best known as a location for a huge range of second-hand bookshops, Hay on Wye was served by two pre-Grouping railway companies — the Midland's route between Three Cocks Junction and Hereford and the Great Western's branch from Pontrilas. The first railway to serve Hay was the appropriately-named Hereford, Hay & Brecon Railway, which was incorporated on 8 August 1859, although ultimately it only constructed the section as far as Three Cocks Junction, with the line onward to Talyllyn passing to the Mid-Wales Railway and the Neath & Brecon completing the line to Brecon. The section from Eardisley to Hay opened on 11 July 1864 and from Hay to Three Cocks Junction on the following 19 September. The line was leased by the Midland Railway in 1868 and absorbed by it eight years later. Hay became a junction with the completion of the Golden Valley Railway, which opened from Pontrilas to Dorstone on 1 September 1881 and thence to Hay on 27 May 1889. Following financial difficulties, the line was closed in 1897/8, but was acquired by the Great Western Railway and reopened in 1901. At the time of the aerial photograph, the Golden Valley route still retained its passenger services but these were to be withdrawn on 15 December 1941. The line from Hay eastwards to Dorstone closed completely on 2 January 1950. Passenger services between Three Cocks Junction and Hereford, via Hay, were withdrawn on 31 December 1962 and the line was closed completely between Three Cocks Junction and Eardisley on 4 May 1964.

31 May 1932 (38160)

Pictured in 1933, this view of Hay station looking eastwards shows the station as it existed after a decade of LMS ownership. Note on the extreme left the milk churns.
Ian Allan Library

Almost 20 years later, in 1950, the Midland Railway presence is still evident in this view looking westwards, most clearly demonstrated in the design of the signalbox, although 'ownership' had passed to the Western Region.
Ian Allan Library.

[1904]

Henley-on-Thames

Situated at the end of end of a 4.5-mile long branch from Twyford, Henley-on-Thames was considered by the Great Western Railway to be a most prestigious destination and was thus provided with a significant array of facilities. As a commuter town and as host of the annual Henley Regatta, these facilities were probably essential. Although the GWR received authorisation for the construction of the broad-gauge branch in 1847, it was not until 1 June 1857 that the line was actually opened. It was converted to standard gauge in 1876 and doubled in 1897. The station building was provided with an overall roof at the buffer stops, which extended along the platforms. Shortly before the outbreak of World War 1 this provision was extended by the addition of 200ft long platform canopies. Other facilities at the station included an engine shed, with a 55ft diameter turntable, and carriage sidings at the country end of the station. These sidings were regularly used in later years for the storage of spare rakes of coaches. The aerial photograph shows the station in 1957, the year of the branch's centenary, shortly before rationalisation set in. The engine shed was closed in 1958 and its associated sidings were removed in 1963. The line reverted to single track in 1961. Freight facilities at Henley were withdrawn on 7 September 1964 and the sidings were removed in 1967 as were the carriage sidings in 1969. Platform 3, the southernmost, was also taken out of use in 1969 and, in 1972, the signalbox was abolished, with control being transferred to Reading.

2 July 1957 (A68184)

This good general view of Henley-on-Thames, taken looking towards the buffer stops on 5 October 1948, sees ex-GWR 4-6-0 No 4019 *Knight Templar* about to depart with the 10.20am service to London Paddington. Outside the small locomotive shed in the background is 0-6-0PT No 4688. *SLS Collection*

Taken on 21 June 1969, this view portrays well the overall roof at Henley-on-Thames. A single-car diesel unit stands in the platform awaiting departure with the 13.06 service to Twyford. *John A. M. Vaughan*

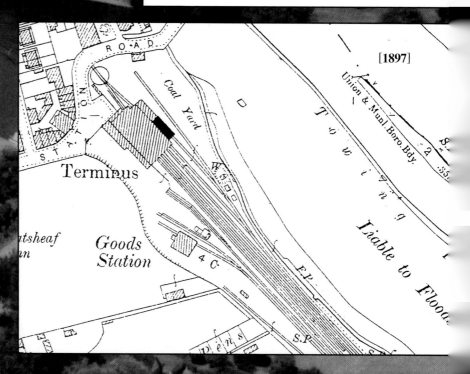

[1897]

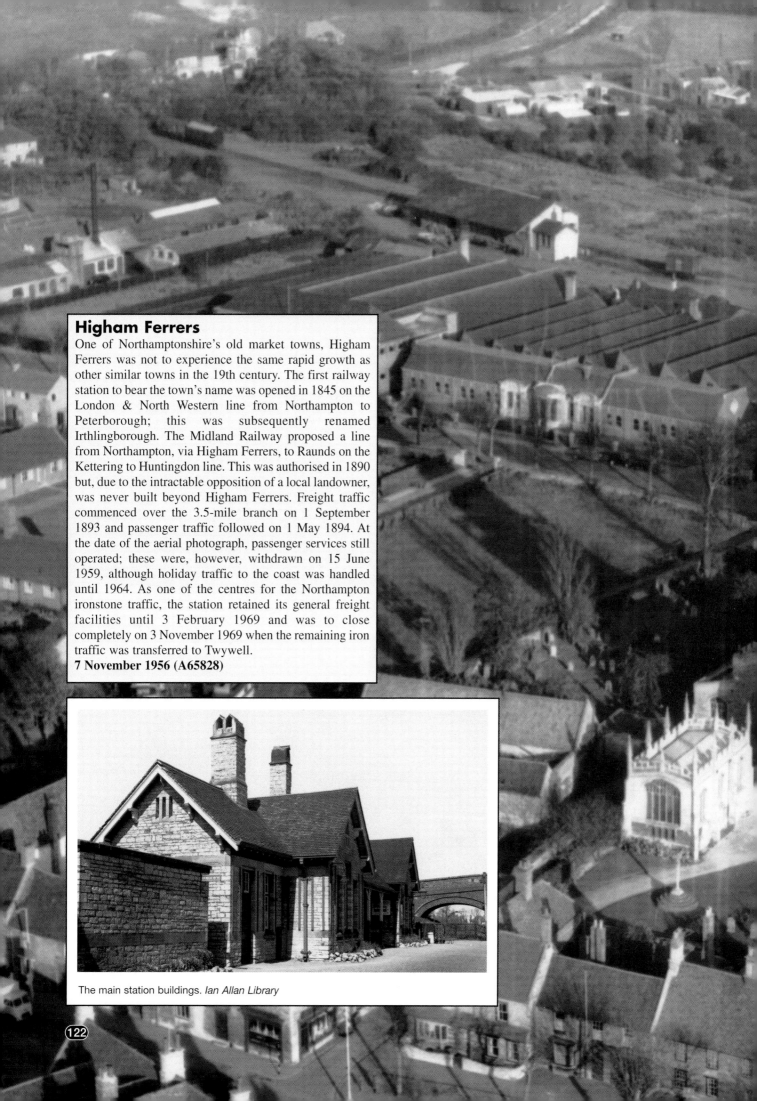

Higham Ferrers

One of Northamptonshire's old market towns, Higham Ferrers was not to experience the same rapid growth as other similar towns in the 19th century. The first railway station to bear the town's name was opened in 1845 on the London & North Western line from Northampton to Peterborough; this was subsequently renamed Irthlingborough. The Midland Railway proposed a line from Northampton, via Higham Ferrers, to Raunds on the Kettering to Huntingdon line. This was authorised in 1890 but, due to the intractable opposition of a local landowner, was never built beyond Higham Ferrers. Freight traffic commenced over the 3.5-mile branch on 1 September 1893 and passenger traffic followed on 1 May 1894. At the date of the aerial photograph, passenger services still operated; these were, however, withdrawn on 15 June 1959, although holiday traffic to the coast was handled until 1964. As one of the centres for the Northampton ironstone traffic, the station retained its general freight facilities until 3 February 1969 and was to close completely on 3 November 1969 when the remaining iron traffic was transferred to Twywell.

7 November 1956 (A65828)

The main station buildings. *Ian Allan Library*

Higham Ferrers & Irthlingborough Station

Fitzwilliam Arms (P.H.)

123

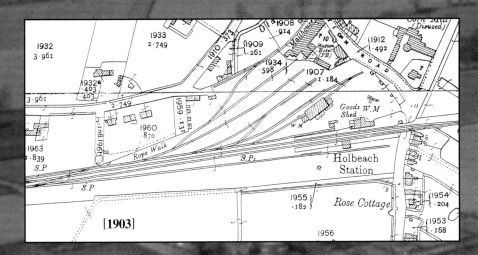

[1903]

Holbeach

Located on the erstwhile Midland & Great Northern line from Spalding to Sutton Bridge, Holbeach was one of the most important intermediate stations on the line. The line through Holbeach opened on 15 November 1858 but was only to become a passing place in 1890, at which time the second platform with its timber shelter was added. The station possessed a goods yard and two signalboxes (East and West). The scale of the goods yard can be seen to good effect in this aerial photograph; much of the freight traffic, as would be expected, was agricultural with potatoes and fruit being particularly significant. The station was to suffer the fate of much of the M&GN network, with its passenger services being withdrawn on 28 February 1959. The station retained its freight facilities until 1 May 1965, when they succumbed at the same time as the line between Spalding and Sutton Bridge was closed completely.

29 April 1930 (31775)

On 9 August 1953, ex-LMS Class 4F 0-6-0 No 44122 approaches Holbeach station with a service from Birmingham and Leicester to Cromer, Norwich and Yarmouth Beach.
Frank Church

By August 1958, when this view of Holbeach was taken looking westwards, the station had less than 12 months to go before passenger services were withdrawn. This view shows well the combination of old signage alongside that of British Railways; note the BR totem, for example, on the lamp-post on the extreme left. *SLS Collection*

Hornsea

The Hull & Hornsea Railway, which was worked by the North Eastern Railway from the outset, was authorised by an act of 30 June 1862 and opened throughout on 28 March 1864. The NER formally took over on 16 July 1866. Services to Hornsea were transferred to Hull Paragon on 1 June 1864. The line passed to the LNER in 1923 and to British Railways (North Eastern Region) in 1948. During the 1950s, diesel multiple-units were introduced to the line and, in 1960, further cost cutting measures were introduced, including the sale of tickets on the train to passengers by guards. The cost saving measures proved unsuccessful and the line lost its passenger services on 19 October 1964, at the same time as these were withdrawn from the Withernsea branch, and was to close completely between Hornsea Bridge and the terminus at Hornsea Town (illustrated) at the same time. The section to Hornsea Bridge was to close completely on 3 May 1965. As can be seen from the aerial photograph, by August 1966 the track is overgrown but still in situ, whilst the signalbox, station platform, buildings and water tower are also still extant.

18 August 1966 (A165896)

On 2 August 1949 ex-NER Class A6 4-6-2T No 9796 shunts a Bank Holiday relief train at Hornsea. *SLS Collection*

An ex-NER Class A6 awaits departure from Hornsea station. *SLS Collection*

127

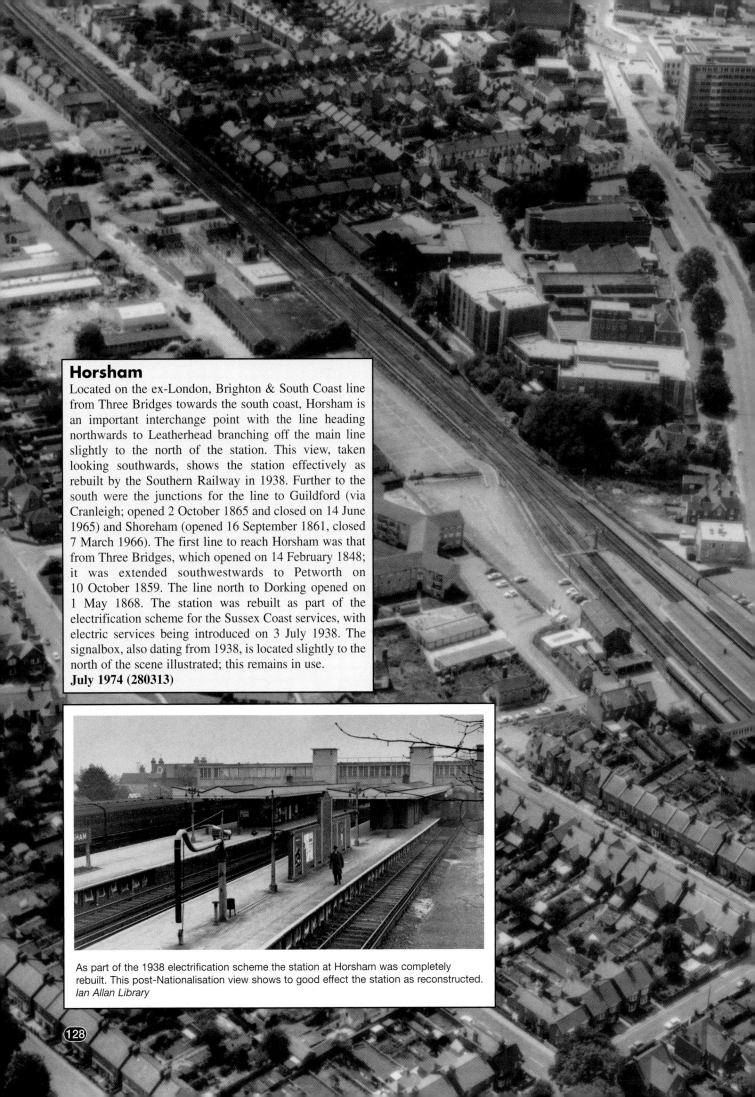

Horsham

Located on the ex-London, Brighton & South Coast line from Three Bridges towards the south coast, Horsham is an important interchange point with the line heading northwards to Leatherhead branching off the main line slightly to the north of the station. This view, taken looking southwards, shows the station effectively as rebuilt by the Southern Railway in 1938. Further to the south were the junctions for the line to Guildford (via Cranleigh; opened 2 October 1865 and closed on 14 June 1965) and Shoreham (opened 16 September 1861, closed 7 March 1966). The first line to reach Horsham was that from Three Bridges, which opened on 14 February 1848; it was extended southwestwards to Petworth on 10 October 1859. The line north to Dorking opened on 1 May 1868. The station was rebuilt as part of the electrification scheme for the Sussex Coast services, with electric services being introduced on 3 July 1938. The signalbox, also dating from 1938, is located slightly to the north of the scene illustrated; this remains in use.

July 1974 (280313)

As part of the 1938 electrification scheme the station at Horsham was completely rebuilt. This post-Nationalisation view shows to good effect the station as reconstructed.
Ian Allan Library

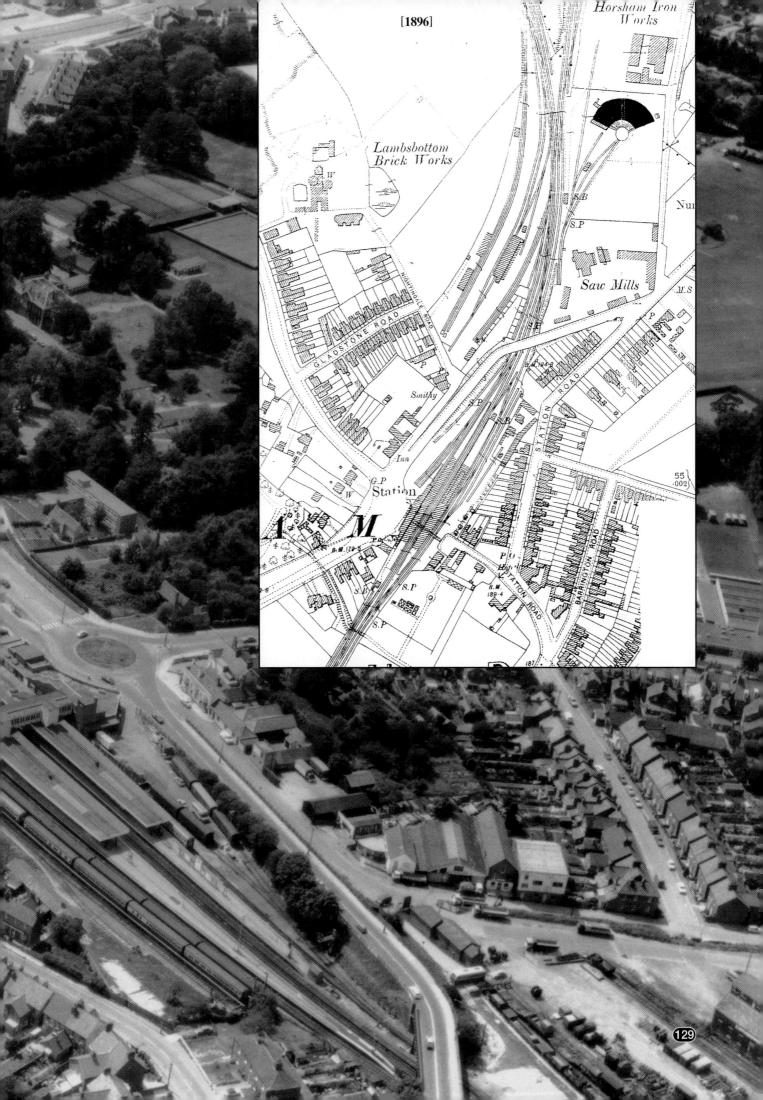

[1896]

Horsham Iron Works

Lambsbottom Brick Works

Saw Mills

GLADSTONE ROAD

NIGHTINGALE ROAD

Smithy

Inn

Station

STATION ROAD

BARRINGTON ROAD

129

Horwich

The short, 1.25-mile long, branch from Blackrod to Horwich was opened for freight traffic on 15 July 1868 and to passenger traffic on 14 February 1870. As can be seen in this aerial view (taken looking westwards), the terminus was provided with a single platform and goods shed with yard. However, the importance of the town for the railway industry came from the fact that the Lancashire & Yorkshire Railway constructed its main locomotive works slightly to the south of the terminus. The works were opened in 1887 and by the date of the aerial photograph were engaged in the production of BR Standard locomotives; the last steam locomotive to be constructed at the works was No 76099 in November 1957. Locomotive overhauls continued until 1962, when the works took on maintenance of carriages and wagons; this continued until complete closure, apart from the foundry, in 1982. Passenger services between Blackrod and Horwich ceased on 27 September 1965 and freight facilities were withdrawn on 25 April 1966. The line remained to serve the works and then foundry.
14 July 1955 (R24855)

On 13 June 1953 ex-L&YR 2-4-2T No 50646 awaits departure from Horwich station with a service to Blackrod. *N. R. Knight*

A decade later, on 12 July 1961, BR Standard Class 2MT 2-6-2T No 84013 stands at the platform at Horwich with a two-coach train, having formed the 5.15pm (SX) railmotor service from Blackrod. *A. Moyes*

On 16 September 1965 BR Standard Class 2MT 2-6-2T No 84025 shunts the auto train alongside the goods shed. *B. Walker*

Hungerford

Now an intermediate station on the Berks & Hants route to the West Country, the broad-gauge line from Newbury opened to a temporary terminus here on 21 December 1847. The line was extended westwards to Devizes and thence to Holt Junction on 11 November 1862. The opening of the through route resulted in the construction of a new station and the closure of the original. Apart from the station building, Hungerford was also provided with two signalboxes (East and West) and a goods shed. Freight facilities were withdrawn from the station shortly after the aerial photograph was taken, on 1 July 1970. The line through Hungerford to Holt Junction was converted to standard gauge between 26 June and 1 July 1874. East signalbox was demolished by the mid-1950s, with control of the goods yard passing to West box.

9 June 1967 (A172585)

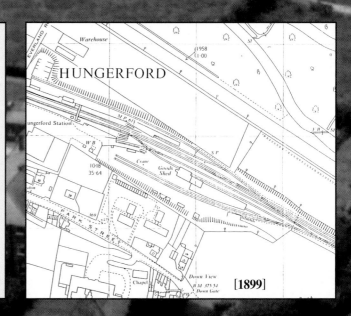

[1899]

It's April 1970 and Hungerford looks as though it's the station that corporate identity missed. More than 20 years after Nationalisation, the station is still replete with GWR pattern signage ... *Andrew Muckley*

... An impression heightened by this view, also taken in April 1970, of the signalbox. Note, in particular, the GWR notice on the extreme left. *Andrew Muckley*

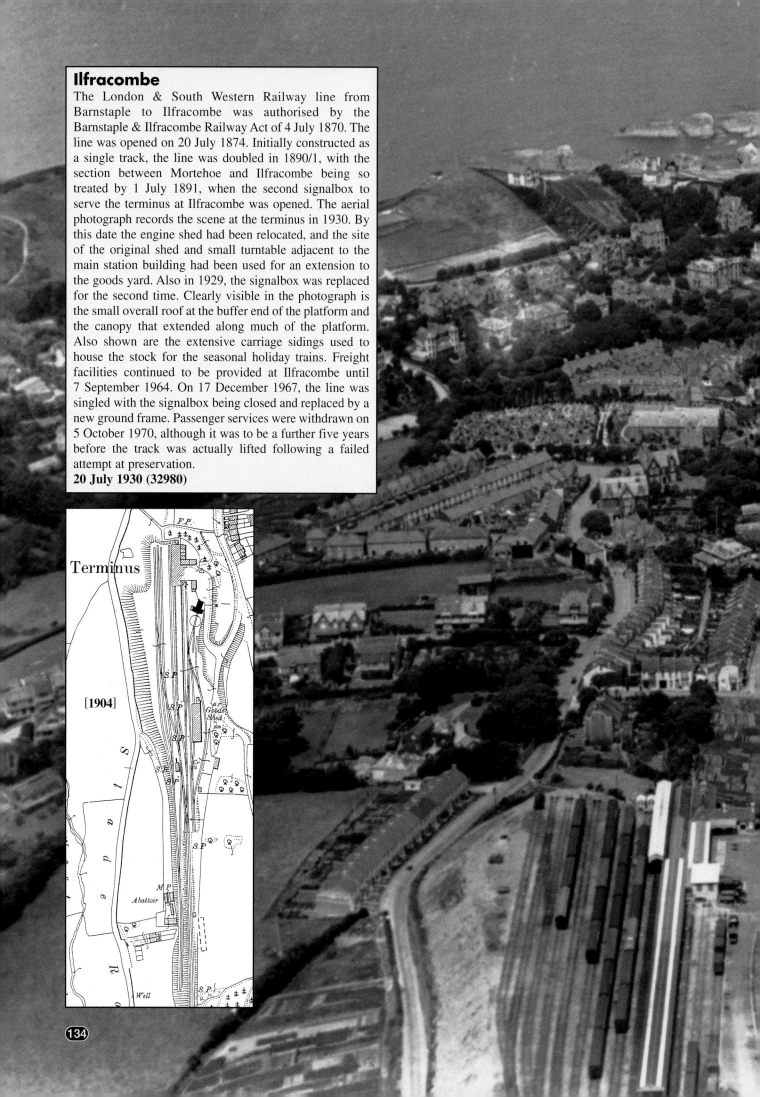

Ilfracombe

The London & South Western Railway line from
Barnstaple to Ilfracombe was authorised by the
Barnstaple & Ilfracombe Railway Act of 4 July 1870. The
line was opened on 20 July 1874. Initially constructed as
a single track, the line was doubled in 1890/1, with the
section between Mortehoe and Ilfracombe being so
treated by 1 July 1891, when the second signalbox to
serve the terminus at Ilfracombe was opened. The aerial
photograph records the scene at the terminus in 1930. By
this date the engine shed had been relocated, and the site
of the original shed and small turntable adjacent to the
main station building had been used for an extension to
the goods yard. Also in 1929, the signalbox was replaced
for the second time. Clearly visible in the photograph is
the small overall roof at the buffer end of the platform and
the canopy that extended along much of the platform.
Also shown are the extensive carriage sidings used to
house the stock for the seasonal holiday trains. Freight
facilities continued to be provided at Ilfracombe until
7 September 1964. On 17 December 1967, the line was
singled with the signalbox being closed and replaced by a
new ground frame. Passenger services were withdrawn on
5 October 1970, although it was to be a further five years
before the track was actually lifted following a failed
attempt at preservation.
20 July 1930 (32980)

Terminus

[1904]

Viewed looking from the turntable pit towards the station, this view of Ilfracombe, taken on 18 May 1959, shows the relationship between locomotive shed, signalbox, goods shed and main station to good effect. Adjacent to the shed can be seen 'N' class 2-6-0 No 31835. *K. L. Cook*

A decade after the earlier shot and rationalisation has already impacted heavily on the facilities at Ilfracombe, with freight traffic having been withdrawn and evidence of other track alterations. On 10 August 1968 'Warship' No D820 *Grenville* departs from an otherwise deserted terminus with the 11.10 service to Paddington. *M. Edwards*

On 13 June 1947 ex-L&YR Class 2P 2-4-2T No 10636, then shedded at Manningham, stands in platform 1 at Ilkley with the 1.37pm service to Bradford Forster Square. *SLS Collection*

Ilkley

Although it retained its passenger services to Leeds and Bradford, Ilkley presented a sorry sight to the photographer on 8 August 1976, with a general air of dereliction. Platforms 1 and 2, to the left, were terminating whilst 3 and 4, to the right, originally served the through lines to Skipton. In platform 2 is the 10.12 arrival from Bradford Forster Square whilst on platform 3 is the 10.35 departure to Bradford.
David Bailey

The town of Ilkley in Wharfedale grew significantly during the 19th century, its prosperity increasing as the result of its growth as a dormitory town for Leeds and Bradford. Although there were proposals in the 1840s for the construction of a line through Wharfedale, it was not until an agreement in 1859 between the Midland and North Eastern railways that the valley was to see a line constructed. Authorised by an act of 11 July 1861, lines were to be constructed from Arthington (on the Leeds-Harrogate line) via Otley to Ilkley and from Apperley Bridge (on the Leeds-Shipley line) to meet it at Burley in Wharfedale. The section between Otley and Ilkley was to be owned by the MR and NER as the Otley & Ilkley Joint, whilst the section from Apperley Bridge to Burley was MR and that from Otley to Arthington belonged to the NER. The lines opened for passenger service on 1 August 1865 and to freight on 1 October 1866. Access for trains from Bradford came in December 1876 with the opening of the Shipley to Esholt line. Ilkley became a through station, as illustrated in the aerial photograph, on 16 May 1888 with the opening of the section to Bolton Abbey of the extension to Skipton. Although the Skipton-Ilkley-Leeds line was a secondary route, it was a useful diversionary line for services over the main line between Leeds and Skipton. The station, which was provided with both terminal and through platforms, was rebuilt in 1887/8 when the through lines were constructed. Apart from the station, Ilkley also possessed an engine shed; this was originally located close to the main station building and opened on 1 July 1866. It was replaced by a new structure in 1892, located further to the east which was to close on 5 January 1959. Passenger services between Ilkley and Skipton were withdrawn on 22 March 1965 and the line was to be closed completely between Embsay and Ilkley on the following 5 July. The road bridge to the west of the station was demolished shortly after closure. Today, Ilkley plays host to electric services to both Leeds and Bradford.
10 September 1928 (24364)

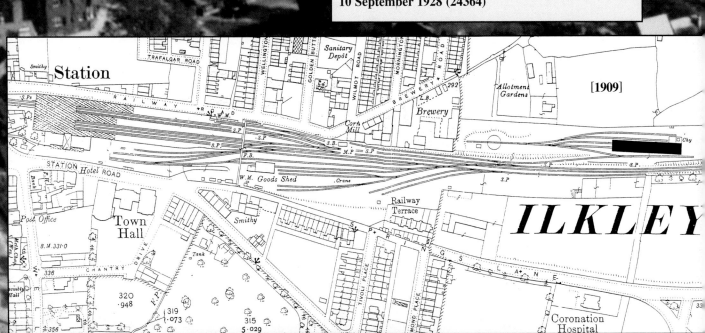

Ironbridge

Iron Bridge & Broseley station was situated on the south side of the River Severn as it passed through the Ironbridge Gorge, close to the famous iron bridge which gave the location its name. The Severn Valley line opened on 1 February 1862 and the station was provided with small goods shed and signalbox adjacent to the level crossing at the west end of the station. Passenger services over the section of line between Bewdley and Shrewsbury ceased on 9 September 1963 and the line was to close completely between Buildwas and Alveley Sidings on 2 December of the same year, at which time freight facilities were withdrawn from Iron Bridge.

October 1934 (46398)

One of the '81xx' class 2-6-2Ts rebuilt from '51xx' class locomotives in 1938, No 8105, stands in Iron Bridge & Broseley station with a service from Hartlebury to Shrewsbury. *SLS Collection*

[1902]

Kidderminster

Taken looking westwards, the aerial view of Kidderminster shows, on the extreme right, the passenger station, but dominating the scene in the centre are the extensive freight facilities once provided for this important manufacturing town. Today, the scene would be radically different with the construction of the Severn Valley Railway's Kidderminster Town station, but in the mid-1970s, the SVR extension into the town was still some years away as freight traffic continued to operate over the remains of the line to Bewdley — to the sugar works at Foley Park — until 1982. The first line to serve Kidderminster was the Oxford, Worcester & Wolverhampton Railway, later to form part of the Great Western Railway, which was incorporated on 3 August 1846 and opened from Droitwich to Stourbridge on 1 May 1852. Kidderminster became a junction with the opening of the three-mile branch to Bewdley, on the Severn Valley line from Hartlebury to Shrewsbury, on 1 June 1878. Although passenger services north of Bewdley ceased on 9 September 1963, those from Bewdley to Kidderminster and Hartlebury survived until 5 January 1970.

9 June 1976 (324842)

[1924]

On 11 July 1961 ex-GWR 2-6-2T No 4114 takes water at Kidderminster before taking a train of empty stock to the carriage sidings whilst railcar No W24W arrives at the station with a service from Wooferton. Note the single wagon attached to the rear of the railcar.
R. James-Robertson

On 28 April 1964, the local service to Dumfries awaits departure from Kirkcudbright behind BR Standard Class 4MT 2-6-4T No 80023. *Derek Cross*

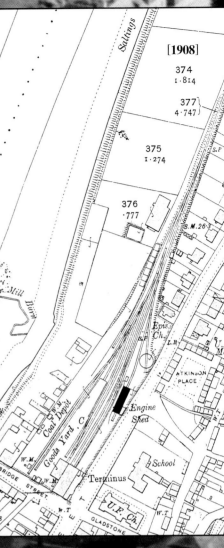

A year later, on 16 April 1965, BR Standard Class 4MT tanks are still providing the motive power from Kirkcudbright, as No 80117 stands at the station with the 8am service to Dumfries. *W. G. Sumner*

Kirkcudbright

The Kirkcudbright Railway was authorised by an act of 1861 to construct the 10.25-mile long line from Castle Douglas. The route was opened to freight traffic on 17 February 1864 and to passenger traffic on 7 March 1864. The line was worked from the start by the Glasgow & South Western Railway; the following year the Kirkcudbright Railway became part of the G&SWR. The parallel development of the line from Castle Douglas to Portpatrick, opened from Castle Douglas to Stranraer on 12 March 1861, resulted in the Kirkcudbright line eventually being relegated to the role of a branch. The aerial view shows the facilities provided at Kirkcudbright almost a decade after the creation of the LMS. Apart from the main station buildings and goods shed, there was also a small engine shed. This was opened simultaneously with the branch and was provided with a 42ft turntable, which was later replaced by one of 44ft 6in. The shed, a sub-shed of Dumfries, was closed in 1955. Passenger services between Castle Douglas and Kirkcudbright were withdrawn on 3 May 1965 and the line was to close completely on the following 14 June.
August 1930 (34427)

Ex-GWR diesel railcar No 19 is seen at Lambourn station on 4 October 1948 prior to forming the 3.10pm service to Newbury. Four months after Nationalisation, little has happened at the station to indicate the change of ownership. *SLS Collection*

Lambourn

Although work started in 1888 on the construction of the 12.75-mile Lambourn Valley Railway — it maintained an independent existence until take-over by the Great Western Railway on 1 July 1905 — it was not until 4 April 1898 that the line was completed through to Lambourn. In order to save money, the line obtained a Light Railway Order in 1903. Under both the LVR and the GWR initially, the line was not provided with passing loops and signalling, being operated under the one loco in steam principle. However, the GWR introduced a crossing loop at Welford Park and signalling shortly after its take-over and in 1910/11 rebuilt the station building. This new building was situated behind the original structure and allowed for the construction of a new goods siding when the original structure was demolished. Lambourn was provided with a small locomotive shed, although this was to be closed in 1937 when branch line services were taken over by GWR diesel railcars (with the exception of one service for schoolchildren). The regular diesel railcars were Nos 18 and 19, but steam, in the guise of '57xx' class 0-6-0PTs, reappeared in later years. The goods shed remained extant throughout the life of the branch. A short spur existed behind the signalbox, but this was removed in 1938. The aerial photograph was taken towards the end of the branch's life, by which date the passenger service was formed of six down and five up services daily with no Sunday service; the branch closed to all services beyond Welford Park on 4 January 1960.
31 July 1958 (A72726)

Again a view from the early post-Nationalisation era, here ex-GWR '2301' class No 2579 stands at the station with a three-coach service to Newbury. *SLS Collection*

Station

Cattle Pens   Crane

[1899]

446   XXV. 7.   445

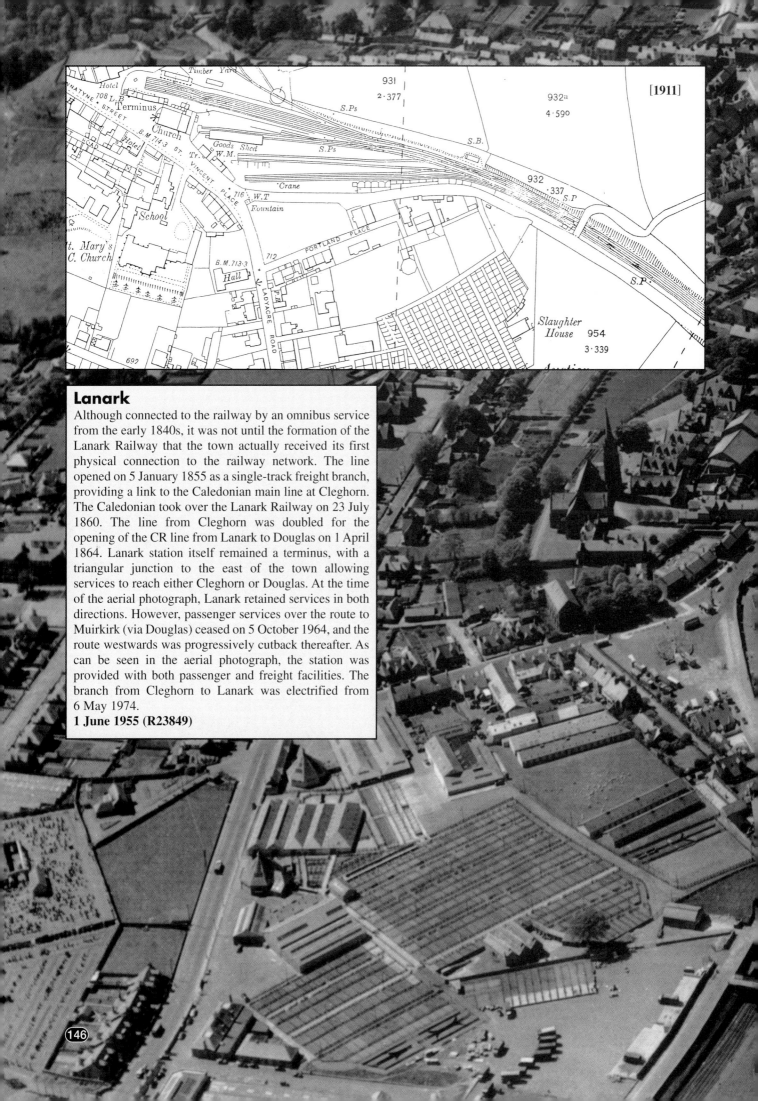

[1911]

Lanark

Although connected to the railway by an omnibus service from the early 1840s, it was not until the formation of the Lanark Railway that the town actually received its first physical connection to the railway network. The line opened on 5 January 1855 as a single-track freight branch, providing a link to the Caledonian main line at Cleghorn. The Caledonian took over the Lanark Railway on 23 July 1860. The line from Cleghorn was doubled for the opening of the CR line from Lanark to Douglas on 1 April 1864. Lanark station itself remained a terminus, with a triangular junction to the east of the town allowing services to reach either Cleghorn or Douglas. At the time of the aerial photograph, Lanark retained services in both directions. However, passenger services over the route to Muirkirk (via Douglas) ceased on 5 October 1964, and the route westwards was progressively cutback thereafter. As can be seen in the aerial photograph, the station was provided with both passenger and freight facilities. The branch from Cleghorn to Lanark was electrified from 6 May 1974.

1 June 1955 (R23849)

On 9 June 1949 ex-CR 4-4-0 No 14474, still bearing its LMS number and livery, is seen at the head of the 4.15pm service to Edinburgh whilst alongside is ex-LMS Class 2P 4-4-0 No 645, which is awaiting departure with the 4.10pm service to Muirkirk. *SLS Collection*

On 18 September 1954 ex-CR 0-4-4T No 55264 is pictured at Lanark awaiting departure with the 8.20am service to Muirkirk. *L. King*

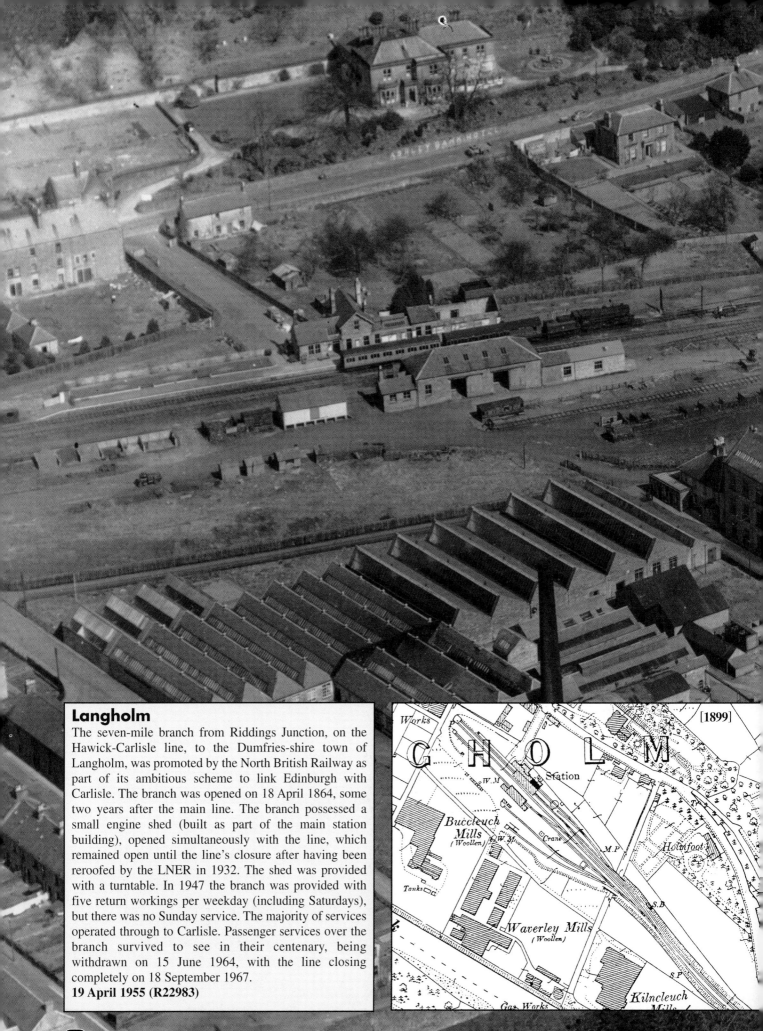

Langholm

The seven-mile branch from Riddings Junction, on the Hawick-Carlisle line, to the Dumfries-shire town of Langholm, was promoted by the North British Railway as part of its ambitious scheme to link Edinburgh with Carlisle. The branch was opened on 18 April 1864, some two years after the main line. The branch possessed a small engine shed (built as part of the main station building), opened simultaneously with the line, which remained open until the line's closure after having been reroofed by the LNER in 1932. The shed was provided with a turntable. In 1947 the branch was provided with five return workings per weekday (including Saturdays), but there was no Sunday service. The majority of services operated through to Carlisle. Passenger services over the branch survived to see in their centenary, being withdrawn on 15 June 1964, with the line closing completely on 18 September 1967.

19 April 1955 (R22983)

The station buildings at Langholm viewed looking northwards in 1935. *Ian Allan Library*

A second view taken in 1935, this time showing the station buildings looking south towards Riddings Junction. *Ian Allan Library*

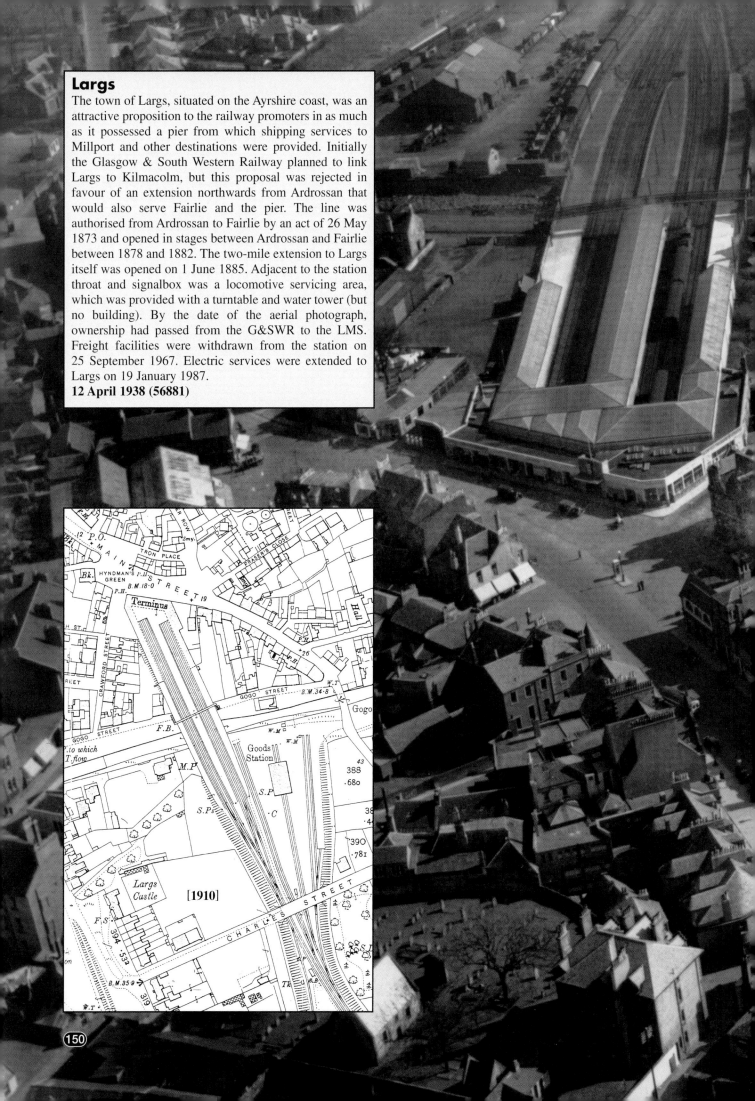

Largs

The town of Largs, situated on the Ayrshire coast, was an attractive proposition to the railway promoters in as much as it possessed a pier from which shipping services to Millport and other destinations were provided. Initially the Glasgow & South Western Railway planned to link Largs to Kilmacolm, but this proposal was rejected in favour of an extension northwards from Ardrossan that would also serve Fairlie and the pier. The line was authorised from Ardrossan to Fairlie by an act of 26 May 1873 and opened in stages between Ardrossan and Fairlie between 1878 and 1882. The two-mile extension to Largs itself was opened on 1 June 1885. Adjacent to the station throat and signalbox was a locomotive servicing area, which was provided with a turntable and water tower (but no building). By the date of the aerial photograph, ownership had passed from the G&SWR to the LMS. Freight facilities were withdrawn from the station on 25 September 1967. Electric services were extended to Largs on 19 January 1987.

12 April 1938 (56881)

[1910]

Terminus

Largs Castle

Goods Station

On 24 May 1960, 'Jubilee' class 4-6-0 No 45697 *Achilles* is seen at Largs at the head of a return Women's Guild excursion to Cumberland. *G. H. Robin*

Looking south from Largs station on 21 April 1962, Class 5 No 45251 is about to proceed on to the turntable, which is located beyond the bridge, whilst BR Standard Class 5 No 73101 awaits its turn. *S. Rickard*

Lavenham

The line from Sudbury, through Long Melford (where a junction was created with the route westwards towards Cambridge), to Bury St Edmunds via Lavenham opened throughout on 9 August 1865, although there had been proposals 20 years earlier for the extension of the Sudbury branch northwards. Lavenham and was perceived to be the major intermediate station on the line was provided with a substantial two-platform passenger station, goods shed and signalbox. The line passed from the GER to the LNER in 1923 and to British Railways (Eastern Region) in 1948. During the 1950s there were efforts to try and encourage increased passenger usage, including, towards the end of the decade, the replacement of steam-hauled services with diesel motive power. However, despite these efforts, passenger traffic did not increase significantly and, on 10 April 1961, passenger services were withdrawn from the Long Melford-Bury St Edmunds route. Freight traffic continued to be handled at Lavenham from the Bury direction, with the line between Lavenham and Long Melford being closed completely on 10 April 1961 and lifted during early 1962. The line from Bury St Edmunds to Lavenham was to be closed completely on 19 April 1965.

3 April 1929 (25907)

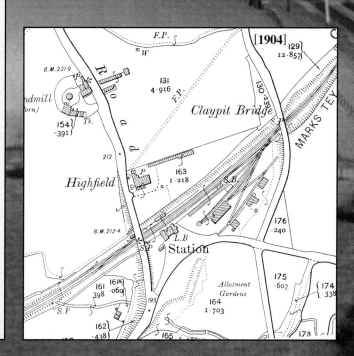

Pictured in 1953, looking northwards, this view of Lavenham station shows well the brick structures provided on both up and down platforms; these were typical of the buildings provided by the GER on lines in the area. *Ian Allan Library*

Ledbury Town Halt viewed through the double track width overbridge in 1959. The ex-GWR railcar service would only last a few more weeks. *Roger Carpenter*

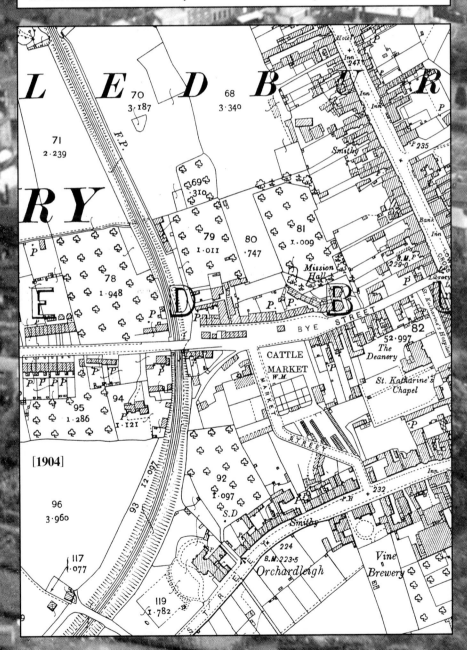

Ledbury

The first railway to serve Ledbury was that opened by the West Midland Railway on 13 September 1861 with a station on its single-track route from Malvern Wells to Hereford. Ledbury passed to the Great Western Railway two years later when the WMR was absorbed by the GWR. The line through Ledbury was doubled, with the exception of Ledbury Tunnel, in 1868 and, on 27 July 1885, the station become a junction with the opening of the line southwards to Gloucester, a route which had been promoted by the Ross & Ledbury Railway. Although the line towards Gloucester was constructed as double track, by the date of the aerial photograph it had been singled (in 1917) from a point some 400yd beyond the junction. The station illustrated here was the station constructed on the route south from the junction, Ledbury Town Halt. The service between Gloucester and Ledbury was relatively sparse with five workings in 1939 each way on Mondays to Fridays with an additional service each way on Saturdays. There was no service on Sundays. Ledbury Town Halt was not provided with freight facilities. Latterly the passenger services over the route were in the hands of ex-GWR diesel railcars. Passenger services over the line to Gloucester were withdrawn on 13 July 1959, at which time the line from Ledbury to Dymock was to close completely. Services continue to serve Ledbury through the erstwhile Junction station.

28 September 1929 (29969)

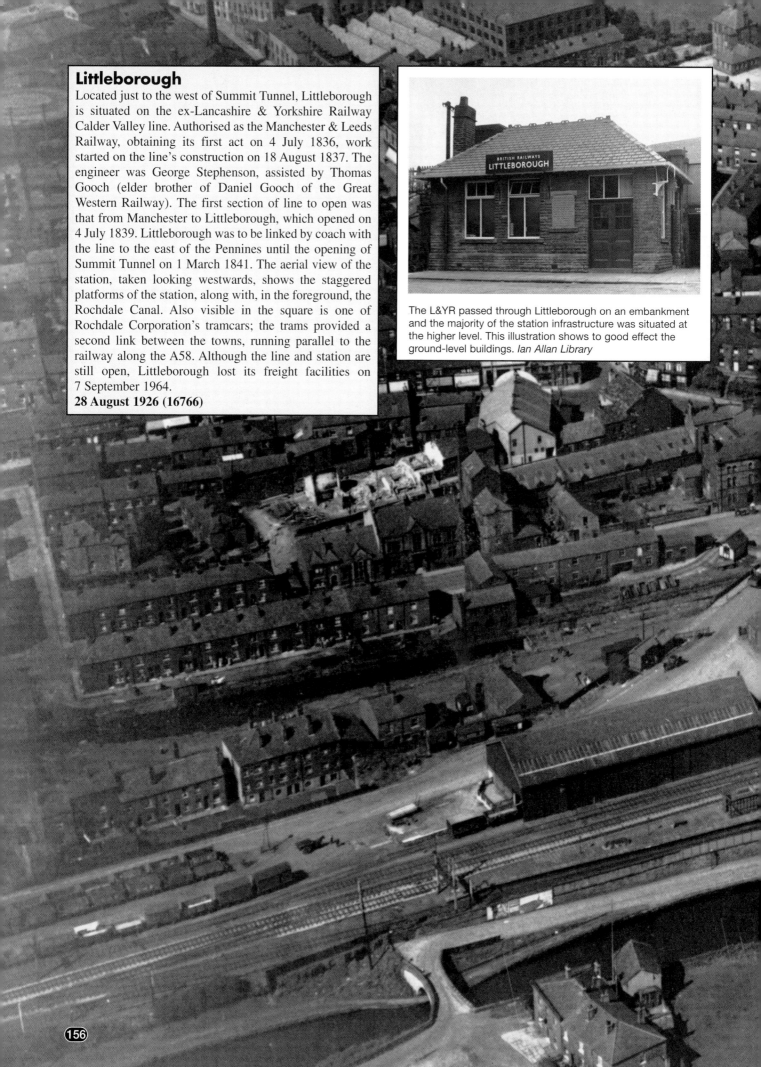

Littleborough

Located just to the west of Summit Tunnel, Littleborough is situated on the ex-Lancashire & Yorkshire Railway Calder Valley line. Authorised as the Manchester & Leeds Railway, obtaining its first act on 4 July 1836, work started on the line's construction on 18 August 1837. The engineer was George Stephenson, assisted by Thomas Gooch (elder brother of Daniel Gooch of the Great Western Railway). The first section of line to open was that from Manchester to Littleborough, which opened on 4 July 1839. Littleborough was to be linked by coach with the line to the east of the Pennines until the opening of Summit Tunnel on 1 March 1841. The aerial view of the station, taken looking westwards, shows the staggered platforms of the station, along with, in the foreground, the Rochdale Canal. Also visible in the square is one of Rochdale Corporation's tramcars; the trams provided a second link between the towns, running parallel to the railway along the A58. Although the line and station are still open, Littleborough lost its freight facilities on 7 September 1964.

28 August 1926 (16766)

The L&YR passed through Littleborough on an embankment and the majority of the station infrastructure was situated at the higher level. This illustration shows to good effect the ground-level buildings. *Ian Allan Library*

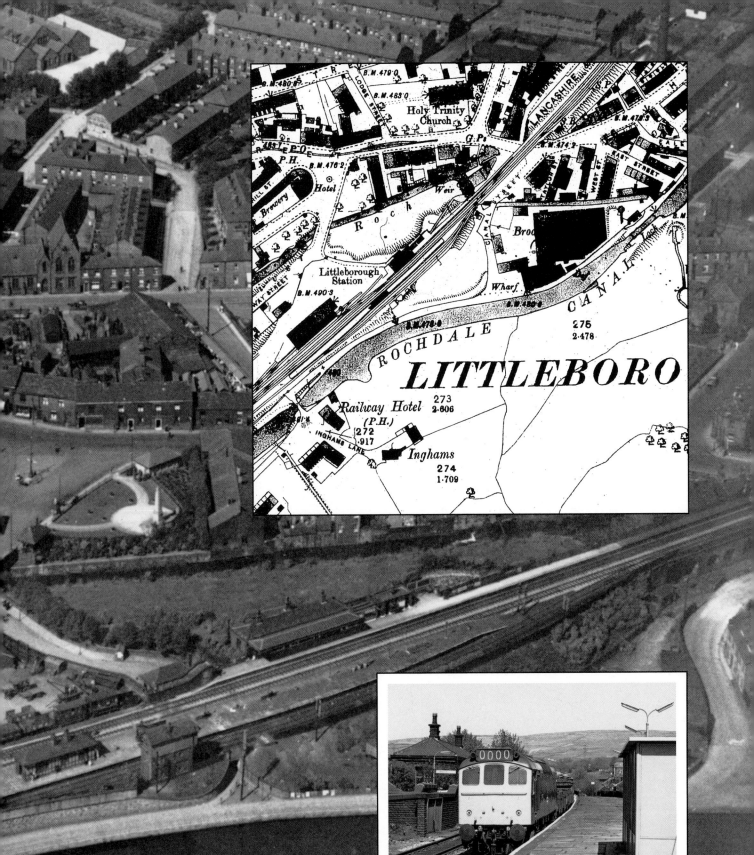

Littleborough was the terminus of the Manchester & Leeds Railway between 1839 and 1841. Although it retained its period buildings on the down platform, by 18 May 1977, when this view of Class 25 No 25172 heading westwards with a freight was taken, the buildings on the up platform had been replaced by a Greater Manchester PTE-style bus shelter. *R. S. Greenwood*

Loanhead

Situated to the south of Edinburgh, Loanhead was on the ex-North British branch from Millerhill Junction to Glencorse. At the heart of the Lothian coalfield, it comes as no surprise that the limited passenger facilities are overshadowed by the coal mine in the aerial view, which was taken looking northwards. The line through Loanhead was promoted by the Edinburgh, Loanhead & Roslin Railway and opened as far as Roslin on 23 July 1874 and was extended to Glencross (later renamed Glencorse) on 2 July 1877. Passenger services over the line were a relatively early casualty, being withdrawn by the LNER on 1 May 1933, but the line was to survive for coal traffic, serving Roslin and Bilston Glen collieries, until the latter was to close; the line from Millerhill Junction closed completely on 5 June 1989. Apart from the loss of passenger traffic in 1933, general freight facilities were withdrawn from Loanhead station on 22 July 1968 and all facilities ceased on 5 August 1968.
11 April 1963 (A109830)

159

Lossiemouth

Situated on the north coast of Morayshire, Lossiemouth was the target of a railway scheme as early as 1846, but it was not until 1851 that construction started. The 5.5-mile long line from Elgin opened on 10 August 1852 under the auspices of the Morayshire Railway, which was later to form part of the Great North of Scotland. From 1903, the branch was one of those on which the GNoSR experimented briefly and unsuccessfully with steam railcars. With Grouping in 1923 came the introduction of a through sleeper service to King's Cross; this service continued until it was suspended in 1939. After passing to British Railways (Scottish Region) in 1948, passenger services were withdrawn on 6 April 1964 and freight ceased on 28 March 1966. Apart from the main station buildings and goods shed, a single line also served the town's fishing harbour. In 1947 there were five services per day between Elgin and Lossiemouth on Mondays to Fridays with two additional trains on Saturdays; from Lossiemouth to Elgin there were four services on Mondays to Fridays, again with an additional two on Saturdays. The normal time allowed for the journey was 12min.

24 September 1932 (C14989)

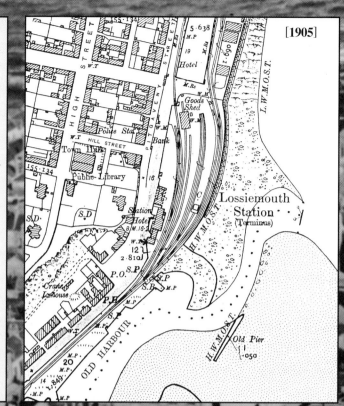

[1905]

On 4 July 1951 the 1.44pm service to Elgin awaits departure from Lossiemouth station. *SLS Collection*

On 29 June 1957 BR Standard Class 2MT 2-6-0 No 78053 is recorded at Lossiemouth station having just arrived with a service from Elgin. By this date the station signage had been replaced with standard Scottish Region blue enamel signs. *SLS Collection*

Louth

Promoted by the East Lincolnshire Railway, the route through Louth was taken over by the Great Northern Railway before completion. The first section to open was that northwards to Grimsby, over which services were introduced on 1 March 1848. The section south to Firsby followed on 3 September 1848 and Louth became a junction with the opening of the line to Bardney on 1 December 1876 and that to Mablethorpe on 17 October 1877. To serve the town, the GNR constructed an impressive station in a Jacobean style; when originally built, the station was provided with a twin-span trainshed supported by iron columns running between the two tracks. Passenger services between Louth and Bardney ceased on 5 November 1951, the line being closed completely between Louth and Donington-on-Bain on 17 September 1956, and those between Louth and Mablethorpe followed on 5 December 1960 (at which time the line to Mablethorpe closed completely). By the date of the aerial photograph, all passenger services through Louth had ceased, on 5 October 1970, at which time the line south to Firsby Junction closed completely, leaving the town's freight traffic to be handled from the Grimsby direction. Final closure of the route to Grimsby came on 3 October 1980. Part of the route is now the target for a preservation scheme.

9 September 1971 (A215261)

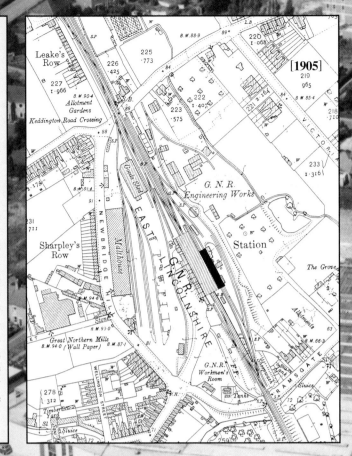

Taken from the south, this view records the scene looking north at Louth on 10 June 1947. Locomotives visible are, in the distance (through the shed door), Class C12 4-4-2T No 7389, in the centre sister locomotive No 7352 and, on the right, ex-GCR Class N5 0-6-2T No 9306. Also present on the day, but not visible in the photograph, were two more 'C12s', Nos 7359 and 7398. *SLS Collection*

The GNR provided Louth with a superb station built in an Jacobean style to a design by Weightman and Hadfield of Sheffield. As can be seen in this view, taken, almost seven years after closure to passenger services, on 29 September 1977, the condition of the building had considerably deteriorated. *Stanley Creer*

[1906]

Mablethorpe

One of the Lincolnshire coastal resorts, unlike Skegness and Cleethorpes, Mablethorpe no longer possesses its railway station. The first line to serve the town was the Louth & East Coast Railway's route, backed by the Great Northern Railway, from Louth, which opened on 17 October 1877. The route was extended southwards from Mablethorpe to Willoughby on 14 July 1888 under the auspices of the Sutton & Willoughby Railway, again backed by the GNR. Mablethorpe never expanded as other East Coast resorts did and, by the early 1960s (at the time the aerial photograph was taken), the position of the railway in the town was under threat. Passenger services over the line to Louth had been withdrawn on 5 December 1960, at which time the line between Mablethorpe Junction and Mablethorpe had closed completely, leaving the town to be served by a single track from the Willoughby direction. DMUs had taken over the operation of the line from

1955 and gradually the number of special summer services disappeared. Virtually all the lines in east Lincolnshire were proposed for closure in the Beeching Report, but there was opposition and the line to Mablethorpe survived until the wholesale closure of much of the ex-GNR empire in the region on 5 October 1970. The aerial photograph shows the station as it existed shortly after the closure of the line to Louth. Clearly visible are the 52ft turntable installed by BR in 1954 (as a replacement for an earlier one), the goods shed and signalbox on the platform. There was originally a small engine shed, opened in 1877, but this had been closed by the LNER in 1924 and subsequently demolished. Steam locomotives, however, continued to use the facilities provided until 1964, with freight facilities being withdrawn on 30 March of that year.

18 July 1962 (A104865)

Seen entering the station from the north is ex-GNR Class C12 4-4-2T No 67398 at the head of the 1.46pm service from Louth to Sutton-on-Sea on 13 September 1954. It was the section northwards from Mablethorpe that would be the first to close, leaving the town to be served by a branch from the south that survived until 1970. Note the well-stocked W. H. Smith station bookstall. *R. J. Buckley*

By 28 March 1970, when this photograph of the 13.20 departure to Willoughby and Boston was taken at Mablethorpe, the line was coming towards the end of its life, although the station remained in good condition. The train was formed of DMU Nos 56442 and 51284. *SLS Collection*

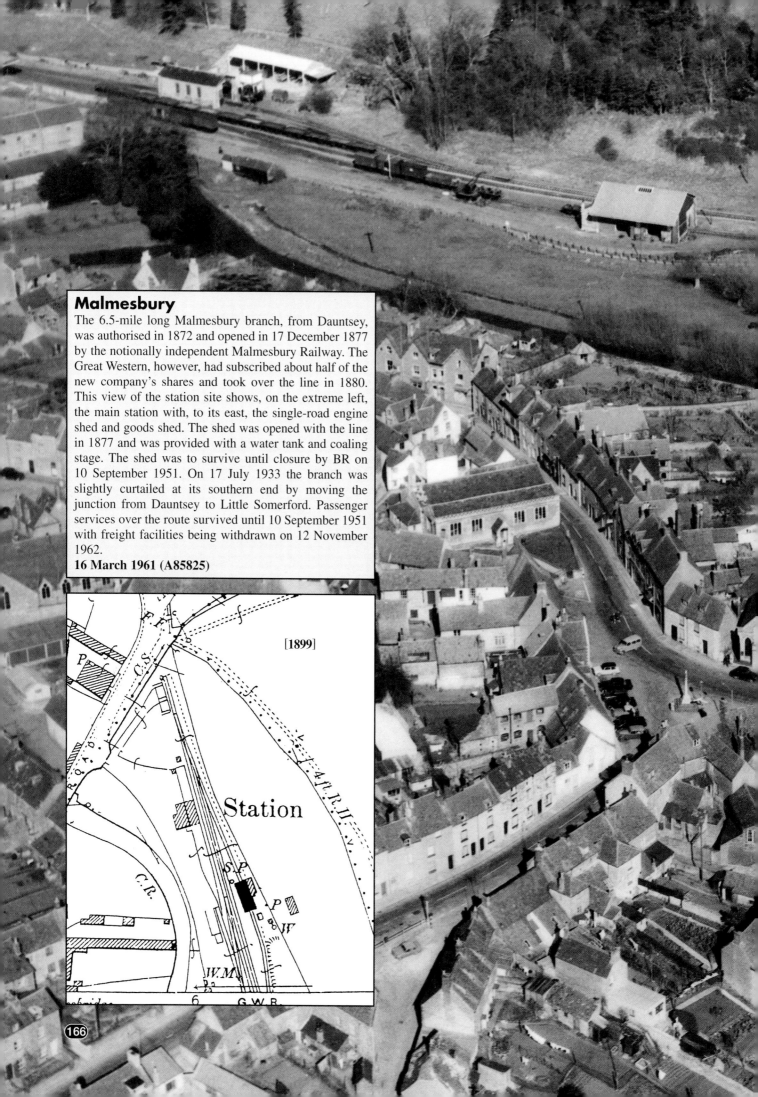

Malmesbury

The 6.5-mile long Malmesbury branch, from Dauntsey, was authorised in 1872 and opened in 17 December 1877 by the notionally independent Malmesbury Railway. The Great Western, however, had subscribed about half of the new company's shares and took over the line in 1880. This view of the station site shows, on the extreme left, the main station with, to its east, the single-road engine shed and goods shed. The shed was opened with the line in 1877 and was provided with a water tank and coaling stage. The shed was to survive until closure by BR on 10 September 1951. On 17 July 1933 the branch was slightly curtailed at its southern end by moving the junction from Dauntsey to Little Somerford. Passenger services over the route survived until 10 September 1951 with freight facilities being withdrawn on 12 November 1962.

16 March 1961 (A85825)

[1899]

Station

An attractive view at Malmesbury on 5 July 1936 looking towards the branch terminus shows to good effect the small locoshed with its coal and water facilities. Although not visible in the photograph, the photographer has recorded the fact that No 4833 was on shed at the time. *SLS Collection*

A decade on from the previous photograph and in the first year of the Nationalised railway industry, little has occurred to alter Malmesbury from the traditional GWR branch terminus. '58xx' class 0-4-2T No 5805 is pictured in the platform awaiting departure with the 2.22pm service to Little Somerford on 4 October 1948. *SLS Collection*

Malton

One of the most important intermediate stations on the ex-North Eastern Railway line between York and Scarborough, Malton was opened with the York & North Midland Railway's route to the coast on 7 July 1845. The station with its trainshed was designed by G. T. Andrews, who was a close colleague of the 'Railway King', George Hudson. The aerial view, taken looking northwards shows to good effect, the station building with its overall roof and platform arrangements; for many years, the only means of accessing the island platform was via a wooden drawbridge lowered over the tracks. Slightly to the east of the station was a curve linking in to the second line to serve Malton, that between Pilmoor and Driffield, which opened on 19 May 1853. This line lost its normal passenger services on 5 June 1950, but was to continue to see summer services from Scarborough to the north, via two reversals at Malton, until 1963. Visible in the foreground is the turntable that served the small engine shed. The shed was built in 1867, replacing an earlier one constructed in 1853 and was to survive until closure on 15 April 1963.

23 April 1960 (A80014)

With Derby class 108 DMU No E50644 leading, the 12.19 York-Scarborough service arrives at Malton on 2 September 1980. The view shows the G. T. Andrews-designed overall roof. Note that the island platform has been demolished. *Brian Morrison*

[1928]

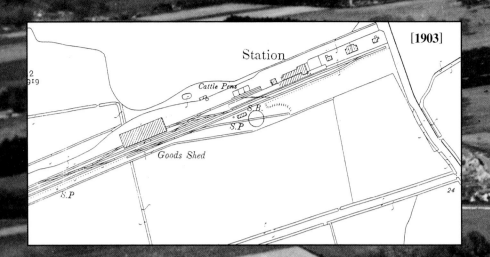
[1903]

Mildenhall

The terminus of the 19-mile long branch from Barnwell Junction, via Fordham Junction, Mildenhall was provided with a passenger station, goods shed, signalbox, turntable and two railway houses. The branch was authorised by the Great Eastern Railway Acts of 18 July 1881 and was opened in two stages: Barnwell Junction-Fordham Junction on 2 June 1884 and Fordham Junction-Mildenhall on 1 April 1885. The line served a predominantly agricultural community and much of the freight traffic comprised agricultural products such as sugar beet. Passenger services over the line were never excessive, with four return workings, for example, in 1949. The route saw the introduction of German-built railbuses in July 1958, but these were soon replaced by two-car DMUs. Following proposals first made in October 1961, passenger services over the route were withdrawn on 18 June 1962. Freight facilities were withdrawn from Mildenhall, and the line closed completely between Fordham Junction and the terminus, on 13 July 1964.

29 April 1930 (31762)

Ex-GER Class E4 2-4-0 No 62781 is pictured at the branch terminus on 18 April 1949 prior to providing the motive power on the 5.48pm service to Cambridge. *SLS Collection*

On 30 November 1957 ex-GER Class J15 0-6-0 No 65438 stands at Mildenhall with a two-coach train for Cambridge. *L. King*

171

Minehead

A popular holiday destination, which gained a significant increase in traffic during the summer months, Minehead was served by a branch off the Bristol-Exeter main line just to the west of Taunton at Norton Fitzwarren. The original West Somerset Railway was authorised in 1857 to construct a line from Norton Fitzwarren to Watchet; this line, following delays, was not opened until 31 March 1862. The extension — the Minehead Railway — was not to be opened until 16 July 1874. Both lines were operated by the Bristol & Exeter — later the GWR — and were built to the broad gauge, being converted to standard gauge in October 1882. Minehead was provided with a single, double-faced, platform, a goods shed, signalbox and a small wooden engine shed with turntable. The engine shed had originally been erected at Watchet and had been moved to Minehead for the opening of the extension. At the date of the aerial photograph, the line was still under GWR control; it passed to British Railways (Western Region) in 1948. The shed was to close on 3 November 1956. On the west side of the station site, adjacent to the turntable road, a further siding was added in 1928. Although there was a harbour at Minehead, this resulted in little traffic to the railway. Minehead lost its freight facilities on 6 July 1964 with the decision to concentrate all services at Taunton, whilst the line was to close completely on 4 January 1971. Subsequently, Minehead and the line to Norton Fitzwarren was preserved by the West Somerset Railway and regular passenger services reintroduced between Minehead and Bishops Lydeard with occasional specials via Norton Fitzwarren junction to and from the national network.

16 August 1947 (R9090)

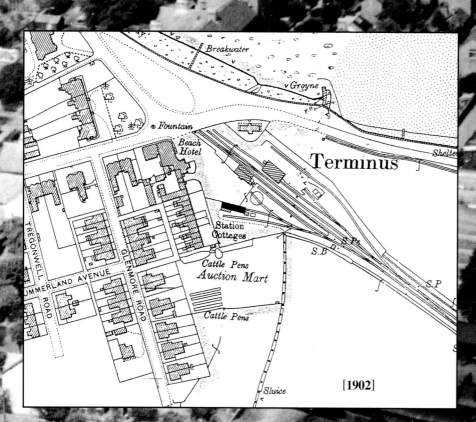

[1902]

On 7 April 1959 0-6-0PT No 9732 is seen at Minehead station awaiting departure with a service to Taunton. *R. N. Joanes*

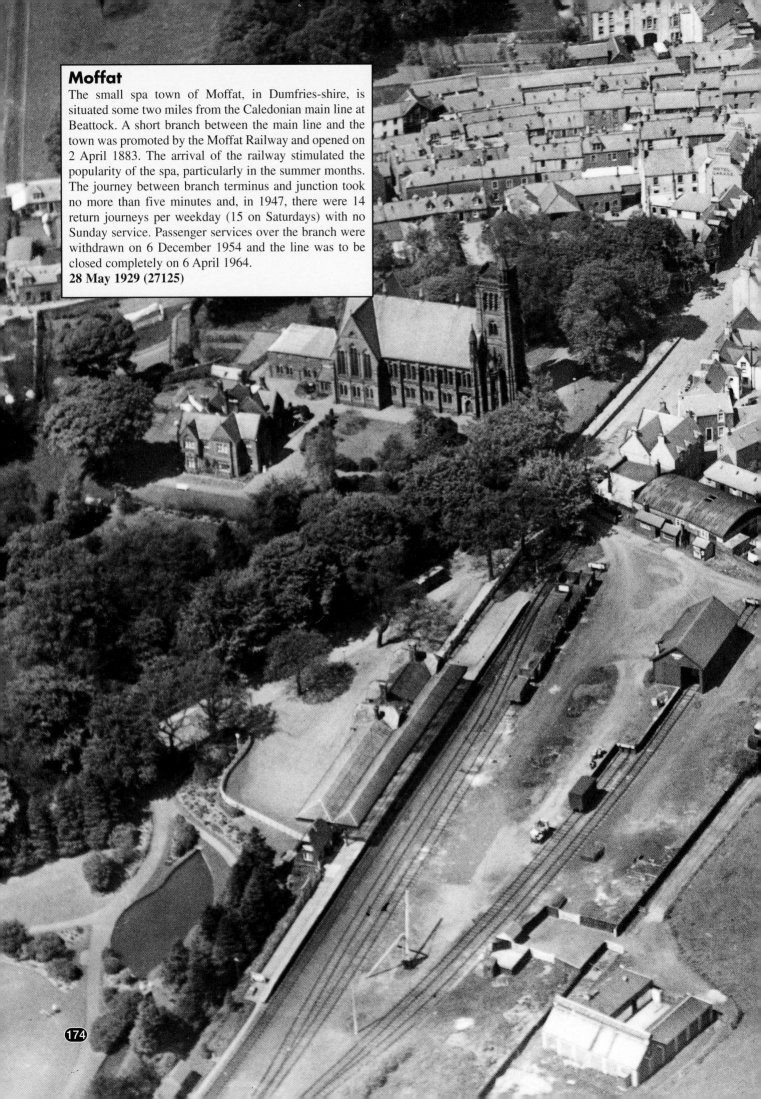

Moffat

The small spa town of Moffat, in Dumfries-shire, is situated some two miles from the Caledonian main line at Beattock. A short branch between the main line and the town was promoted by the Moffat Railway and opened on 2 April 1883. The arrival of the railway stimulated the popularity of the spa, particularly in the summer months. The journey between branch terminus and junction took no more than five minutes and, in 1947, there were 14 return journeys per weekday (15 on Saturdays) with no Sunday service. Passenger services over the branch were withdrawn on 6 December 1954 and the line was to be closed completely on 6 April 1964.
28 May 1929 (27125)

On the map inset:

526
1·652

Manse

527
1·223

Station

528

516
3·204
3·204

517

515
1·522

513
1·471

514
·550

Smithy

Gas Work

Lady
Knowe

530
4·932

[1899]

Slaughter
House

25·018

529
2·479

Police Burgh Boundary

Sluice

On 26 June 1954 the single-coach with locomotive forming the 12.20pm (SO) service from Moffat to Beattock awaits departure from the branch terminus. *SLS Collection.*

Mold

Situated in the Alyn Valley to the northwest of Wrexham, Mold was located within the North Wales coalfield and be part of the country where the London & North Western and Great Western railways competed strongly for the traffic. In the case of Mold it was the former that predominated. The first line to serve the town was the 10-mile branch from Saltney which was opened by the Mold Railway (authorised by an Act of 9 July 1847) on 14 August 1849. Although the bulk of the route, which was operated by the LNWR from the outset, was constructed as double track, the final 2.75 miles into Mold was single track; it would not be doubled until 1870. The line beyond Mold, towards Denbigh, was promoted by the Mold & Denbigh Junction Railway, which was authorised by Act on 6 August 1861 to construct the line. Opened in September 1869, the company's line was operated by the LNWR but was to retain its notional independence until the Grouping. The aerial photograph, taken looking westwards shortly after Nationalisation, shows the station in the centre. From 1849 until 1890 there was a small two-road engine shed on the south side of the line just to the east of the station; after closure it was used as a grain warehouse, but it is now demolished. Passenger services between Denbigh and Chester via Mold were withdrawn on 30 April 1962, with the line closing completely west of Mold at that time, except for occassional MoD traffic to Rhydymwyn which ended in 1983. The line closed between Mold Synthite Siding and Penyffordd Junction on 9 September 1984.

14 August 1954 (A56430)

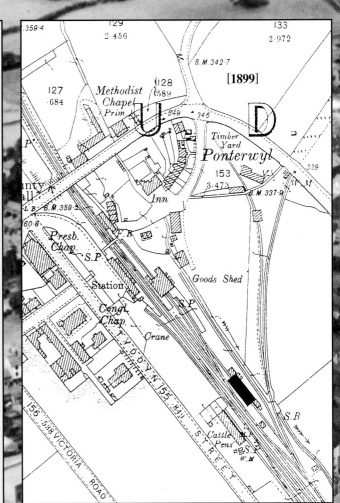

[1899]

In October 1955, an RCTS special headed by Stanier-designed 2-6-4T No 42461 awaits departure from Mold station. *Ian Allan Library*

Montrose

The town of Montrose, situated on the east coast of Scotland, possessed two railway stations: the ex-Caledonian Railway terminus (which had closed to passenger services in April 1934 when services were diverted to the second station) and the ex-North British station situated on the through route between Arbroath and Kinnaber Junction. By the date of the aerial photograph, the once-extensive network of lines serving the town had been reduced solely to the main line between Aberdeen and Dundee. The NBR's presence north of the River Tay was cemented with the opening of the first Tay Bridge on 1 January 1878 (although the collapse of the bridge on 28 December 1879 meant that the fixed link was severed until the opening of the second bridge on 11 July 1887). Through its share in the Dundee & Arbroath Joint line, the NBR gained access to Arbroath and from there promoted its own route northwards towards Aberdeen. The line from Arbroath to Kinnaber Junction, where it met the existing CR line towards Aberdeen, opened in three phases: Arbroath-Inverkeilor on 1 October 1880; Inverkeilor-Lunan Bay on 8 October; and, Lunan Bay-Kinnaber, via Montrose, on 1 May 1881. As part of the East Coast main line, the route through Montrose witnessed the express services operated in both 1888 and 1895 during the 'Railway Races to the North'. The line remains operational today, carrying both passenger and freight services. In addition to serving passenger trains, Montrose retains its freight facilities, providing a rail head for traffic destined to and from east Angus.

17 May 1975 (290895)

Montrose South signalbox recorded on 5 February 1979. This is a North British Railway design dating from 1881.
R. E. Ruffell

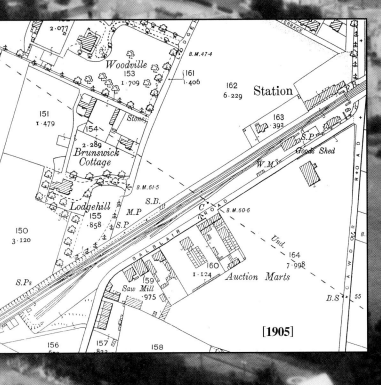

[1905]

Nairn

Viewed looking northwards, the aerial photograph records one of the intermediate stations between Inverness and Aberdeen. The line through Nairn was promoted by two different companies that were ultimately to form part of the Highland Railway. The section from Inverness to Nairn, opened on 5 November 1855, was built by the Inverness & Nairn Railway and that eastwards, opened on 22 September 1857, by the Inverness & Aberdeen Junction Railway. The station was served by two signalboxes, East and West, both of which were built by the Highland Railway in 1891; latterly the boxes were under the control of a single signalman who used a cycle along the platforms to control both sections. By the date of the aerial photograph all services were dieselised; in the May 1971-April 1972 timetable, there were six return workings per day between Inverness and Aberdeen, with an additional early morning service from Elgin to Inverness serving Nairn. There was no Sunday service.

11 July 1972 (235217)

Pictured at Nairn on 28 May 1980 is Class 27 No 27108 with the 10.58 departure to Aberdeen (the 10.39 ex-Inverness). *Peter Harris*

Newcastleton

Located on the ex-North British Waverley route between Riddings Junction and Riccarton Junction, Newcastleton station is pictured in the aerial view looking eastwards. The Border Union (North British) Railway Act received Royal Assent on 21 July 1859 for the construction of a 43-mile long line from the existing NB terminus at Hawick through to Carlisle. The line was opened throughout on 1 July 1862, although (until the completion of the Midland route to Carlisle) the line was not a huge financial success. Of the stations between Hawick and Carlisle, in terms of traffic generated Newcastleton was one of the most important, however. As can be seen in the aerial view, the station was provided with both passenger and freight facilities; the latter were, however, withdrawn on 9 October 1967. The Waverley route was to be closed completely through Newcastleton on 5 January 1969, despite considerable opposition. In Newcastleton, for example, the level crossing gates were padlocked to prevent to movement of the final train.

15 May 1964 (A129581)

[1920]

On 10 June 1968, Newcastleton station had barely six months to go before closure. This view records the scene looking southwards to Carlisle and shows well the station building, signalbox and footbridge. *Andrew Muckley*

The platform accommodation at Newcastleton for Edinburgh-bound passengers was relatively spartan, as shown in this view taken on 10 June 1968. *Andrew Muckley*

On 25 May 1984 Class 31 No 31322 leaves Oakham with the 10.20 from Birmingham New Street to Norwich. *W. A. Sharman.*

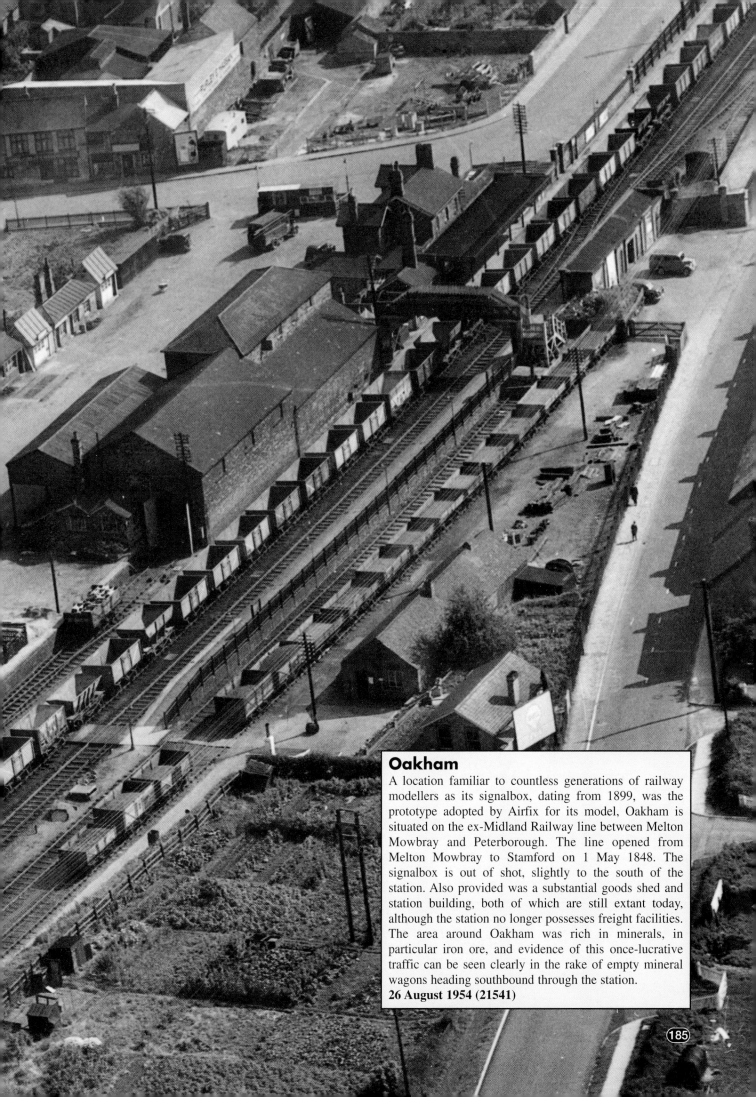

Oakham

A location familiar to countless generations of railway modellers as its signalbox, dating from 1899, was the prototype adopted by Airfix for its model, Oakham is situated on the ex-Midland Railway line between Melton Mowbray and Peterborough. The line opened from Melton Mowbray to Stamford on 1 May 1848. The signalbox is out of shot, slightly to the south of the station. Also provided was a substantial goods shed and station building, both of which are still extant today, although the station no longer possesses freight facilities. The area around Oakham was rich in minerals, in particular iron ore, and evidence of this once-lucrative traffic can be seen clearly in the rake of empty mineral wagons heading southbound through the station.

26 August 1954 (21541)

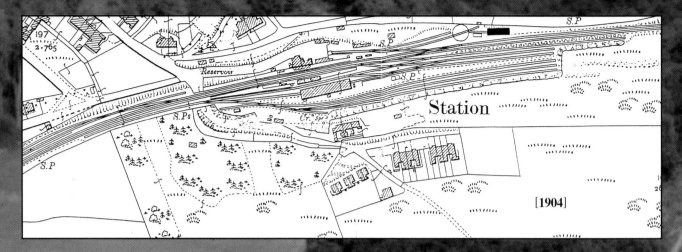

[1904]

Okehampton

Situated on the London & South Western Railway main line from Exeter to Plymouth, Okehampton station, despite serving one of the most important intermediate towns on the route, was actually situated some distance from the town itself. Promoted by the Okehampton Railway (which was incorporated in 1862) to construct a line from Coleford to the town, the plans were amended in 1863 to allow for the construction of an extension to Lydford and thence to Plymouth over the existing broad gauge lines on which mixed gauge track would be constructed. Behind the OR was the LSWR, despite its agreement with the South Devon Railway that it had no interests west of Okehampton. The OR became the Devon & Cornwall Railway in 1865 with the first section of line, from Coleford Junction to North Tawton, opening on 1 November of that year. From North Tawton to Okehampton Road (later known as Sampford Courtenay) the line was opened on 8 January 1867 and thence to Okehampton proper on 3 October 1871 and westwards to Lydford on 12 October 1874. By this date, however, the D&CR had been formally absorbed by the LSWR. The route through Okehampton represented the LSWR's line to the west and as such played host to famous services such as the 'Atlantic Coast Express'. By the date of the aerial photograph passenger services west of Okehampton had ceased (on 6 May 1968) although the line remained open to serve the quarry at Meldon. Passenger services had also been withdrawn eastwards, succumbing on 5 June 1972. The station is still extant and is now used regularly for seasonal services to and from Exeter and is the base for the Dartmoor Railway preservation scheme.
9 August 1973 (269362)

On 30 October 1970, towards the end of the line's passenger service, a single-car diesel unit awaits departure from Okehampton with the 11.40 service to Exeter. *John King*

More than a decade later, on 2 August 1983, Okehampton station remains largely intact although the signage has disappeared and the line is used for freight traffic alone, with the bulk of the movements serving Meldon Quarry. Almost two decades later a seasonal service to Okehampton would be restored and the Dartmoor Railway would provide links on to Meldon. *R. E. Ruffell*

Peebles station seen on 26 August 1960, a year after closure.
Hugh Ballantyne

Peebles

Viewed looking westwards, the aerial view shows the ex-CR station in Peebles shortly before Nationalisation. The first railway to serve the town was the North British, whose route from Eskbank opened on 4 July 1855 and was extended through to Galashiels on 18 June 1866. The Symington, Biggar & Broughton Railway, which was authorised in 1858 and became part of the CR in 1861, was authorised in 1860 to extend its planned route to serve Peebles. The line to Peebles opened on 1 February 1864. A link was constructed from the CR station through to the NBR station, although this never carried normal passenger services and was used primarily for the movement of freight traffic. Passenger services between Symington and Peebles were withdrawn on 3 June 1950 and the line was closed completely between Broughton and Peebles West (as the ex-CR station had become to differentiate it from the ex-NB one) on 7 June 1954. This closure resulted in greater use of the link between the ex-NB line and Peebles West for the period until the complete closure of Peebles West and the line to Peebles Junction on 1 August 1959. The aerial photograph shows the station on the south bank of the River Tweed and the link line heading eastwards. The station was, as is evident in the photographs, an impressive structure with overall roof and the location was also provided with a large goods shed; one of the station's main sources of freight traffic was the movement of carcasses for shipment southwards.
26 September 1947 (A11531/47)

[1908]

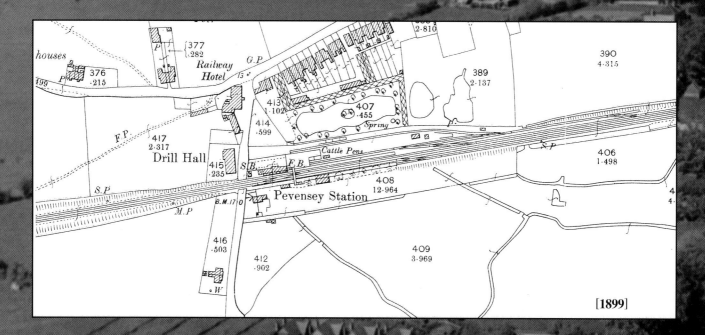

[1899]

Pevensey & Westham

Famous for its castle (seen in the background), Pevensey is served by the ex-London, Brighton & South Coast Railway line between Eastbourne and Hastings. The station, known originally as West Ham & Pevensey, was opened on 27 June 1846. The aerial view is taken looking northwards; slightly out of shot to the west is a level crossing and the location of the 1876-built signalbox (which remains operational). The line the Pevensey was originally promoted by the Brighton, Lewes & Hastings Railway, which was incorporated in 1844; the BL&HR became part of the LBSCR. The line east of Lewes was originally constructed as single track, but was later to be doubled. At the date of the aerial photograph, passenger services through the station were still steam-hauled; the line was electrified in the 1930s with services commencing on 7 July 1935. The station possessed a small goods yard, but freight facilities were withdrawn on 4 September 1961.

25 May 1931 (35327)

191

Ponteland

Located to the northwest of Newcastle, Ponteland was situated at the end of a seven-mile long branch from South Gosforth via Kenton. The line opened, promoted by the North Eastern Railway under a Light Railway Order, on 1 March 1905 to freight and on 1 June 1905 to passenger traffic. Located about 400yd to the south of the terminus at Ponteland was the junction for the 1.25-mile long extension to Darras Hall, which opened on 27 September 1913 to freight and to passenger traffic on the following 1 October. The intention of the NER was eventually to electrify these lines in the expectation that housing development would lead to vastly increased traffic; in the event, World War 1 put paid to these hopes and despite efforts to make the services more cost-effective, including the use of Sentinel steam railcars, passenger services were withdrawn on 17 June 1929. The line from Ponteland to Darras Hall closed completely on 2 August 1954 with the cessation of coal traffic from Kirkheaton Colliery. Ponteland retained its freight facilities until complete closure on 14 August 1967. The line was retained to serve the ICI works at Callerton and much of the route was, ironically, electrified as part of the Tyne & Wear Metro in the early 1980s; in 1991, the Metro was extended over part of the closed route to serve Newcastle Airport.

26 April 1959 (A74863)

Pictured on the occasion of a joint SLS/RCTS tour of the line in late September 1963, Ponteland station is a buzz of activity as enthusiasts record the special, hauled by Class V3 2-6-2T No 67620, at the station. The view affords a good reference to the signalbox and platform. *Ian Allan Library*

[1920]

Pontrilas

Situated on the ex-Great Western line from Buildwas to Abergavenny via Marsh Farm Junction which now forms part of the North & West route from Newport to Hereford, Shrewsbury and Chester, Pontrilas was the junction for the line towards Hay on Wye. The main line through Pontrilas was authorised as part of the Newport, Abergavenny & Hereford Railway on 3 August 1846 and opened for freight on 30 July 1852 and to passenger services on 6 December 1853. The Golden Valley Railway opened from Pontrilas to Dorstone on 1 September 1881 and thence to Hay on 27 May 1889. Following financial difficulties, the line was closed in 1897/8, but was acquired by the Great Western Railway and reopened in 1901. Passenger services were withdrawn between Pontrilas and Hay on 15 December 1941 and the line closed completely between the MoD sidings at Moss and Abbeydore on 3 June 1957. The final section, from Pontrilas to Moss depot closed on 31 March 1969. Although the station looks well kept in the aerial view, it had in fact already lost its passenger service — on 9 June 1958 — and was on the point of losing its regular freight facilities, which were to be withdrawn on 12 October 1964.

17 September 1964 (A139517)

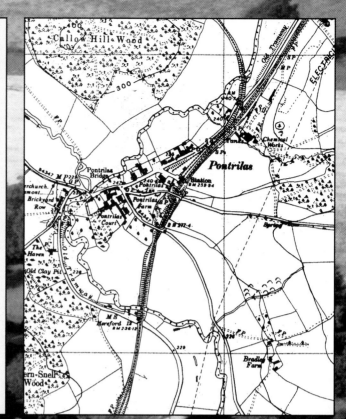

194

'Castle' class 4-6-0 No 5007 *Rougemount Castle* heads south through Pontrilas station on 21 June 1951 with a service from Birmingham Snow Hill to Cardiff. In the bay platform '58xx'class 0-4-2T No 5818 waits at the head of a short freight train. This view shows well the facilities on both platforms in the early years of the post-'Big Four' era. *SLS Collection*

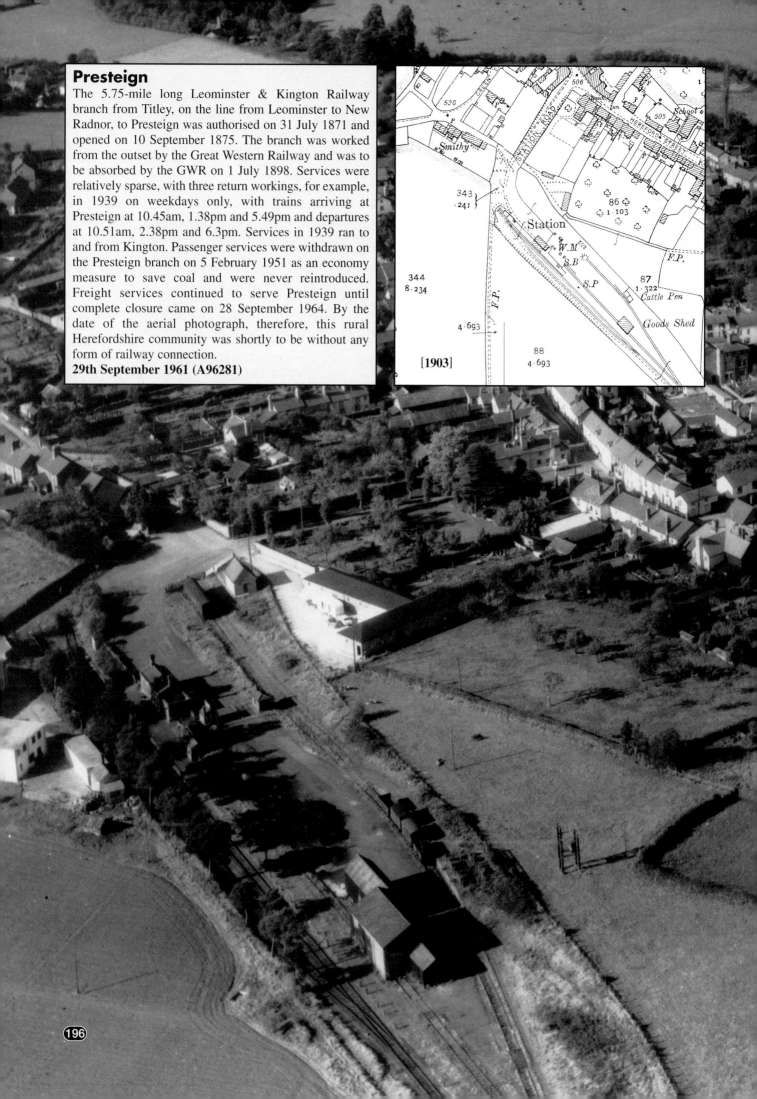

Presteign

The 5.75-mile long Leominster & Kington Railway branch from Titley, on the line from Leominster to New Radnor, to Presteign was authorised on 31 July 1871 and opened on 10 September 1875. The branch was worked from the outset by the Great Western Railway and was to be absorbed by the GWR on 1 July 1898. Services were relatively sparse, with three return workings, for example, in 1939 on weekdays only, with trains arriving at Presteign at 10.45am, 1.38pm and 5.49pm and departures at 10.51am, 2.38pm and 6.3pm. Services in 1939 ran to and from Kington. Passenger services were withdrawn on the Presteign branch on 5 February 1951 as an economy measure to save coal and were never reintroduced. Freight services continued to serve Presteign until complete closure came on 28 September 1964. By the date of the aerial photograph, therefore, this rural Herefordshire community was shortly to be without any form of railway connection.

29th September 1961 (A96281)

[1903]

The view of the main station building from the loading bank on 29 March 1959.
Ian Allan Library

Princetown

Although the Great Western branch from Yelverton to Princetown received the Royal Assent on 13 August 1878 and was opened on 11 August 1883, it was largely constructed over the route of an earlier horse-powered line, the Plymouth & Dartmoor Railway, which had opened as far as King Tor on 26 September 1823 and to Princetown three years later. Princetown is the location of Dartmoor prison, opened in 1809 to house Prisoners of War, and was also perceived as a railhead for the extraction of granite from the moors. Nominally independent until 1922, the Princetown Railway was operated from the outset by the GWR. The line possessed a number of steep gradients and sharp curves, with the result that one class of locomotive — Churchward's '44xx' class 2-6-2Ts of 1905 — became closely associated with the route, particularly once a system of flange lubrication had been perfected. By the mid-1950s, with the withdrawal of the '44xx' class, other classes of locomotive also became regular performers, most notably members of the '45xx' class of 2-6-2T.

When first opened the station was provided with a carriage shed, at the buffer stops, but this had disappeared by the date of the aerial photograph, along with station building, goods shed and engine shed. Passenger services were withdrawn between Yelverton and Princetown on 5 March 1956, at which stage the line was to close completely.

18 April 1952 (R16164)

An undated — but probably early 1920s — view of the station looking westwards. Note the entertaining display of five-bar gates on the platform! *Ian Allan Library*

[1904]

Terminus

In August 1953 ex-GWR Class 44xx 2-6-2T No 4401 awaits departure from Princetown with a service for Yelverton.
Ian Allan Library

Redditch

Now the terminus of the electrified branch from Barnt Green, Redditch was at the time this aerial photograph was taken an important intermediate station on the ex-Midland Railway route southwards via Evesham to Ashchurch. The view shows the approaches to the station from the north; the actual station is just out of frame further to the south. Clearly visible, however, are part of the extensive goods facilities offered by the railway and, in the distance, the small locomotive shed. The shed was opened in 1872 and, prior to 1902, boasted a 42ft turntable. The shed's roof was replaced by the LMS in 1938 and the shed was to close on 1 June 1964. Visible across the line from the engine shed is Redditch North signalbox; this was a replacement box opened on 8 November 1925 which was to survive until 10 August 1986. The line to Dixon's Wharf, with a rake of wagons standing, can be seen to the left of the engine shed. The Redditch Railway, authorised on 23 July 1858, from Barnt Green opened to freight on 19 September 1859 and to passenger services on the following 1 October. The line was extended southwards, at which time the original passenger station was closed and relocated slightly to the south, with the opening of the Ashchurch & Evesham Railway (to freight on 1 July 1864 and to passenger traffic on 1 October 1864). Passenger services south of Redditch were withdrawn officially on 17 June 1963, although since 1 October 1962 these had been provided by buses as a result of the condition of the track and the line south from Redditch to Evesham was effectively closed completely from that date. On 7 February 1972, the 1864 station was replaced by one further to the north and, more recently, the line was electrified as part of the Birmingham Cross-City project.
28 June 1952 (R16970)

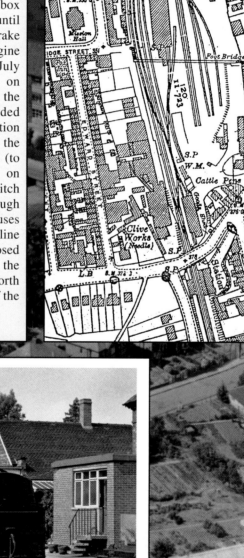

The stock to form the 2.55pm service to Ashchurch arrives at Redditch at 3.59pm — some things don't change! — on 18 June 1960 behind ex-LMS 2-6-4T No 42446. The train had been delayed by an earlier failure and departed from Redditch 65min late; however, more than 16min was recovered by the time it arrived at Ashchurch as a result of some spirited running. *M. Mensing*

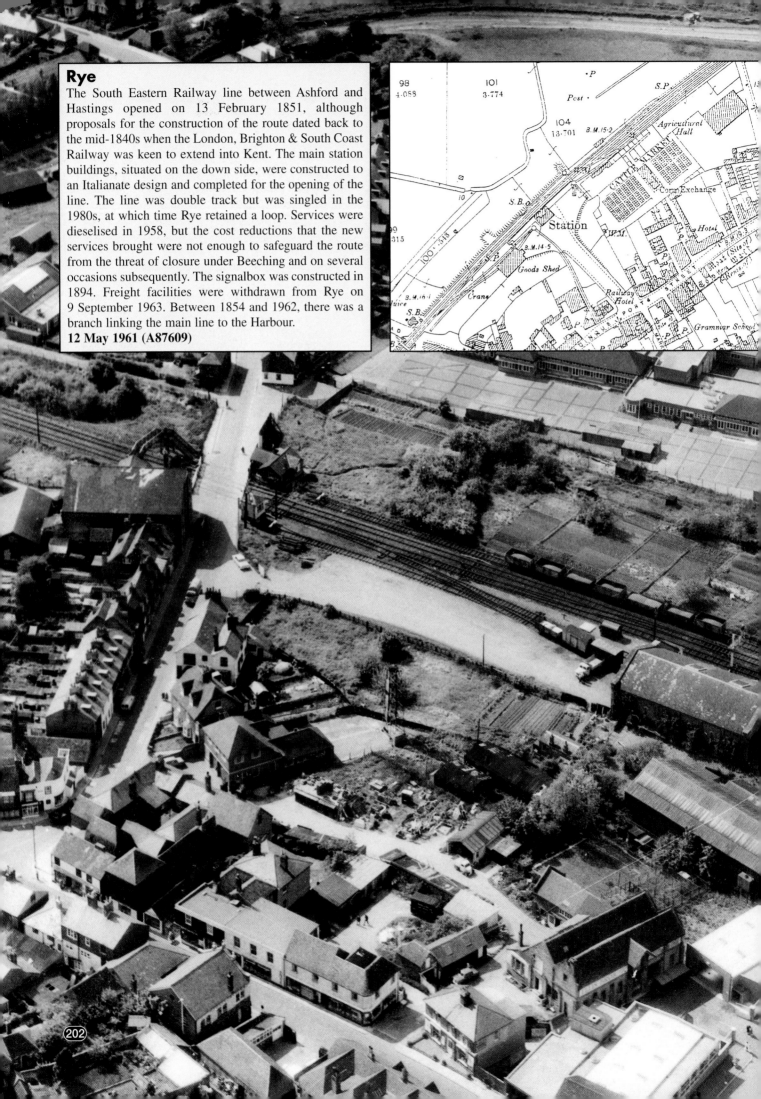

Rye

The South Eastern Railway line between Ashford and Hastings opened on 13 February 1851, although proposals for the construction of the route dated back to the mid-1840s when the London, Brighton & South Coast Railway was keen to extend into Kent. The main station buildings, situated on the down side, were constructed to an Italianate design and completed for the opening of the line. The line was double track but was singled in the 1980s, at which time Rye retained a loop. Services were dieselised in 1958, but the cost reductions that the new services brought were not enough to safeguard the route from the threat of closure under Beeching and on several occasions subsequently. The signalbox was constructed in 1894. Freight facilities were withdrawn from Rye on 9 September 1963. Between 1854 and 1962, there was a branch linking the main line to the Harbour.

12 May 1961 (A87609)

A six-car DEMU set, No 1034, heads eastbound through the station. Note, in particular, the gap between the running line and the signalbox. *Ian Allan library*

The main station buildings at Rye recorded in October 1955. *SLS Collection*

St Ives (Cambs)

The Cambridgeshire town of St Ives was the location of the junction between the Cambridge-Huntingdon and St Ives-March lines. The line from Chesterton to St Ives was authorised in 1845 and opened by the Eastern Counties (later Great Eastern) Railway on 17 August 1847. On the same day, the line from Ely to Huntingdon via St Ives was opened by the Ely & Huntingdon Railway and the station was shared between the two railways. The station became a junction with the opening of the line to March on 1 February 1848. The aerial view of the station, taken looking towards the southwest shows well the substantial station building constructed on the March side of the junction. On 1 February 1883, the line between St Ives and Huntingdon was transferred to the control of the Great Northern & Great Eastern Joint Committee. The whole network of lines passed to the LNER in 1923, but the service to Ely was withdrawn on 2 February 1931. Passenger services were withdrawn between St Ives and Huntingdon East on 15 June 1959, at which time the section of line between St Ives and Godmanchester closed completely. DMU operation had already been introduced on the Cambridge-St Ives-March line, but these services were withdrawn north of St Ives on 6 March 1967, the economies that DMU operation offered had failed to save the services. At the same time pay trains were introduced on the remaining services between St Ives and Cambridge. Passenger services were withdrawn between Cambridge and St Ives on 5 October 1970, although the line remained open for freight traffic thereafter. The line is now out of use, although, given the growth of Cambridge's economy and traffic problems, there have been plans for its reopening to passenger services.

4 September 1929 (28938C)

[1902]

Although by the date of this photograph, 2 October 1970, St Ives was but a shadow of its former importance as a railway junction, this view shows well the location of the signalbox and its relationship with the main station building. A DMU awaits departure with a service to Cambridge whilst alongside Class 31 No 5532 sits amongst rakes of mineral wagons. *G. R. Mortimer*

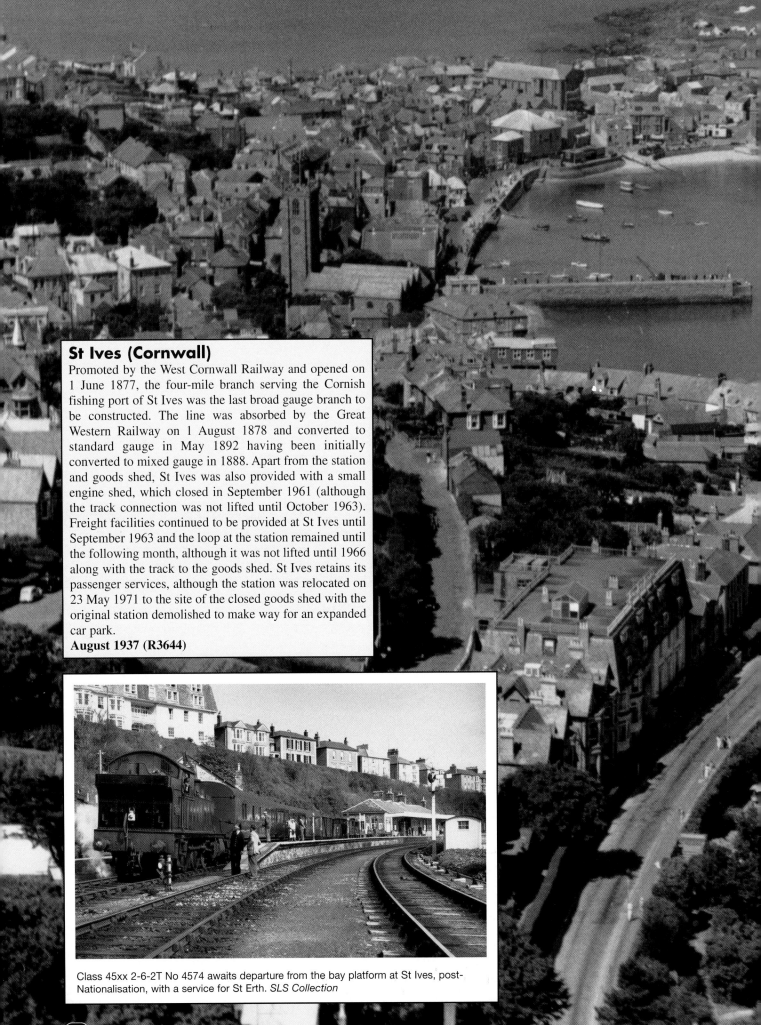

St Ives (Cornwall)

Promoted by the West Cornwall Railway and opened on 1 June 1877, the four-mile branch serving the Cornish fishing port of St Ives was the last broad gauge branch to be constructed. The line was absorbed by the Great Western Railway on 1 August 1878 and converted to standard gauge in May 1892 having been initially converted to mixed gauge in 1888. Apart from the station and goods shed, St Ives was also provided with a small engine shed, which closed in September 1961 (although the track connection was not lifted until October 1963). Freight facilities continued to be provided at St Ives until September 1963 and the loop at the station remained until the following month, although it was not lifted until 1966 along with the track to the goods shed. St Ives retains its passenger services, although the station was relocated on 23 May 1971 to the site of the closed goods shed with the original station demolished to make way for an expanded car park.

August 1937 (R3644)

Class 45xx 2-6-2T No 4574 awaits departure from the bay platform at St Ives, post-Nationalisation, with a service for St Erth. *SLS Collection*

[1906]

Pedn Olva

Low Water Mark of Ordinary Tides

Porthminster Be

High Water Mark of Ordinary Tides

Sand

Sand

Station

Posts

Capstan

Capstans

Capstan

Capstan

Capstan

Capstans

Tallund

Viaduct

TALLAND ROAD

Saltcoats station on 30 September 1973 looking in the Glasgow direction.
R. F. Roberts/SLS Collection

Saltcoats

The port of Ardrossan was the target for both the Glasgow & South Western and Caledonian railways and, en route to the port, both served the town of Saltcoats about a mile to the east. This view shows the ex-G&SWR station looking westwards. Authorised in 1827, the Ardrossan & Johnstone Railway was one of the earliest in Scotland and was promoted as a result of the investment made earlier in the 19th century by the Earl of Eglington in trying to turn Ardrossan into the foremost harbour serving Glasgow. The railway was designed to be linked to a canal running from Glasgow to Johnstone but this concept proved impractical and the railway was recreated as the Ardrossan Railway Company in 1840; at this time the line was rebuilt as standard gauge and the alignment was modified to allow for the use of steam locomotives. As such the line fell under the influence of the Glasgow, Paisley, Kilmarnock & Ayr Railway, and thus, ultimately, the G&SWR. The station illustrated here was the third to be constructed to serve the town and dated from 1882; although freight facilities were provided, these had been withdrawn before the aerial photograph was taken, on 5 April 1965. At the time of the main photograph services were operated by DMUs, but 25kV EMU services over the line to Ardrossan were introduced on 24 November 1986.
28 June 1972 (A236514)

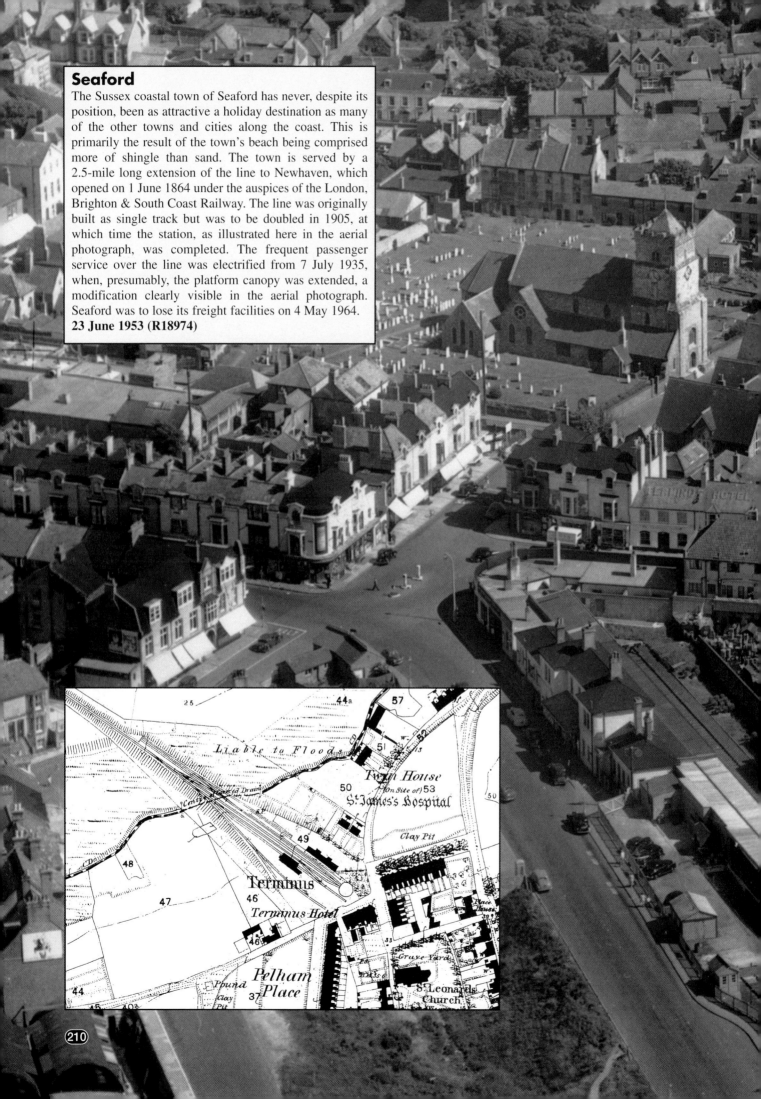

Seaford

The Sussex coastal town of Seaford has never, despite its position, been as attractive a holiday destination as many of the other towns and cities along the coast. This is primarily the result of the town's beach being comprised more of shingle than sand. The town is served by a 2.5-mile long extension of the line to Newhaven, which opened on 1 June 1864 under the auspices of the London, Brighton & South Coast Railway. The line was originally built as single track but was to be doubled in 1905, at which time the station, as illustrated here in the aerial photograph, was completed. The frequent passenger service over the line was electrified from 7 July 1935, when, presumably, the platform canopy was extended, a modification clearly visible in the aerial photograph. Seaford was to lose its freight facilities on 4 May 1964.

23 June 1953 (R18974)

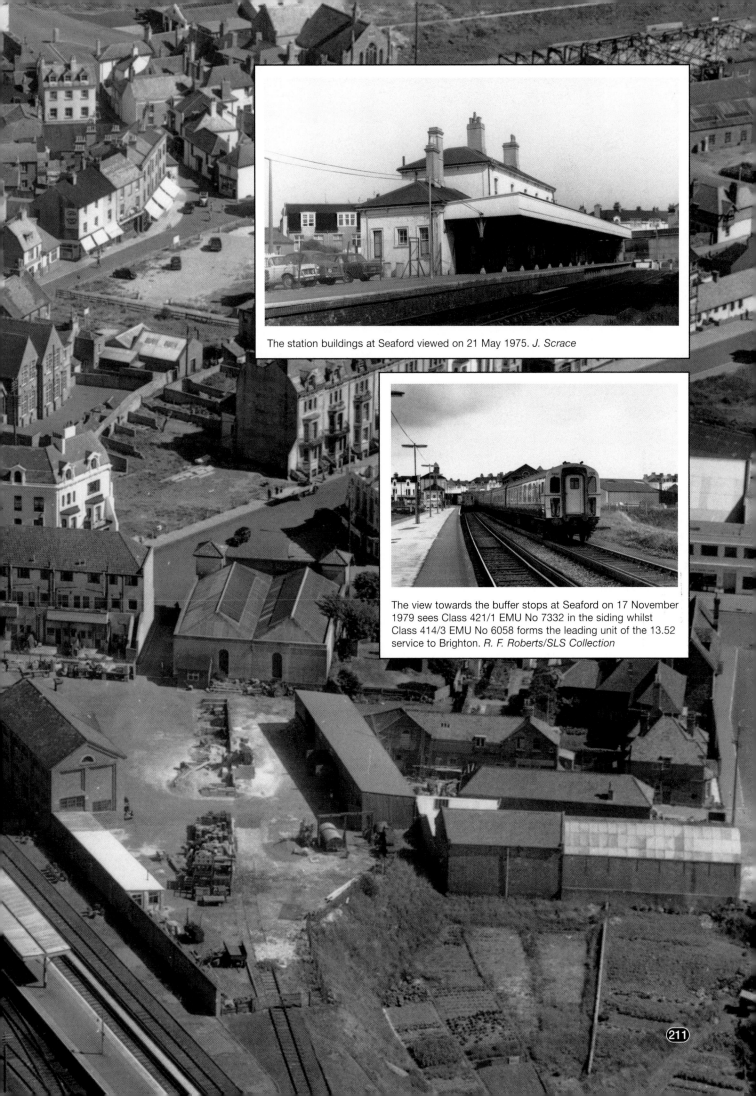

The station buildings at Seaford viewed on 21 May 1975. *J. Scrace*

The view towards the buffer stops at Seaford on 17 November 1979 sees Class 421/1 EMU No 7332 in the siding whilst Class 414/3 EMU No 6058 forms the leading unit of the 13.52 service to Brighton. *R. F. Roberts/SLS Collection*

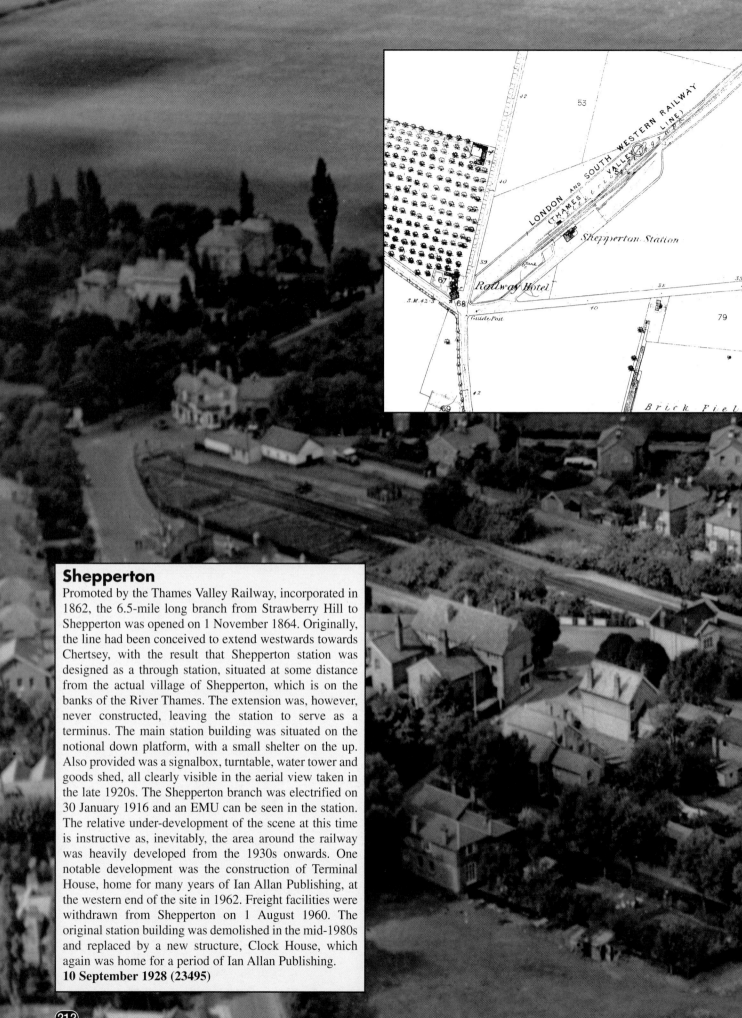

Shepperton

Promoted by the Thames Valley Railway, incorporated in 1862, the 6.5-mile long branch from Strawberry Hill to Shepperton was opened on 1 November 1864. Originally, the line had been conceived to extend westwards towards Chertsey, with the result that Shepperton station was designed as a through station, situated at some distance from the actual village of Shepperton, which is on the banks of the River Thames. The extension was, however, never constructed, leaving the station to serve as a terminus. The main station building was situated on the notional down platform, with a small shelter on the up. Also provided was a signalbox, turntable, water tower and goods shed, all clearly visible in the aerial view taken in the late 1920s. The Shepperton branch was electrified on 30 January 1916 and an EMU can be seen in the station. The relative under-development of the scene at this time is instructive as, inevitably, the area around the railway was heavily developed from the 1930s onwards. One notable development was the construction of Terminal House, home for many years of Ian Allan Publishing, at the western end of the site in 1962. Freight facilities were withdrawn from Shepperton on 1 August 1960. The original station building was demolished in the mid-1980s and replaced by a new structure, Clock House, which again was home for a period of Ian Allan Publishing.

10 September 1928 (23495)

When constructed, it was anticipated that Shepperton would form a through station, with the line extended ultimately to link up with the Weybridge-Virginia Water line. In the event, the station has remained a terminus throughout although rudimentary, but unused, facilities were provided on the up platform. This view shows well the main station building with, in the distance, Terminal House, the offices of the Ian Allan Group. *Ian Allan Library*

With the bridge of Terminal House visible in the background, the mail is loaded on board '4-SUB' No 4671 at Shepperton on 18 December 1970. *R. E. Ruffell*

Stanmore

Although the first railway to serve Stanmore was the London & North Western from Harrow & Wealdstone, a line which was opened under the aegis of the Harrow & Stanmore Railway on 18 December 1890 and closed on 15 September 1952, the second line to serve the town was much more conveniently sited. The station illustrated here with its extensive sidings is that constructed for the Metropolitan Railway's extension from Wembley Park, which opened on 10 December 1932. Following the reorganisation of routes resulting from the creation of the London Passenger Transport Board in 1933, from 20 November 1939 services to Stanmore were taken over by the Bakerloo line. In 1977, with the opening of the Jubilee Line, its trains replaced Bakerloo stock on the route. One consequence of the opening of the line was the dramatic increase in the construction of houses in the area, an aspect made all to evident in the aerial view taken looking southwards in 1963. The original LNWR terminus was about one mile to the southwest.

7 July 1963 (A116093)

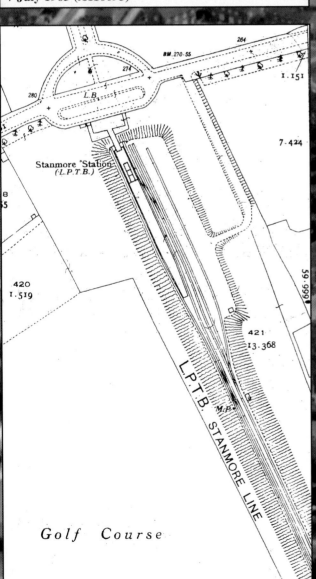

Stanmore "Station" (L.P.T.B.)

L.P.T.B. STANMORE LINE

Golf Course

Pictured on 24 February 1986, two rakes of Jubilee Line stock stand in the platform at Stanmore station. *R. F. Roberts*

The exterior of Stanmore station pictured on 24 February 1996 shows well its origins as part of the expansion of the Underground network during the 1930s. *R. F. Roberts*

On 19 July 1981 two 'Hastings' DEMUs, Nos 1012 and 1005, stand at Stonegate station with the 17.44 service from Hastings to Charing Cross. *Les Bertram*

Viewed from the up platform at Stonegate (formerly Ticehurst Road), the staggered platforms provided at this location are clearly evident. *P. J. Sharpe*

Stonegate

One of the intermediate stations between Tonbridge and Hastings on the South Eastern & Chatham Railway route, Stonegate was originally known as Withernden, then Ticehurst Road. The line between Tunbridge Wells and Bopeep Junction at Hastings was opened in three stages by the South Eastern Railway: from Tunbridge Wells to Robertsbridge, via Stonegate, on 1 September 1851; Robertsbridge to Battle on 1 January 1852; and from Battle to Hastings on 1 February 1852. Three tunnels along the route were constructed with restricted loading gauge, which resulted in specially-constructed DEMUs when the line was dieselised in 1957. By the date of the aerial photograph, freight facilities were in their final months; they were withdrawn completely on 6 November 1961. The line was electrified in the mid-1980s, with electric services being introduced on 27 April 1986.

6 March 1961 (A85755)

Stourbridge Town

Bypassed by the Oxford, Worcester & Wolverhampton
Railway by less than a mile, the town of Stourbridge was
provided with a short branch linking it to Stourbridge
Junction. The line, originally authorised with the rest of
the OWW on 4 August 1845, was not built at that time,
but was finally authorised on 30 June 1874 and opened on
1 October 1879, with freight following on 1 January
1880. The new line allowed for the closure of the branch
opened in 1859 to serve the Lower High Street canal
basin, over which passenger trains had never operated.
The new goods shed and canal basin were served by a line
running beyond the passenger terminus. On 25 August
1935 the branch was effectively converted into two single
track branches: the former down line being exclusively
used for passenger trains and the former up line for freight
traffic only. From 1935 also the passenger service was
largely in the hands of GWR diesel railcars; these were
replaced by BR diesel railcars in the late 1950s. By the
date that the aerial photograph was taken, the freight
facilities had been withdrawn from both Stourbridge
Basin and Stourbridge Town and the line had been singled
(the old up line having been closed on 5 July 1965). As is
evident, part of the formation was converted into a bus
station and the old goods yard has undergone
redevelopment. Subsequent to the date of this photograph,
the traditionally-styled ex-GWR station was demolished
and the terminus provided with more basic facilities.
29 June 1972 (A245065)

By August 1973, when this view of the station was taken, the lines to the goods yard had been lifted and the yard itself redeveloped. Notice the foreshortened platform in the foreground. *SLS Collection*

Stroud

Promoted by the Cheltenham & Great Western Union Railway, but subsumed into the GWR by the time that the line between Kemble and Gloucester was opened on 12 May 1845, the first route through Stroud provided part of the link between Cheltenham and London. This view of the town, looking northwest shows, at its centre, the GWR station with goods yard. On the extreme left can be seen the second railway to serve the town, the Midland Railway branch from Dudbridge, which opened on 16 November 1855. As can be seen in the photograph, there was considerable freight traffic to and from the town over both LMS and GWR routes. Passenger traffic to the ex-MR station ceased on 16 June 1947, but the line was to remain open to freight traffic until 1 June 1966. Normal freight facilities were withdrawn from the ex-GWR station on 10 July 1967, but the line continues to see passenger services between Swindon and Gloucester.
August 1928 (23880)

The LMS station at Stroud, was destined the close to passenger services in June 1947. This view, looking southeast towards the goods shed, was taken in the year of closure. *Ian Allan Library*

[1901]

Swaffham

Viewed looking eastwards, this aerial view of Swaffham in Norfolk shows the ex-Great Eastern Railway route to Dereham heading eastwards whilst the ex-GER line to Roudham Junction, on the Thetford-Norwich line, heads southwards. The first railway to serve the town was the Lynn & Dereham Railway, which was opened on 10 August 1847. Authorised in 1869 as an extension of the line northwards from Watton, the Watton & Swaffham Railway was not be opened for freight traffic until 20 September 1875 and passenger traffic commenced on the following 15 November. Swaffham station was provided with extensive facilities, with sidings on both up and down sides. It was also provided with a 45ft turntable, located towards the junction, where a small two-road engine shed was situated. This opened originally in 1847 and was demolished and replaced, during the 'Big Four' era, by a simple servicing point, which was to last until closure by BR on 2 April 1962. Passenger services over the line to Thetford ceased on 15 June 1964 and the line between Swaffham and Watton was to close completely on 19 April 1965. Passenger services from Dereham to King's Lynn ceased on 9 September 1968, at which time the line from Dereham to Middleton Towers closed completely, freight facilities having been withdrawn from Swaffham on 31 January 1966.

24 July 1964 (A134999)

On 28 May 1950 ex-GER Class J15 0-6-0 No 65479 stands at Swaffham. *SLS Collection*

Towards the end of its life, the line through Swaffham was dieselised and a two-car set stands awaiting departure with a service to Norwich. *SLS Collection*

Cattle Pens

Goods Shed

Tk.

Mission Room

Northwell
Pool

Station

Railway Tavern

P.H.

S.P.

S.B.

Providence Terrace

Baptist Chapel

Cottage

B.M.228·9

229

250
·314

268
1·837

267
6·726

299
·681

298
2·087

304
·646

305
2·932

301
·546

307
2·063

306
1·892

n   e

[1904]

On 9 June 1964 Ivatt Class 2MT 2-6-2T No 41238 is pictured awaiting departure with the 5.38pm service to Wareham. This view, taken from alongside the engine shed shows the overall layout of the station in the early 1960s, with platform, goods shed, signalbox and yard, to good effect. *J. Scrace*

Some five years later, on 22 August 1969, the scene at Swanage is radically different. By this date, steam has been replaced by SR DEMUs and the line was scheduled for abandonment. Shorn of its run round loop, sidings and good facilities, the station has been reduced to a single terminating line on which DEMU No 1128 waits prior to forming the 16.16 service to Wareham. Although passenger services were scheduled for withdrawal on 6 October, this was cancelled as a result of delays in the issuing of the licences for the replacement bus services. *P. Paye*

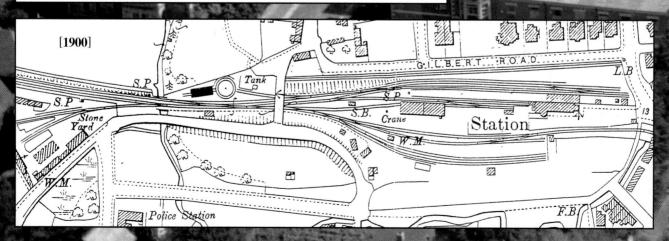

Swanage

The line to Swanage was opened under the aegis of the Swanage Railway on 20 May 1885 and passed to the London & South Western Railway the following year. Although Swanage had a tradition for both quarrying and fishing — indeed the station buildings were constructed out of local Purbeck stone — it was the growth of the town as a seaside resort that was critical for the development of the station, particularly in the interwar years. The aerial photograph shows the station before to the modernisation carried out by the Southern Railway immediately prior to the outbreak of World War 2. As built the station was not provided with a runround loop; this was added in 1897. At the start of the 20th century additional siding accommodation was provided for the freight traffic, but this was increasingly used in the station's heyday for the storage of coaching stock. Swanage was also provided with a small engine shed, again built in Purbeck stone. Freight facilities were withdrawn from Swanage on 4 October 1965 and, thereafter, the process of rationalisation continued, resulting in ultimate closure on 3 January 1972. On 6 June 1967, with diesel-electric multiple-units now providing the passenger stock, the signalbox was closed with the line south of Corfe Castle being operated under the one-engine-in-steam principle. Through carriages to Waterloo were withdrawn from 3 October 1969. Since closure, the preserved Swanage Railway has progressively reopened the line towards Wareham and, in late 2002, the first through train for some 30 years operated to the town.

7 September 1935 (R1037)

Talgarth

One of the southernmost stations of the Cambrian Railways, Talgarth was situated on the section of line between Three Cocks Junction and Talyllyn Junction. This section of line was originally planned to be part of the Hereford, Hay & Brecon Railway, incorporated on 8 August 1859, but was actually to form part of the Mid-Wales Railway. The line opened for freight traffic on 1 September 1864 and to passenger traffic 18 days later. The line was initially operated by the Mid-Wales itself but was operated by the Cambrian Railways from 1888 onwards and absorbed by it 16 years later. The Midland — and later the LMS — had running powers over he section between Three Cocks Junction and Talyllyn Junction. By the date of the aerial photograph, the line was entering its last days. Passenger services between Talyllyn Junction and Moat Lane Junction via Three Cocks Junction were withdrawn on 31 December 1962. At the same time the line between Talyllyn Junction and Llanidloes was to close completely.

26 September 1961 (A96308)

[1904]

227

Teignmouth

Located on the south Devon coast just to the east of Newton Abbot, Teignmouth is one of a number of seaside towns served by the former Great Western main line. Its cramped location sees it effectively located on a shelf cut into the hillside, with a sharp embankment on the northern side. The station was originally opened by the South Devon Railway on 30 May 1846 as a broad-gauge route for passenger services with freight commencing on the following 1 May. From 13 September 1847 the station witnessed the start of the shortlived atmospheric railway promoted by Brunel. The SDR was absorbed by the GWR in 1878 and it was under the auspices of the GWR that the station appearing in the aerial photograph was built in 1884. By the date of this photograph, Teignmouth had been significantly rationalised, with the loss of withdrawal of all freight facilities (with the exception of some short-lived private siding work) on 4 December 1967. By 1971, the track rationalisation at the station had resulted in Teignmouth possessing two through roads and a single trailing cross-over at the western end.

7 September 1971 (A214721)

[1904]

228

The ex-GWR lower quadrant up starter at Teignmouth station viewed in August 1962. *Ian Allan Library*

With the station cut into the hillside, the station at Teignmouth was always a confined location, as clearly shown in this view taking looking westwards in 1921. *Ian Allan Library*

Tenterden

Incorporated in 1896 as the Rother Valley Railway (it became the Kent & East Sussex in 1904), the line from Robertsbridge to Rolvenden (or Tenterden as it was initially called) opened, under the provisions of the Light Railway Act, on 29 March 1900 to freight traffic and to passenger traffic on the following 2 April. The line was extended to Tenterden Town on 15 April 1903; in the same year a Light Railway Order covering the construction northwards to Headcorn was granted. This final extension was opened on 15 May 1905. The date of the aerial photograph is shortly before the death of the line's engineer and Managing Director, Holman Stephens, who was to die two years later. The station building at Tenterden was unique on the line in being constructed in brick; Stephens' more usual materials were wood and corrugated iron. The approach to the station, which was provided with a single platform, from the south was controlled by an unusual three-arm signal. The K&ESR remained independent in 1923, but went into receivership in 1932 and into government control as a result of the outbreak of World War 2 in 1939. The line's independence ceased in 1948 when it passed to British Railways (Southern Region). Passenger services, with the exception of specials, ceased on 4 January 1954, at which time the section between Tenterden and Headcorn closed completely. The line between Robertsbridge and Tenterden was to close completely on 12 June 1961. After closure, Tenterden station passed into preservation and after much controversy and effort, the preservationists have succeeded in reopening the line as far as Bodiam. However, as a result of considerable work at Tenterden, the station site there is now radically different to that portrayed in 1929.

21 June 1929 (27693)

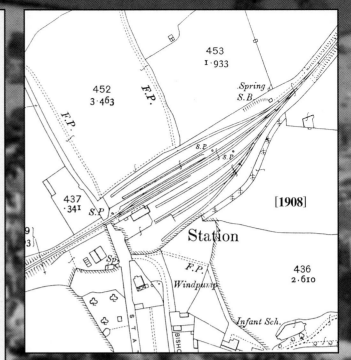

In September 1946, a one-coach train is seen departing from the station with a service for Rolvenden. Note the cattle guard, level crossing and whistle sign. *J. F. Taylor*

On 12 August 1953 'O1' class 0-6-0 No 31065 is pictured at Tenterden with the 3.30pm mixed train to Headcorn. *Geoffrey F. Bannister*

Gas Works

Sta.

239
2·615

...te to Floods

1·415

B.M.37·5

B.M.37·9

264
·852

265
·801

Allotment Gardens

F.P.

241
2·768

40 + 2·768

40·2

242
1·420

266
·223

Allotment Gardens

267
2·136

270
2·810

Science Hall

Howell's
Gardens

F.P.

Hospital

F.P.

COTSWOLD ROAD

B.M. 47·7

W

F.P.

243
·155

40

268
1·256

S.P

S.B.

S.P

Station

P

269
3·745

B.M. 51·9

F.P.

Almshouses

F.P. Cotswold Place

B.M. 46·7

Tank

273
4·555

...ttle
Yard

...tion STREET

L.B.

Malthouse

47

Goods Shed

Cattle Pens

·Crane

B.M. 48·6

45

275
5·126

[1900]

Almshouses

Urinal.

P

STREET

Sidings

5·126

274
1·119

Munl. Boro. Bdy.

...ty Church

ROPEWALK ROAD

43

B.M. 41·7

39

A...sh

·Pump

P

F.P. Liable

C.S.

On 22 September 1951, the 5.16pm service from Tewkesbury to Great Malvern — the 5.10pm service from Ashchurch — is pictured in Tewkesbury station behind ex-MR Class 3F 0-6-0 No 43373. *S. H. Keyse*

Tewkesbury

Taken looking eastwards, this aerial view of Tewkesbury shows to good effect the relationship between the old (right, and now serving as the goods yard) and new stations in this Gloucestershire town. The first line to serve the town was a 1.75-mile-long branch off the Birmingham & Gloucester Railway from Ashchurch that opened officially on 21 July 1840. From the junction visible in the distance, a new line, opened under the auspices of the Tewkesbury & Malvern Railway on 16 May 1864, provided a link with the GWR at Malvern. The T&MR became part of the Midland Railway in 1877. Passenger services were withdrawn between Upton-on-Severn and Malvern on 1 December 1952 and between Ashchurch, Tewkesbury and Upton on 14 August 1961. There was a small engine shed provided at Tewkesbury, located slightly to the west of the malthouse (the large building in the foreground), which was to close on 7 September 1962. The short section beyond the engine shed, serving Tewkesbury Quay, closed completely on 1 February 1957. The line was to close completely between Tewkesbury and Upton on 1 July 1963 and between Ashchurch and Tewkesbury Goods on 2 November 1964.
August 1928 (23942)

The view, looking southwards, at Truro Newham on 6 June 1970. *R. F. Roberts/SLS Collection*

Truro Newham

The 2.5-mile long line from Penwithers Junction to Newham opened under the auspices of the West Cornwall Railway on 16 April 1855. It was, however, to have a relatively short life as a passenger station, with the majority of passenger trains being diverted to the site of the present Truro station four years later and all passenger services ceasing on 16 September 1863. The line, however, remained open for freight services for more than 100 years, before final closure on 6 November 1971. In its later years much of line's traffic was to the siding constructed in April 1955 to serve Truro's gas works; it was the loss of this traffic, in December 1970, that was the major cause of the branch's closure. The gas works siding was located about half-a-mile towards Penwithers Junction. As a passenger station, Newham was provided with a small passenger station with wooden overall roof alongside which was a warehouse that had been rail connected until the early years of the 20th century. Apart from the traffic to and from the gasworks, Newham also provided facilities for domestic coal traffic and the quay alongside the Truro River. Amongst locomotive types to be seen at Newham included 0-6-0PTs and 2-6-2Ts.

16 June 1959 (A76306)

[1906]

Twyford

Situated on the Great Western main line between Maidenhead and Reading, the broad-gauge reached Twyford on 1 July 1839 when the stretch westwards from Maidenhead opened. For a brief period, until 30 March 1840 when the line was extended to Reading, Twyford was the terminus. Twyford became a junction when, on 1 June 1857, the branch to Henley was opened. This was initially single track and broad gauge, but was converted to standard gauge in 1876 and doubled in 1897. The main line remained broad gauge alone until 1 October 1861 when it was converted to mixed gauge. The station that appears in the aerial photograph is, however, very much a product of the 1890s. During that decade, the broad gauge was finally eliminated and the route through Twyford quadrupled. Initially Twyford was provided with two signalboxes — East and West — but these were to close on 23 October 1961, when they were replaced by a single box located in the 'v' between the Henley branch and the main lines. The Henley branch was also singled in 1961. Twyford was provided with a goods shed, but freight facilities were withdrawn from the station on 7 September 1964. The station remains open, with services between Reading and London as well as those on the Henley branch, although inevitably there has been considerable rationalisation.

14 September 1929 (29339)

Taken on a wintry 10 February 1969, an unidentified 'Western' heads eastbound with an up service from South Wales through Twyford station whilst a DMU awaits departure with a down service. *J. H. Cooper-Smith*

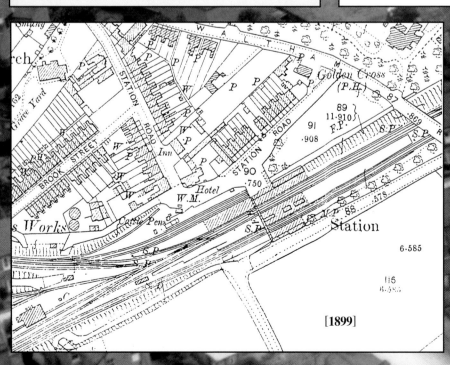

[1899]

In August 1947, a Great Western Railway diesel railcar awaits departure from the Henley on Thames bay platform at Twyford. *R. F. Roberts/SLS Collection*

Terminus
(Met. Ry.)

Heath
Lodge

Coaxden

Goods Shed

Church

238

Uxbridge

Although slightly damaged, this aerial view is of interest in that it portrays the original Metropolitan Railway terminus in Uxbridge on Belmont Road. Whilst the town was ultimately to possess two Great Western branches — serving High Street and Vine Street (both of which are now closed) — it was the town's second railway that was to be the most important, providing as it did a direct connection with central London. The Harrow & Uxbridge Railway, incorporated on 6 August 1897, was promoted by the District Railway as an extension of its existing line, but the District's inability to raise the capital resulted in the line passing instead to the Metropolitan, with the District Railway having running powers. The line was opened on 4 July 1904 and was initially operated by steam. Electrification, clearly visible in the photograph by examining the track, was inaugurated on 1 January 1905, although District Railway services did not commence until 1 March 1910. The station was provided initially with a brick building on the down side and the shelter on the up platform, which was used by District and later Piccadilly trains, was added later. The station was closed on 4 December 1938 when services were relocated to a new station on the High Street.

5 March 1929 (25812)

Judging by the lack of crowds and the general emptiness of the scene, this commercial postcard was probably produced roughly contemporaneously with the opening of the line. *SLS Collection*

Wadebridge

The first railway to serve Wadebridge was the Bodmin & Wenford, which opened in 1834, but by the date of the aerial photograph all traces of this original line had been removed by the London & South Western Railway's development of the line. The LSWR's first station was developed in the 1880s and was provided with a single platform; this proved adequate even after the opening of the line towards Launceston on 1 June 1895. However, with the opening of the extension to Padstow on 27 March 1899, the opportunity was taken to extend considerably the facilities. This work included the construction of a second platform and the replacement of the original signalbox with the new East and West boxes. In 1907 both these boxes were modified when the junction between the Boscarne and Launceston lines was brought to the station throat. The other facilities provided at Wadebridge included an engine shed, first opened in 1895, and a 50ft turntable. The shed was extended in 1908 when rail-motors took over operation of the line to Bodmin. The 1932 aerial photograph was taken shortly after the SR had both replaced the original wooden footbridge with a concrete structure and also extended the goods shed. In 1937, after the date of the photograph, the scissors crossing at the station throat was replaced by two cross-overs. Despite holiday traffic, the network of lines in North Cornwall was to be virtually eradicated in the 1960s. Control of the station was transferred to Western Region on 1 January 1963. The shed was closed in 1964 and demolished five years later. The line to Launceston was to lose its passenger services on 3 October 1966, at which time the line closed completely. Passenger services through the station to Padstow were withdrawn on 31 January 1967, at which stage the line to Padstow was closed completely. Wadebridge's two boxes remained open until the end of that year, whilst Wadebridge itself retained freight facilities until complete closure on 4 September 1978. Since closure the station site has been largely cleared, although with the preserved Bodmin & Wenford's plans for reopening the line to Boscarne Junction, Wadebridge may yet be reconnected to the railway network.

16 August 1932 (39812)

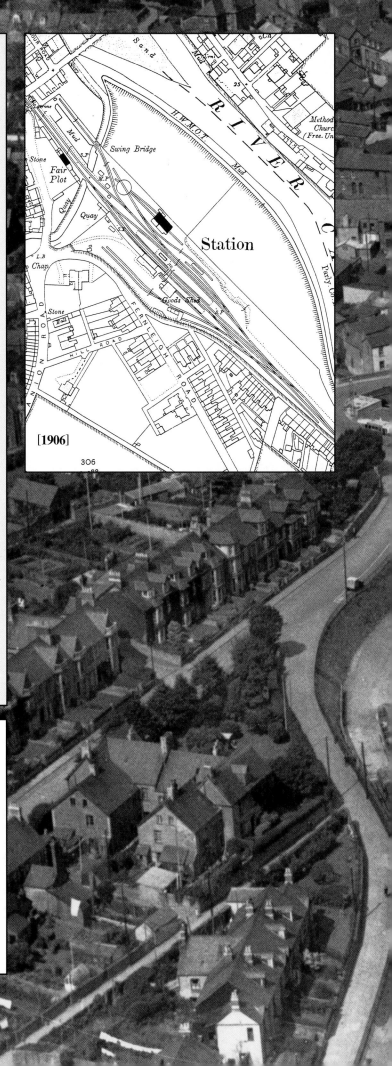

[1906]

Wadebridge shed pictured on 11 April 1938. Outside the shed are 'N' class 2-6-0 No 1837 and '0298' 2-4-0T class E0314. Inside were three locomotives: a second '0298' No 3329, an 'O2' 0-4-4T No 216 and a 'T9' 4-4-0 No 117. *SLS Collection*

On 18 May 1959, Class T9 4-4-0 No 30711 shunts the empty stock of a train from Okehampton at Wadebridge.
J. Spencer-Gilks

An unidentified ex-GWR 'Castle' 4-6-0 stands at Wellington with a Wolverhampton-bound service, whilst an 0-6-0PT awaits its next duty outside the small engine shed that served the station. *P. Ward*

Wellington (Salop)

Wellington in Shropshire was a major junction on the line between Wolverhampton and Shrewsbury. From Wellington to Shrewsbury the line was jointly controlled by the Great Western and London & North Western Railways; the GWR controlled the lines east to Wolverhampton, south to Buildwas and northwest to Market Drayton, whilst the LNWR owned the line that ran northeast to Stafford. A branch from the Wellington-Stafford line headed southwards to Coalport. The lines from Shrewsbury to Oakengates (east of Wellington) and from Wellington to Stafford opened on 1 June 1849; the line from Oakengates to Wolverhampton opened on the following 12 November. The route towards Stafford was to lose its passenger services on 7 September 1964 and was progressively cut back to all traffic, the last section at the Wellington end (serving a military store at Donnington) closed in the 1980s (although there are currently proposals for its reopening). The line southwards from Wellington was to open in 1857 with passenger services commencing on 2 May 1859; the line from Much Wenlock to Wellington lost its passenger services on 23 July 1962, at which time the line south from Wellington to Ketley closed completely. The ex-LNWR Coalport branch opened on 17 June 1861; it was to close its passenger services on 2 June 1952 and to close completely between Stirchley and Coalport on 5 December 1960. The remains of the line, from Hadley Junction to Stirchley, closed completely on 6 July 1964. The final addition to the local network came with the opening of the Wellington & Drayton Railway on 16 October 1867. This line was to lose its passenger services on 9 September 1963 and close completely on 8 May 1967.

Today, Wellington is one of the major districts of the new town of Telford although, as can be seen clearly, its railway facilities have been much reduced. The engine shed, which opened in 1876 and which was provided with a turntable until the 1940s, was coded 84H (1959) by British Railways and was to close on 10 August 1964.
9 October 1963 (A121546)

Although the shed and coaling facilities have long gone, the bulk of Wellington station remains largely unchanged. On 13 April 1986 two Class 37s, Nos 37426 and 37427, head westwards through the station with the 'Barmouth Bridge Express'. On arrival at Barmouth, No 37427 had its new nameplates officially unveiled. *Brian Robbins*

Recorded on 4 September 1952, this view shows the terminus at West Bay looking towards Bridport. By this date passenger services over the section between Bridport and West Bay had not operated for more than 20 years, but it was a further decade before the line closed completely. Today, the station has been restored and provided with a short section of track; the trackbed beyond has been converted to a cycleway. *Ian Allan Library*

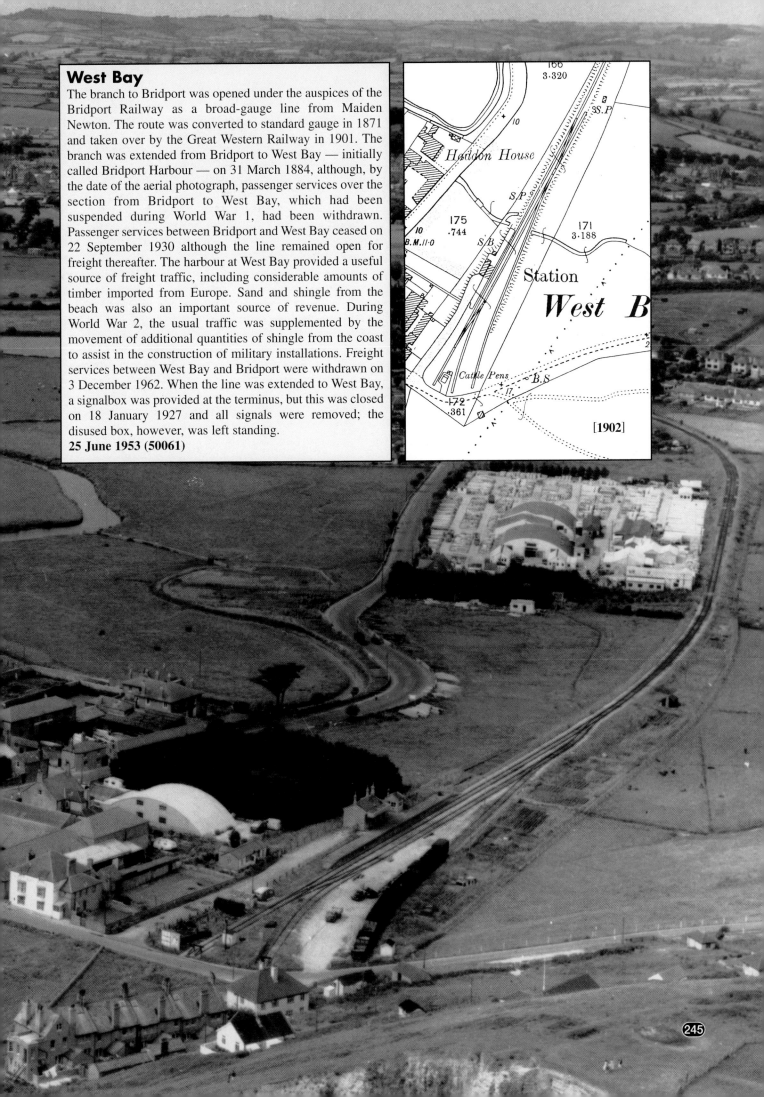

West Bay

The branch to Bridport was opened under the auspices of the Bridport Railway as a broad-gauge line from Maiden Newton. The route was converted to standard gauge in 1871 and taken over by the Great Western Railway in 1901. The branch was extended from Bridport to West Bay — initially called Bridport Harbour — on 31 March 1884, although, by the date of the aerial photograph, passenger services over the section from Bridport to West Bay, which had been suspended during World War 1, had been withdrawn. Passenger services between Bridport and West Bay ceased on 22 September 1930 although the line remained open for freight thereafter. The harbour at West Bay provided a useful source of freight traffic, including considerable amounts of timber imported from Europe. Sand and shingle from the beach was also an important source of revenue. During World War 2, the usual traffic was supplemented by the movement of additional quantities of shingle from the coast to assist in the construction of military installations. Freight services between West Bay and Bridport were withdrawn on 3 December 1962. When the line was extended to West Bay, a signalbox was provided at the terminus, but this was closed on 18 January 1927 and all signals were removed; the disused box, however, was left standing.

25 June 1953 (50061)

166
3·320

SS.P

Haddon House

10

S.P

175
·744

10

B.M.11·0

S.B

171
3·188

Station

West B

Cattle Pens

B.S

172
·361

17

[1902]

Whitland

Located on the line between Carmarthen and Fishguard,
Whitland is the junction station for the line towards
Pembroke Dock. The first station at Whitland opened with
the broad gauge line constructed by the South Wales
Railway between Carmarthen and Milford Haven on
2 January 1854. The line was originally single track but
was doubled on 1 July 1857. The standard gauge line to
Pembroke opened on 4 September 1866 under the aegis of
the Pembroke & Tenby Railway (incorporated into the
Great Western Railway in 1897). The up line between
Whitland and Carmarthen was converted to standard
gauge on 1 June 1868 (freight) and in August 1869
(passenger). The down line was converted to standard
gauge on 11/12 May 1872. In addition to the main station
building, Whitland was also provided with two
signalboxes (West and East), a goods shed and engine
shed with turntable. The shed was opened by the P&TR
and was rebuilt by the GWR in 1901. The shed was again
rebuilt, c1948, when the turntable was removed. The shed
was closed on 9 September 1963.
26 September 1961 (A96215)

Station

Engine Shed

[1907]

A commercial postcard, produced (given the date on the reverse of 2 October 1940) during the 1930s, shows Whitland station during the last full decade of GWR ownership. One of the platform staff apparently eyes the photographer with suspicion. Note in the background the variation in platform heights clearly evident. *SLS Collection*

WAY OUT

PARCELS & CLOAK ROOM

In July 1953, an ex-LMS 2-6-4T No 42456 awaits departure from Wigan Central with a service for Manchester.
Ian Allan Library

Wigan

Although the ex-LNWR and ex-LYR stations in Wigan still serve the national network, the terminus of the third pre-Grouping company to serve the town — the Great Central — has now disappeared. When recorded in the aerial photograph, however, the terminus of the 6.25-mile long branch from Lowton St Mary's was still busy with both passenger and freight services. Promoted as part of the Wigan Junction Railway, incorporated on 16 July, and backed by the Manchester, Sheffield & Lincolnshire Railway, the first section of the branch opened for freight only in 1879. Passenger services were first introduced with the line's extension to Darlington Street, Wigan on 1 April 1894. The final extension, to Wigan Central, was opened on 3 October 1892. The WJR was taken over by the Great Central on 1 January 1906. Passenger services were withdrawn to Wigan Central on 2 November 1964 and freight facilities were withdrawn on 5 April 1965.
13 March 1959 (A74415)

An excellent view of the main station buildings at Wigan Central recorded in July 1939, shortly before the outbreak of World War 2. *R. F. Roberts/SLS Collection*

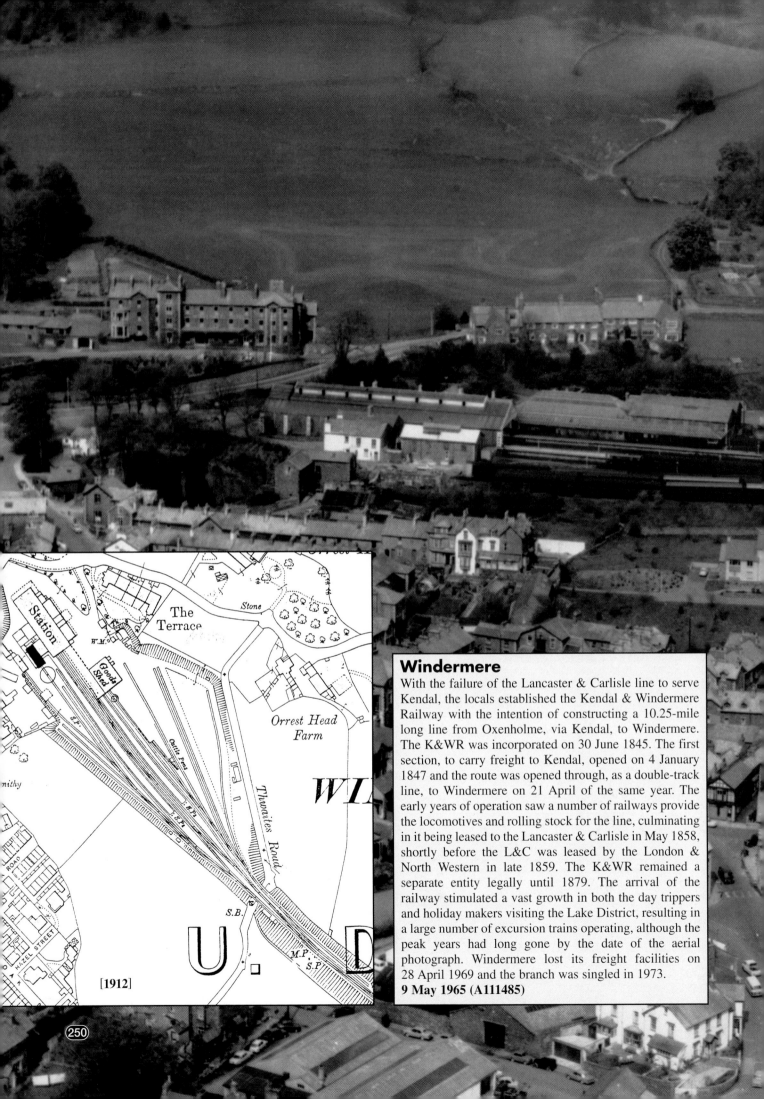

Windermere

With the failure of the Lancaster & Carlisle line to serve
Kendal, the locals established the Kendal & Windermere
Railway with the intention of constructing a 10.25-mile
long line from Oxenholme, via Kendal, to Windermere.
The K&WR was incorporated on 30 June 1845. The first
section, to carry freight to Kendal, opened on 4 January
1847 and the route was opened through, as a double-track
line, to Windermere on 21 April of the same year. The
early years of operation saw a number of railways provide
the locomotives and rolling stock for the line, culminating
in it being leased to the Lancaster & Carlisle in May 1858,
shortly before the L&C was leased by the London &
North Western in late 1859. The K&WR remained a
separate entity legally until 1879. The arrival of the
railway stimulated a vast growth in both the day trippers
and holiday makers visiting the Lake District, resulting in
a large number of excursion trains operating, although the
peak years had long gone by the date of the aerial
photograph. Windermere lost its freight facilities on
28 April 1969 and the branch was singled in 1973.
9 May 1965 (A111485)

The impressive facilities provided at Windermere are shown to good effect in this view of 2-6-4T No 42299 awaiting departure from the station with the 2pm stopping service to Oxenholme. *R. E. Toop*

In 1971, although services were by this date provided by DMUs, the station retained its overall roof and was in many respects unchanged from the steam era. However, a new station was constructed in the mid-1980s, replacing the structure shown here. *Peter W. Robinson*

Withernsea

The branch line from Hull to Withernsea opened on 27 June 1854 under the auspices of the independent Hull & Holderness Railway, which had obtained its act on 8 July 1853. Initially passenger trains served Hull (Victoria Dock) station, which the H&HR shared with the York & North Midland. However, from 1 November 1854 the H&HR had sole occupation of the Victoria Dock station as Y&NM trains were diverted to Paragon, but it was not until 1 June 1864 that Withernsea trains served Paragon. Operated by the North Eastern Railway, the Withernsea branch passed to the LNER in 1948 and to British Railways (North Eastern Region) in 1948. Despite the introduction of diesel multiple-units in the 1950s, the line was to close to passenger services on 19 October 1964 and completely between Hedon and Withernsea on 3 May 1965.

6 May 1925 (12684)

A view of the main station building at Withernsea with platform canopy looking towards the station throat. *Neville Stead Collection*

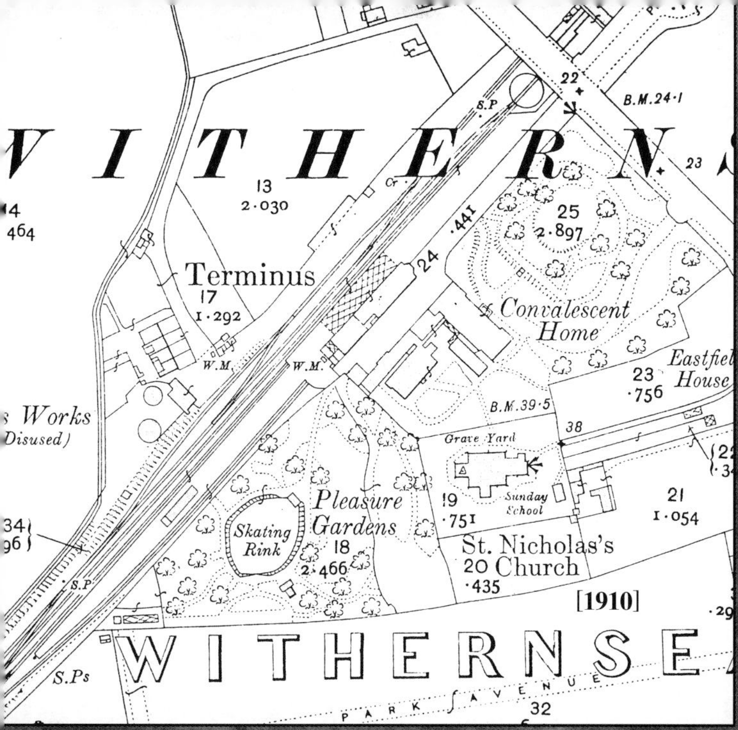
VITHERN
Terminus
Convalescent Home
Eastfie
House
Works
Disused)
Grave Yard
Sunday School
Pleasure Gardens
Skating Rink
St. Nicholas's Church
[1910]
WITHERNSE
PARK AVENUE

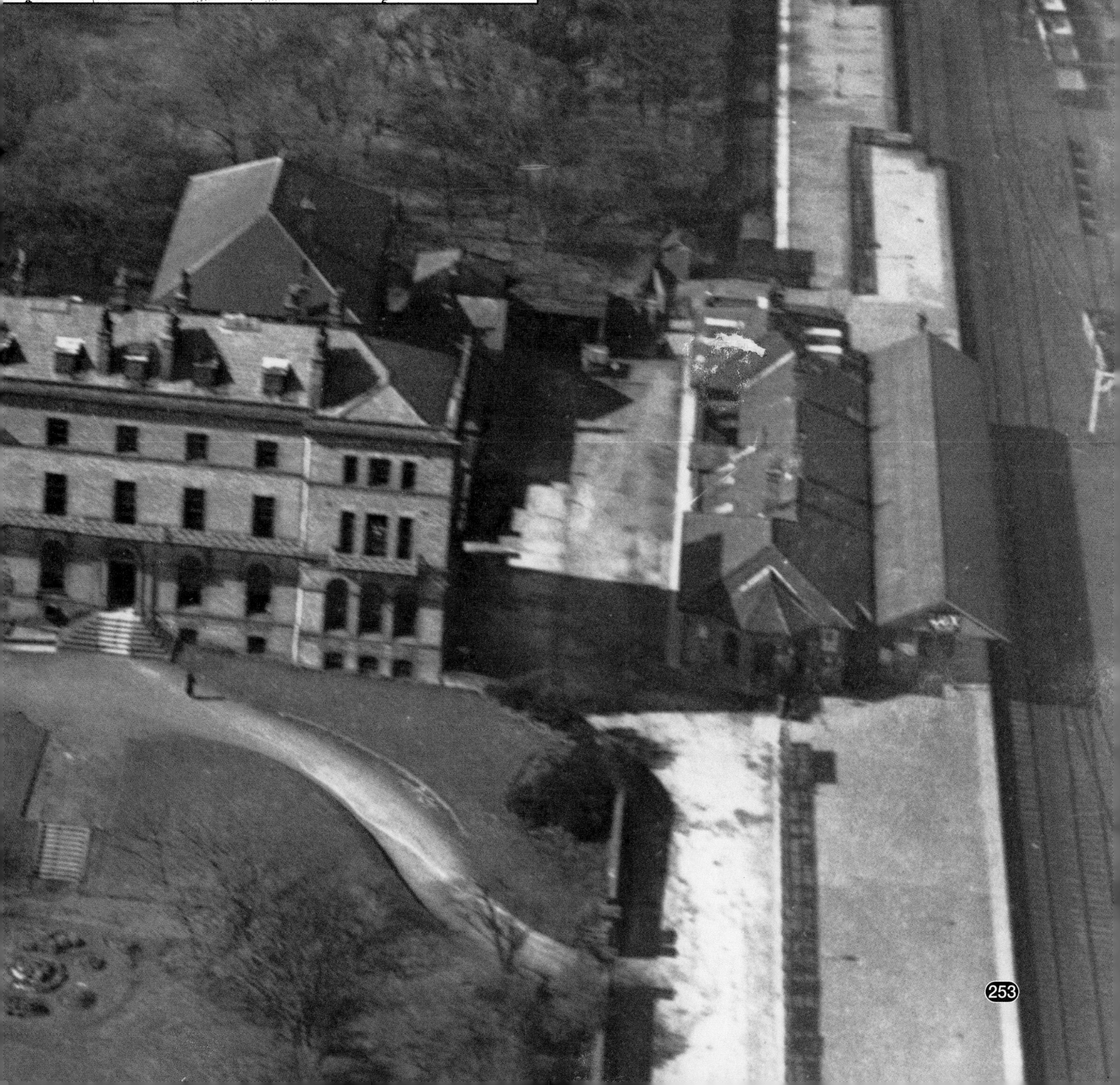

Wrexham Central

Viewed looking east, Wrexham Central station represented the point where the Great Central's line from the Wirral Peninsula met the Cambrian Railways' line from Ellesmere. The Wrexham, Mold & Connah's Quay Railway was authorised by an Act of 7 July 1862 and was opened from Wrexham to Buckley for freight on 1 January 1866 and to passenger traffic on 1 May 1866. Although only single track, the route was built to accommodate double track when required. In 1882 an extension to a new station in Wrexham, Wrexham Central, was authorised and the 0.5-mile long, single-track, extension was opened on 1 November 1887; at this stage the original WM&CQR station was renamed Wrexham Exchange. The new line to Central station was doubled in 1888. The WM&CQR was to be taken over by the Great Central and thus, after 1923, brought LNER services to the Welsh borders. The Cambrian was brought to Wrexham courtesy of the Wrexham & Ellesmere Railway, which was authorised on 31 July 1885 and opened on 11 July 1892. At this stage a new island platform and footbridge were added to the original WM&CQR terminus. The platform arrangements are clearly visible in the aerial photograph as are the extensive freight facilities to the west of the station; in the foreground can be seen the lines of the ex-GWR Chester-Shrewsbury line. By the date of the aerial photograph, passenger services had ceased between Central and Ellesmere, on 10 September 1962, but the line was still open, from the Wrexham end, to serve a number of freight facilities along the route. The ex-Cambrian line closed progressively to freight, the last section, from Central to Abenbury, succumbing on 4 May 1981. Although Wrexham Central is still served by services to the north, the station has more recently been relocated slightly to the west to allow redevelopment of the station site. Freight facilities were withdrawn from the joint GC/Cambrian yard on 7 December 1964.

3 April 1963 (A109169)

[1909]

The island platform building is shown to good effect in this view of Wrexham Central station taken on 7 October 1958. The view is taken from the east end of the station looking westwards in the direction of the ex-GWR line between Shrewsbury and Chester. *R. J. Buckley*

254

This platform level view at Wrexham Central shows the station looking eastwards. The station was jointly controlled by the Great Central and Cambrian railways at this time. *SLS Collection*

Further Reading

A Guide to the Midland & Great Northern Joint Railway; Nigel Digby; Ian Allan Publishing 1993

An Historical Survey of Selected Great Western Stations — Layouts and Illustrations Volume 1; R. H. Clark; OPC 1976

An Historical Survey of Selected Great Western Stations — Layouts and Illustrations Volume 2; R. H. Clark; OPC 1979

An Historical Survey of Selected Great Western Stations — Layouts and Illustrations Volume 3;
   R. H. Clark and C. R. Potts; OPC 1981

An Historical Survey of Selected Great Western Stations Layouts and Illustrations Volume 4;
   R. H. Clark and C. R. Potts; OPC 1981

An Historical Survey of Selected Southern Stations; G. A. Pryer and G. J. Bowring; OPC 1980

An Historical Survey of Southern Sheds; C. Hawkins and G. Reeve; OPC 1979

An Historical Survey of the Didcot, Newbury and Southampton Railway — Layouts and Illustrations;
   C. W. Judge; OPC 1984

An Illustrated History of the Ashchurch to Barnt Green Line — The Evesham Route; R. J. Essery; OPC 2002

Branch Line to Lambourn; V. Mitchell, K. Smith and K. Robertson; Middleton Press 2001

Branch Lines to Falmouth, Helston and St Ives; V. Mitchell and K. Smith; Middleton Press 2001

Branches & Byways: Cornwall; J. Vaughan; OPC 2002

Branches & Byways: East Anglia; John Brodribb; OPC 2000

Britain's Rail Super Centres: Birmingham; Paul Collins; Ian Allan Publishing 1992

By Rail to Mildenhall: The Story of the Cambridge to Mildenhall Railway;
   Peter Turner; Mildenhall Museum Publications 1978

Great Western Branch Line Termini; Paul Karau; OPC 1985

On Didcot, Newbury & Southampton Lines; K. Robertson; Ian Allan Publishing 2002

On the North and West Route; C. R. L. Coles; Ian Allan Publishing 1984

On the Waverley Route; Robert Robotham; Ian Allan Publishing 1995

Portrait of the Isle of Wight Railways; Handel Kardas; Ian Allan Publishing 1998

Railways through Airedale & Wharfedale; Martin Bairstow; Martin Bairstow 1985

Scottish Branch Lines; C. Gammell; OPC 1999

Southern Main Lines: Waterloo to Windsor via Richmond; V. Mitchell & K. Smith; Middleton Press 1988

Steam Days; October 2002; *Castle Douglas and the Kirkcudbright Branch*; Stanley C. Jenkins

Steam Days: December 2002; *The Peebles and Dolphinton Branches*; David Anderson

Steam on the Cambrian; Rex Kennedy; Ian Allan Publishing 1990

Steaming through the Cheddar Valley: D. Phillips; OPC 2001

The Bridport Branch; B. L. Jackson & M. J. Tattershall; OPC 1976

The Bude Branch; D. J. Wroe; Kingfisher 1988

The Cambrian Railways: Portrait of a Welsh Railway Network; Ian Allan Publishing 1999

The Colonel Stephens' Railways: A View from the Past; J. S. Morgan; Ian Allan Publishing 1999

The Ilfracombe Line; John Nicholas; Irwell Press 1998

The Newcastle & Carlisle Railway; G. Whittle; David & Charles 1979

The Queensbury Lines: A Pictorial Centenary Edition; A. Whitaker and B. Cryer; Dalesman 1984

The Railways of Brechin; W. Simms; Angus District Libraries 1985

The Railways of Purbeck; R. W. Kidner; Oakwood Press (Third Edition) 2000

The Waverley Route: The Postwar Years; Robert Robotham; Ian Allan Publishing 1999

The Woodstock Branch; R. Lingard; OPC 1973

The Woodstock Branch; S. C. Jenkins; Wild Swan 1987

effective publicity & design

effective publicity & design

designed and written by
Jonathan Zeitlyn.

Typeset from disk and printed by

Lithosphere Printing Co - operative Limited,
203 – 205 Pentonville Road,
London N1 9NF.
Tel: 01- 833 2526

Cover by Graham Betts

Published by InterChange Books, the publishing
unit of InterChange Studios, 15 Wilkin Street,
London NW5 3NG.

```
Zeitlyn, Jonathan
    Effective publicity and design : a do-it-
yourself guide.
1. Publicity  2. Publicity——Audio-visual
aids.
I. Title
659.2    HM263

ISBN 0-948309-03-2
```

Copies from the publishers, payment with order,
plus postage and packing.

Trade Distribution in the UK by:Turnaround
Distribution, 27 Horsell Road, London, N5 IXL.

Contents

introduction

Anyone can now get into print, make a photocopy or a display, paint a sign or use a video or computer. All of these involve making choices about how information and images are to be arranged. They involve designing. More and more people have gained access to print and other visual media. Problems arise as to how people can best use those media to get their own messages over clearly and with impact. In other words how to make their own publicity effective.

Photo copying and offset litho printing are photographic processes offering total flexibility in terms of images. Electronic, computer and video technology can also give greater freedom, but they also create new design needs.

Graphic Design has become a skill that everyone, has or could have, a need for. Getting to the basics of what design is and how it can be useful for everyone is what 'radical design' is all about. This involves a radical re·examination of design and stripping it of its professional mystifications. It needs saving from the worst excesses of advertising and fashion. When it is freed from the useless clichés of the commercial and the professional, a way of design can be created that is useful for everyone.

This will enable people to communicate their own material directly and in their own ways. Instead of being processed and translated by others, people can express themselves. Media can be created that is local and appropriate to any community, or any need. This can be part of changing where our media comes from. People who are not normally in the 'media' will find a new form in which to communicate their own ideas and experiences.

By trying to isolate and explain the ideas and techniques that design uses, it is hoped to create a practical step-by-step guide. This is based on working out the approaches and techniques that I have found useful in my own design work. It comes from the experience of being both a designer and a teacher, working with community groups and individuals to enable them to have their say. This handbook is aimed at all groups and individuals who want help in putting over their message effectively so that other people will take notice.

It will meet all kinds of needs; from the very simple leaflet or sign, to the complex jobs of designing TV credits, magazines and large exhibitions. It argues that everyone should have the confidence and the

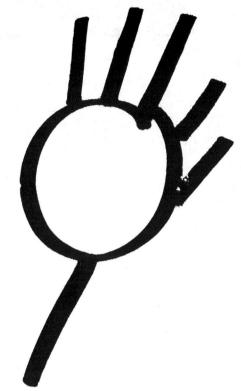

interest to spend time and energy thinking about, and using, visual ways of expressing themselves. Media may need as much time spent on the visual side, as in the words used. People say 'Oh, I can't draw', 'I'm not good at art', but design is part of a different form of expression. We all have a graphic ability but it is educated out of us by schooling. Children draw ideas before they learn to draw representational images. Before they can write, they work out things by putting images on paper. They draw hands as round blobs with five lines for fingers, in fact they draw their idea of a hand. If we can regain this lost ability to put down our ideas in this way, we will be able to design. This involves thinking visually and graphically; a skill that is not usually encouraged. Words predominate in education and in society generally.

If design is made accessible to people, they can evolve their own way of graphically expressing themselves, and design itself will change. Instead of one consistent style and norm of 'good' design, a variety of visual forms can be created that reflects the variety of cultures, classes and interests we have in society today. The aim is to free the imaginative and creative capabilities we all have, and enable them to be used in our everyday surroundings and lives.

message & form

It is useful to ask yourself or to discuss as a group, what you are really trying to get over. To work out how that message can be communicated requires you to choose between different media, and finding the one that is most suitable for your particular need.

Make sure of a pause between formulating the design 'brief' and doing the design work. Formulating the design problems and the aim of the product you are to design, can be a very difficult but necessary part of the job. This is obvious when employing a designer, and it can be a most important part of the process.

What is the best media for your message?

Consider what access you have to any media. Is it really appropriate for what you are trying to get over? Often people are used to producing exhibitions, for example, and so every year they do so without questioning if they would be better off to put this particular message in a booklet, or...a bottle?

Who is it for?

In terms of media, language and design, it is important to work out who you are really trying to reach. This can involve you in carefully looking at your market. Are you really trying to reach everyone? A more specialised target may be more successfully reached and communicated with.

It can be useful to consider what your readership is like. Where they go, what they do and what other things they read and see. If they are used to 'Mirror' typography, with lots of pictures, your 'Guardian' style may not work.

And how will it get there?

This is often the question left until last, or ignored. It may be the vital one for the design and the success of the publication or product. Thinking about the 'distribution' of your product can immediately give clear guidelines to specify what is needed in terms of design. A cover that will work on the newsagents stand, or a placard that will reproduce in newspaper photos; both have particular design requirements.

Cost

Consider what you can afford to put your message across and how much time you can devote to getting the message out. An advert may be cheaper in time, though expensive in money.

Organisation

This handbook argues that design needn't be a specialised and individual activity. It can be done by anyone who needs to put over their own views. Usually, it is easier and better to produce a publication or product with a group. This can be far simpler in terms of expense, distribution and production. Some people may not be good at writing, but capable at drawing. Others could contribute by doing headlines, or just folding the finished newspaper. Some may be able to sell it, when all the others may not.

It is important to involve everyone in the design decisions. This is often the first time that people see how the results of their work will look. It gives them a feeling of power, as they have produced something, and can see how it will look. It becomes their own product, their own work, their own mouth-piece.

By making a large rough version, or copies of the artwork or storyboard, you can make sure that everyone sees what is being proposed. A dummy, or rough, in pencil can be easily changed. And everyone's ideas can be used. This is the initial test for the design ideas - seeing if they work with the whole group.

Designing and producing a publication, or other product, will usually involve working with other people, groups or suppliers. It can involve giving instructions to typesetters, printers and other professionals. These people will have a professional jargon and distrust the amateur. Care, and a certain knowledge, is needed to ask the right questions and to learn from professionals. It may be necessary to get quotes and time-commitments from them. It is useful to get this in writing but it is also important to get to know them, and build up a relationship. This relationship can be a problem if you are not sure what you want, and keep changing your mind. It may be better to ask questions and advice, and then decide. Some resource centres, typesetters, suppliers and printers are sympathetic to your aims. It may be easier to deal with them than the usual commercial ones. See the listings for some places to start.

The design stage can be fun and exciting, though it shouldn't be forgotten that the distribution and marketing stage is the vital one, for the success or failure of your message. Try and organise involvement in this stage, as well as in the design.

politics of design

Designs and images have a political dimension. How they are used is political. Is it to exploit people, or to inform them? Does the design clarify the real aim of the message?

Who produces a design is political – so is why. Is the design done just for money? Or is it done by people to get their own message across?

Often design is part of a complex division of labour so that no one group has control over it, or involvement with its use. Designers design for their clients — who pay—not for the readers or consumers who see or buy it.

Design is usually in the hands of just a few people. Their training and background means they are far more likely to design to impress other designers, than for the consumers.

Design is political in its very choice of images, some images are sexist, others are racist; and some are both. Many present a never - changing vision of the world based on a materialist and stereotypical view of the family, of fashion and so forth. All these images need to be analysed politically and discussed so that they can been seen critically for what they are.

Images can reinforce passivity when they are meant to be promoting active involvement. They can present an authoritive voice, when they are meant to be presenting anti - authoritarian ideas.

Images can become ossified cliches rather than new ways of presenting new ideas.

Images can be created and sum up by a movement. The imaginative use and development of such images can give that movement identity.

By designing your own publication or product you can gain an experience of creative power, a group power that can be seen and can work.

This handbook is meant to be usefully political. It aims to help you design your own message yourselves — changing not just how you represent yourselves but also your own ideas about the value of your own message.

Words

In writing this handbook I've come across several problems with words:

To start with, design is mystified by a professional jargon. The aim of this handbook is to explain

Susan Irvine

design and do away with the jargon — using technical terms where necessary — and explaining them (see glossary). But there is also a scarcity of words suitable for some of the new activities described here.

'Publishing' for example suggests a substantial business producing large tomes and volumes. What word can you use to describe a group getting together to get out a photocopied leaflet, badge or even a video?

The accessible, small scale, instant media requires a new term to describe producing or getting it out. You can't really 'publish' a badge, can you?

'Information' as in 'information technology' suggests that what is published is 'the truth' — 'objective information' rather than somebody's ideas, or just one view of reality. 'Information' suggests a 'stock exchange' approach to media where everything can be reduced to figures. Reality is far more complex, and the new electronic media require a more complex view of what they can be used for. Ideas, messages, creative writing, news — with all its biases — are all the products of people. They are not in themselves commodities, they are not pure information or 'the truth' — but cultural inputs to which everyone can contribute.

Often design happens after its information content has been established. This reflects the division of labour between word people and visual people. This book is about creating a different sort of relationship, between those who do the work; but it is also about the relationship between all the different people who produce, and those who read or watch…

In reading this book and working on these ideas in practice you may come up with alternative terms that usefully clarify activities. I would be interested in your suggestions.

design ideas

It is useful to separate the process of working out the design idea, from the actual techniques of making the design. So don't worry about the practical problems of producing headlines or images etc. First let your imagination free-wheel, and try and sort out what you would like ideally.

To help you do this, I have sorted out six basic approaches that I use when I'm stuck for an idea.

It is difficult to think graphically, without using a pencil on paper. Play around with your ideas on paper, so that you can see what they actually look like. In words, visual ideas may sound silly or absurd. On paper, they may make excellent design.

Many people find it difficult to sort out their ideas clearly. It is a good approach to force yourself to produce at least six different ideas for any one design job. This way you have to put only one idea into one design. Too many ideas, in a design, will conflict while one good one will work with clarity and impact.

Draw small, rough drawings – little thumb nail sketches – of your ideas. You can put, say four on an A4 sheet of paper. Use squiggles as headlines, and lines as lines of type. Pictures can be drawn as boxes, or outlines. Once you have got down six, or at least quite a few, you can compare them and select the best one. Elements can be used from each to create a final design, if no one idea is obviously the best.

It can be quite good to go through this exercise of sorting out your ideas as a group. Each person can work out their ideas individually and then explain, and show them, to everyone else. It is interesting, when ten individuals come up with ten very different designs, each claiming that theirs is the clearest, or most interesting. You may all come up with the same basic idea, which obviously will be the one the whole group can relate to.

When starting, it can be useful to try simple information, and try to work out ideas for a very simple product. For example if nothing comes from your own work, try working on a leaflet design for a jumble sale. If you can think of six different and interesting designs for this, you will find designing something for a more interesting project far easier.

Exercise text:
Fleet Community Education Centre's Summer Jumble Sale is to raise money for the new music building. It will be on Saturday 20th July, between 2 and 4pm. Entrance 5p. Tea, cakes, bric-a-brac, badge-making, face-painting. Fleet Community Education Centre, Agincourt Road. NW3. 485 9988.

6 rough ideas. Which one works best?

The following six design approaches are useful in working out your design ideas.

design approach 1 Visualising

Design is about imagining the information in visual form.

Imagine the page as if it were a picture. Try to get a visual impression, of the whole design on paper.

The idea behind the information could be visualised. It can be useful to ignore the exact information and work out an image that gets over the spirit, or idea, of the message. The poster or publicity for a festival, for example, needs to have a festive and fun feel. Working out what style is appropriate to this initial concept can lead to the visualising of a good design idea. A picture may illustrate this idea and so become the basis for the design. If an image can sum up what the message is all about, use it boldly and consistently.

You may need to edit and rewrite the information to fit the design idea. Writing for a poster, or for other media, is different to other writing. Editing it for the particular media you are working in, can be vital. An idea that has come from visualising the whole design, may require this more than other ways of working. If the idea is strong enough it will not matter.

If this visualisation doesn't produce any design ideas, try to sort out just one part of the message, and work out an image or style from this.

In any given space, pictures can get over far more than words, and have much greater impact. They can be very useful in getting over some sorts of information, but they can also mislead or emphasise the wrong element in other messages.

Headlines and captions can give images all kinds of meanings. Putting words and images into context can become the basis of a whole design idea. Although images do not convey meaning as precisely as words, they do work very effectively in that they attract attention and help people to remember the message. Do not presume that you read an image or react to a style in the same way that your readers do. (see testing, page 14).

Visualise a design idea that has impact. What can make people stop and look? Each person may have their own ideas. They may find some images make them look, while others put them off. Ideas about which designs are attractive or exciting vary from one individual to another. However it can be an important aim for your design thinking. So many people flick through life, that you need an effective way of encouraging them to stop, and to concentrate on the particular message you are designing.

A 'festive' poster for a Festival.

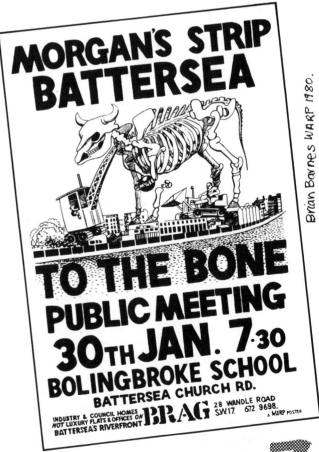

Brian Baynes WARP 1980.

Battersea portrayed as a cow, one of a series of posters

7

Design is about clarifying the information and making it easier to read.

One of the easiest approaches is to analyse the information and sort it out into a series of levels of importance. Number each level of information. The first level is the most important heading or group of information, number two is the next level of importance, and so on. It may be difficult to have more than 4 or 5 levels.

The simplest way to make a design idea, from this analysis, is to make the information contained in number one much larger than everything else. But there are many other ways of emphasising information.

To emphasise a particular bit of information you can use: **the weight of the lettering.**

the style of lettering, like italic
<u>underlining</u>
CAPITALS
colour

space

background
and alignment

A picture can emphasis a point, or part of the information and this can be the basis of the design idea.

Aligning information-making lists, can sort and clarify information very usefully. The bit that is to be emphasised can be set to the left, or to the right. The margin of the list, will create an undrawn line through the design which can then be used to make it feel consistent throughout.

Quotations should be consistently indented to differentiate them from the main text, in the same way.

Information analysis can lead into a useful exercise, in designing the simplest possible design solution. Reduce the design to the barest minimum that will still work. Try to design with only 2 levels of importance and one means of emphasis. The most economic design may well be the best. You will have to work out very clearly what is essential.

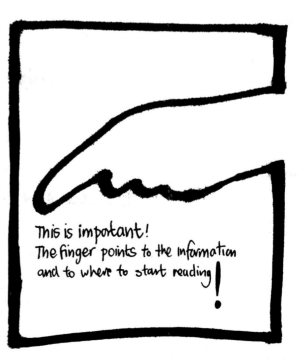

This is important!
The finger points to the information and to where to start reading!

Can you work out any other ways of emphasising information? Work out how these ways could help in doing your design.

design approach 3
problem solving

Design is about solving problems. Look critically at your information and try to work out what problem it is trying to solve. How can the design help solve that problem?

There are some mathematical problems that can only be solved by arranging the numbers on paper. Once this is done you can see the solution clearly. Design should be like this.

Some design problems involve direction. People need to read the text or exhibition in the correct order. To go through it in the right order, you need to consider where people should start. How can you help them visually go in the right direction, find the starting place, and get to the end in the right order? Once formulated, this problem suggests its own answer.

Some design problems are to do with connections. Contents pages, for example, need to connect the page numbers with the chapter titles. How can the design help this connection be made easily? People should be able to look down the list of chapters easily to find the one they are interested in.

Conflicting problems need to be worked out and prioritised. If it becomes clear that the most important problem is for people to be able to find one sort of information, before others, then the design can be worked out and adjusted to meet this requirement. Is the cover of the catalogue intended to tell people what is inside it, or to make sure they know it is this year's issue?

Which connection between chapter name and page number works best.

with a newspaper where does the main article start?

How will it flow? Can you read the article that continues after an illustration. easily?

Maps contain a useful set of graphic conventions that can be used in many different ways. They solve the problem of explaining how to get to places and explain where things are in relation to each other. They can form the basis of a graphic idea for the whole design as well as being useful guides to how to get to a place.

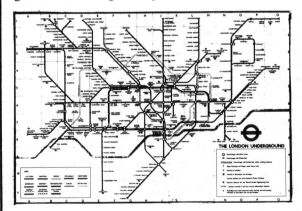

Work out what the map is explaining. What the problem is. The London Tube map is a graphic example: it explains connections, lines, how many stops and where your station is on the system. It is not really a geographical map and it doesn't explain where things are in overground terms. Nevertheless it does work well in solving the problem it was designed to tackle - millions of people getting to the right place.

Work out the problem clearly enough and the solution will suggest itself.

chapter name.........No.

chapter name ————No.

chapter name   No.

chapter name No.

chapter name **No.**

chapter name   *No.*

chapter name   No.

design approach 4
Conventional format

Designing is about using conventional formats in an appropriate way.

People relate to, and understand, conventional design that they have seen and read before. The shape and design of the publication or product, fits with the sort of information it contains.

People know what to expect, and look for a particular format if they want a particular sort of information. This conventionality is both useful, and a restriction that can be broken with, at the same time.

You can use it to work out what a typical sort of newspaper, or other product, is like. If you follow this conventional format, you can establish a credibility for your newspaper, as its design will fit into the convention and tradition of newspapers.

Examine what a 'real' newspaper, or other product, looks like. Draw out a typical format based on good examples that you like. Draw a simple rough, trying to generalise the format. Try to use these models to produce your own design. With some publications it is possible to trace off the grid or layout used, and just change the information by putting in your own. (See page 33 for more details on Grids.)

The format in terms of the shape of the paper and its size can be a starting point in itself. A card or a newspaper has different uses, folds and storage possibilities. The formal outline parameters can be used to create a design idea by showing people the format in which you are working.

It is important not to be restricted by the format. You can play with it and subvert it. Try changing formats — how would the college prospectus work as a newspaper? Is any format really appropriate for your information? Is there a new way of organising and designing things, that works better for you and for your message.?

Creating your own conventions and formats that people relate to is what successful design is all about. Use existing formats to start from, for your own benefit but don't get tied down.

It is fun to use the same style and format as a conventional publication for a very unconventional message. A poster design, for example, used the layout of a newspaper to tell people about a book. The cliches that newspapers had used against teachers were used the other way round against Fleet Street journalists, reflecting the subject of the book. Stickers with the same typography as official signs have been used for unofficial messages. Leaflets about transport, have used the ticket format to get their message over.

PASSENGER CONTROL

Passengers may have wondered what would happen if the controls of this train refused to function. Such an occurence might well result in passengers being forced to remain on the train, possibly under emergency conditions, for some time. In such a situation, passengers would be thrown much closer together; this would naturally cause some difficulties. You would tend to respond by recognising your common situation, and unusual feelings of sympathy and solidarity would be established. In this case you would draw strength from communicating with other people, perhaps for the first time.

Now, suppose our own controls, just like the trains, refused to function. What would happen if we simply smashed those controls. Refused to pay the fare on this train for instance or when we got to work, took the place over collectivly and ran it as WE wanted it. We could even abolish boring work altogether now that the advance in technology has exposed work for what it really is - a means of keeping our minds unquestioning of our desires and in chains. We could do ANYTHING. Completely abolish hierarchial society and change the whole fabric of human relationships. The setting up of workers and neighbourhood councils would be the first step towards a total revolution of everyday life and liberation from the boredom and alienation exemplified by this train journey.

Why not talk to the person next to you about taking over the controls?

design approach 5
popular imagery

Design is about developing the popular imagery and conventions that everyone relates to and understands.

The familiar images are the ones people find easy to understand. They find what they relate to acceptable, because they are part of them, their culture and their surroundings.

Design has to use and be aware of this limitation. It can also be stimulating to work within. However, there are all kinds of popular conventions to use; many are rich sources of inspiration. Work out which one is suitable for your message.

What does your readership relate to and see most? Research the appropriate and popular conventions used, that are familiar to your particular readership. Conventions, and references to the right culture, can make a design very successful.

Our culture is rich in all kinds of visual conventions and references. The form and the message can inter - relate, creating a useful design idea. You have a freedom to adapt and use almost any form or convention. You can make your leaflet in a cartoon strip, or your poster could work as a pub sign − or an estate agent's 'For Sale' sign.

Work out the various popular forms and conventions that could be useful. Try them out on your message. The styles of mass culture have lots of different conventions to choose from. Cartoon conventions can be used as elements in a design as well as in full cartoon strips. A bubble of the 'speech' or 'thinks' sort can be used to make any one or anything speak or think. The advertising conventions of the supermarket can be used as full posters, or just as a burst in the corner.

Popular styles, such as punk and other pop music references, can be easily used for quite different messages. Idioms of speech or other specialised references, can be used to develop a design idea.

These popular forms and conventions will be far closer to particular sections of the community than normal general design. A punk style may not go down well with old people. It may therefore be important to consider a more specialised design for any particular audience. Older people may

design their own publications in a very different way to young people or designers. They may like larger type and clearer images just because they don't see so well. They may also have a different style, and way of ordering things, that relates to a different culture and which needs respect, so that it can be viewed and considered.

Mechanically there are very few limitations to the sort of images you can use. The interesting limitations and positive reactions are in the minds of the readers or audience.

11

design approach 6
word images

Design is a way of getting words to convey visual meaning as well as just being read.

It is quite fun to try to draw out simple words to reflect their meaning visually. These 'word images' must be able to be read as well as visually making their meaning clear:

There are all kinds of ways of doing this.
Try and play with this idea.
Make a list of words and try to produce word images for all of them.

You can use this technique to make a very simple and effective design, or at least start an idea for a design. It can be used for the design of your organisation's name. This design is called a logo. Logos can be made in all kinds of ways using all kinds of design techniques. But generally they try graphically to suggest something about the organisation. The logo is used on everything that the organisation produces so that it becomes associated with it. A logo can be a simple word image or a standard sort of lettering. It can include the way of arranging the lettering or a symbol. Used consistently and successfully they will enable people to pick out your organisation's poster, banner, video etc. at a quick glance.

This can be more difficult than it sounds as there are so many logos, symbols etc. A symbol, for example, will have to compete with lots of others. So, for it to work by itself, it will have to be very commonly used if it is to be understood. Behind this idea of design is the corporatist idea of large corporations who own and run everything. So when people see their symbol everyday they quickly relate that service to the organisation. Many people don't design for large organisations or even share the idea behind this approach.

But some symbols and logos can be useful in design to a limited extent. They can be played with, developed and brought to life. They can be the start to some good design ideas. Most organisations do have a logo or symbol which can be used. Try experimenting with changing its size. Most logos are small and discreet: try making it very large. You could use the style of lettering or the general style to design the new message.

Information Design Workshop from Growing old in Britain Today. CSV advisory service.

Pictograms are simple images that you can use instead of words. They too can be useful to play with and to form the basis of a design idea. Pictograms are used quite a lot in everyday use. Public lavatories are usually distinguished by a male or female pictogram: and not a symbol:

These sorts of pictograms can be usefully adapted for some designs by using them as a visual reference. Or you could design your own that can be used as a basis for a design. Try and design a pictogram for 'sharing', 'dialoque' or 'organisation' or even 'news'.

With electronic and animated media, it may be possible to change a word into an image instantaneously. This could give the production of word images a whole new meaning.

legibility

Your message needs to be readable whatever you design and regardless of the medium you use. Scientific research into legibility has uncovered only a few guides to design. In fact people can read suprisingly difficult and unclear images – if they want to.

It is still an important question though, in design. What makes things clearer and easier to read?

Some guidelines do exist that are useful:
● It is difficult to read lines of words in CAPITALS. We read the shapes of words not letters themselves. So try to keep headlines and text in lower case with just some capital letters.

● Older people find it difficult to read small letters. Some young designers with good eyesight like small type.

IT CAN BE DIFFICULT TO READ LINES OF WORDS IN CAPITALS.
It is easier to read text and headlines in lower case and capital letters.

If a line of text is too long it can be difficult to find the start of the next line.

● When reading text it can be difficult to find the start of the next line if the line is too long. Popular newspapers stick to 5 words a line. Over 15 words a line can make a line very difficult to read.

● With very short lines it can be difficult to set without having to break words in the middle or have large spaces between words. Both will create problems in reading.

● Columns of text that are 'justified' have straight edges at both the left and right-hand side. This looks neat but it doesn't aid legibility. Unjustified text with a straight left hand margin is just as clear and easy to read.

● The ability to 'read' images has to be learnt just like learning to read words. The more familiar you are with a visual convention the easier it is to read it. Care should be taken that you are using conventions people understand and relate to.

● Some photos can be quite unclear and contain useless background details. By removing this,the images become clearer and more legible.

● Over–printing images or colour onto text can make the text unreadable. It is often difficult to judge this until it is printed. So be careful.

● Some uncommon and decorative typefaces are also very difficult to read.

Popular newspapers stick to 5 words a line.

With very short lines it can be difficult to set with out having to break words in the middle or have large spaces between words.

● Text in two columns may not be divided well enough to stop people reading straight across instead of down the column. To avoid this make sure the gap is big enough for all the lines. Or rule a line in between the columns. A thin line will not break up the page very much but will ensure that people can read down the columns.

● Coloured type on coloured backgrounds can interrelate badly making it difficult to look at and hard to read. It is important to assure enough contrast between the two. But it is also necessary to experiment with the colour combinations to make sure they don't hinder legibility.

● Particular media have there own particular problems with legibility and colours.

Decorative typefaces can be difficult to read.

13

testing

Don't assume that your taste for design – or what you find clear – is true for your readership.

It can be useful to try out your ideas and get feedback on them from a sample of people who are not involved in the product. They should be a part of the readership you are aiming at.

This testing can be quite informal but it can point out the weaknesses of your design before you've finally committed yourself. Being close to the ideas, you may wrongly asssume that people can follow them in the same way as you can.

You should check that people pick up precisely the information intended from reading and looking at the design. Try testing the words and the illustrations separately and then together. If people react to the picture and assume that the person is a different sort of person to the subject of the poster then you may have to change the picture.

As well as understanding the exact meaning, people frequently make assumptions about images and associate all kinds of things with them. Try and ask about the associations or impression people have to the design you are testing. The understand-

ing of the message may conflict with the overall association people have to the design. They may find it serious instead of funny, passive instead of active and so on.

Try presenting two or three alternative designs and get preferences. By comparing designs people will be able to convey their reactions far more easily.

People have all kinds of associations with colour. So try to use a coloured rough to test. Colour can give people an association that is political, or just personal. Some advertisers of food products avoid green as they say people associate it with decaying food or tend not to buy green food packs.

It is possible to produce a limited version of your product which you can use and test at the same time. You can then amend it and produce an improved version on a larger scale. Most people respond passively to design and if they don't understand or respond, they move on to the next thing rather than go to the bother to tell you your product doesn't work. To get things right therefore, requires considerable energy in questioning people and in being sensitive to the responses you get.

First version

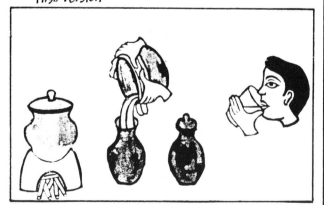

'boil water before drinking it'.

Improved version

Two poster design produced in a poster workshop in Calcutta with Bob Linney & Ken Meharg

media

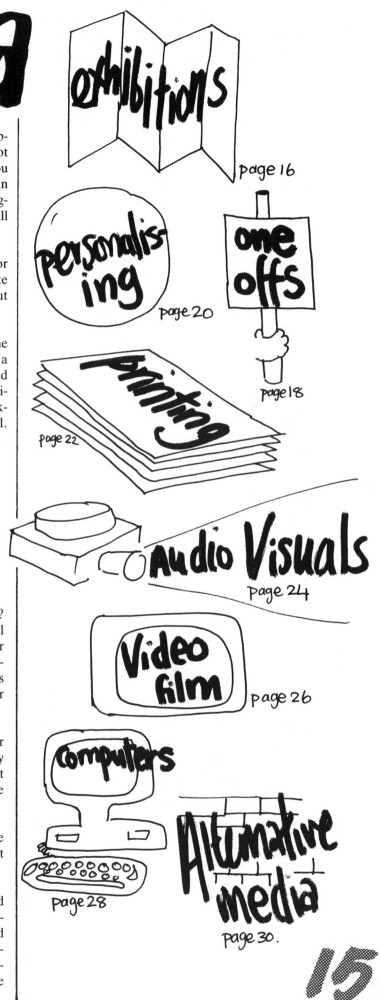

exhibitions

page 16

personalising

page 20

one offs

page 18

printing

page 22

Audio Visuals

page 24

Video film

page 26

Computers

page 28

Alternative media

page 30.

Each 'product' or medium has its own design problems and capabilities. Ideally you should have got your information and design ideas clear before you need to look at the particular medium you have in mind. Working out the design may involve changing your basic idea once you get to know how it will or will not work in the medium of your choice.

Design is about choosing the right medium for your message and also the one that is apropriate for your audience. Keep an open mind about which medium to choose.

This section is only an introduction to some of the design issues in working in these media. It is not a full description of how to use them. You can build on this by using other books, courses and experience. Receiving help from people who have worked with the medium themselves is always useful. See the lists of resource centres in the directory.

Are there any alternatives?
Do you really have to produce anything at all? Sometimes it is possible to improve inter-personal communications, so that having to design, print or produce any media is not really necessary. A telephone tree, where each person in the group phones three other people, for example, could get over news rapidly and effectively.

In some cases producing a poster, newsletter or video is a clear and visible part of a campaign. They show that the campaign exists. But it is important not to be confused between the media and the campaign itself.

Paying a worker actually to talk to people may be more effective than making any media product at all.

So, if you do decide to design anything, you should be able to work out the specifications for the design. Each question discussed and answered should have implications for your design. A properly formulated design brief can be a crucial element in doing the design. Done well, it can make the design work effectively.

exhibitions

Exhibition design involves two problems: firstly the design of the images and information and secondly the design of the space and physical lay-out that the exhibition is to occupy.

People will walk around and in front of the displays, so that the space in which it is located will dictate the sequence in which it is read. It can be vital to work out this ordering so that people start at the point you want them to. Your design can help this and make sure that there is a continuity and style linking the entire exhibition into a unity.

You can use the ambiguity of seeing the whole exhibition and just parts of it at the same time. People can glance up and down, as well as along it, which means more possibilities than the normal linear way of reading.

The space where an exhibition is put is not usually usually flat. It may involve using two sides of stands or two walls. This breaks it up and involves you in designing it in a way that maintains continuity. You may have to re·label it so that there is a clear title on both sides of the exhibition.

You also have to be careful to make sure that the display can physically fit or be fastened onto walls. A mobile exhibition needs to be mounted on boards that are not to large or heavy to move so that it can be put up in a variety of places.

It is best to mount the exhibits on large sheets of cardboard. This enables you to place pictures and text together in the way you want them, so that they will stay in place. It also enables you to move the exhibition around and store it easily. The boards on which the material is to be mounted could be printed with borders or a logo. This gives the exhibits a visual continuity and a strong and colorful identity. Borders can be screen printed quite easily, but be careful, if you are going to have the boards heat-sealed or laminated: the screen inks may react with the heat and ruin the laminating!

Once you have mounted all the text and illustrations onto the boards for your exhibition it is a good idea to protect them. Laminating will do this and will also improve the look and feel of the exhibition (see page 61).

exhibitions can be free standing & walked around.

Mount exhibits on piece of card.

exhibits can be mounted at different heights & angles.

Aligning exhibits on a grid can give them unity. A line the same height all the way round a room can be used as the top line and all the exhibits can be aligned down from it.

You can use exhibitions with other media. For example people may gain some ideas from the exhibition and will want a leaflet with the details to take home. This can be simply done by incorporating into the exhibition, a little box or holder for the leaflets. Some exhibitions have a computer accessible at the end with a view-data program, which can test what you have learned from the exhibition, or give you further details. There may well be other interesting ways of mixing media using exhibition displays, with projectors, computer technology etc.

Thinking of exhibitions or displays as if they were newspapers can be useful. A wall newspaper can have all the impact and topicality of a distributed newspaper, but without the necessity of reproducing it. You can paint a name and border onto the notice board and design it with columns or areas of regular text. Headlines, hand-written text, photos and cuttings etc, can be used. People can add their own news, ads or announcements. With a bit of regular work it can be kept up-to-date, neat and clear. The simple use of coloured backgrounds can help differentiate parts of the display. Decide on one prominent, well-lit wall (or notice board) to be your wall newspaper. It works well and makes the designing and production of news far simpler.

Exhibitions and displays need care and effort in designing, as much as any other 'product'. They need to be kept up to date and changed regularly so that they don't become wall paper to the eye. A clear signing system can help people find the information they want, and keep the displays useful. Using a free-standing display board can avoid this problem as it is only put up when there is an exhibition but make sure that it can stand up safely. Some are not too strong, and can fall down if they get knocked or pushed. It may be worth thinking in terms of designing the whole stand as well as the information.

For details on mounting exhibitions see the mounting section in design techniques (page 60).

add a box for people to take leaflets.

One offs

Design isn't only useful with 'proper' media. It can make simple things far more effective. One off, everyday products such as hand drawn notices, signs and so on, can be made differently and into images that make a visual point. With care, these emphemeral media can be transformed.

Notices, notice boards, placards, signs, directions, name boards and banners can all be made easily, by hand, and to a high standard. Using clear and simple design ideas, even the simplest notice can be improved.

Placards/Notices

Placards and other hand drawn notices can be designed bearing in mind their use. They can be made for a demonstration by the person carrying them with a message and design that is appropriate to that person. Placards should be made so that when the demonstration is photographed the message will be readable in the small black and white photos of a newspaper report.

You can use printed borders or spray stencils for the placards, leaving room for the particular message to be put in by hand. This will give an idea of who the demonstrators are.

Placards, notices or other one offs can be cut into a suitable shape. Card, or hardboard can be cut and an image stuck on, in all kinds of shapes and designs. Notices and other one offs in paper, can also be cut into a shape. This may be a way of stopping people as they walk past,drawing their attention to your news, rather than looking at all the other rectangles of news. You could produce leaf shapes for garden news; placards in the shape of houses or even free-standing people shapes, to welcome people into the theatre. One-offs could be photocopied and coloured in by hand - each in a different colour.

a photocopied placard made by community copyart.

Signs

You may have seen good publicity for an event but then had difficulty finding the place or its entrance. It can be hard for people who live in or know a place well, to imagine that others don't know the way. Signs are vital to help newcomers, and so they have to be carefully designed and put in the right places. To design a sign system, involves envisaging the problems of the person who has never been to the place before. It involves taking into account all their different reasons to be there, and their different heights and means of transport. They may be in a wheel chair or they may come on a bike. Signs can graphically show what is different about a place, and why people should come and visit it. They should look consistent graphically so that, at a glance, they can guide people right to the door.

You can use all kinds of methods to make signs. Large transfer lettering is made to stick on glass or paint, or you can screen print the signs. Hand-painted signs can be made by drawing the words or images in chalk outline, and then painting them in with special 'sign painters' paint. Sign painters use special chalked paper to leave a chalk image, when they draw out the sign,on the surface to be painted. They also support the painting brush with a stick that has a soft ball at the end. With this they can

The Fleet Community Education's banner on the march.

paint a steady line, and rounded curves, without wobbling. Sign-writing is expensive to have done for you, but is quite simple if you do it yourself.

Start looking at how sign systems work, or don't work, when you are visiting a place for the first time.

Banners

Banners can be made with a variety of materials. The best method, though, is to sew fabric in the shape of the design, onto a fabric base. You can paint the image or use sticky plastic, or even screen print images, straight onto the fabric. Whatever you decide to do, the banner needs working out and designing.

Banners, especially trades union banners, have a traditional and symbolic style that goes back to the foundations of the trades union movement and beyond. Your design could take into account these traditions. They can do more than just have your name and slogan. The potential of photo-quality screen printing can enable you to print a number of banners with different images. You could also scale up images and paint them onto the banners with fabric paint. (see page 54).

When banners are carried, they may need to have holes in to allow the wind through as this makes them far easier to carry. You can cover these holes with gauze the same colour as the background and continue the image across them.

When larger banners are to be carried, they need support at the top as well as at the sides. Banners can be supported with tent poles that are slotted together and then threaded through the banner material. The top pole needs to be fastened to the two upright poles as well as to the banner itself.

Banners can also be used to decorate walls, act as signs, or change or label places. Designing banners to do these things involves working out how the design will be affected by where they are to be placed. You can use canvas for this sort of banner which will last longer than normal fabric, and which can be covered with primer to take emulsion paint quite easily.

personalising

You can use design to personalise everyday objects. You can make badges, Tee-shirts, stickers, headed notepaper, and cards for yourself or your organisation. These can all reflect your personal style and can be unique. Personalising can be a way of expressing yourself and affecting your environment.

Badges

You can produce your own badges with hand-drawn or painted images, or they can be printed or photocopied for you. They can be made with simple hand-operated machines, which can be borrowed at your local resource centre.

Hand-made images, drawn on badges with coloured felt tips, come out very well as they are covered with shiny plastic when made into a badge. You can make lots of badges from copied or printed images. Making the artwork for this needs a simple grid (see page 68 for a grid for eight 55mm badges on an A4 sheet). You could do black and white line images that can be copied and coloured in by hand. Or you can get the badges copied in colour, or printed in thousands by offset litho.

Once the image is hand drawn or printed, it has to be cut from the paper. This circle of paper is placed on the metal base, under a sheet of clear plastic. The badge machine presses the paper, plastic and base against a ring that fastens the whole badge together. In the process, the paper is bent round the rim of the badge, and so it is vital to have a small margin around the badge image (see grid). It may be necessary to go over this margin, to assure there is no white paper showing at the rim of the badge.

There are specialist badge makers who make badges for you, organising the printing and the badge making. This can be useful if you have to do thousands.

Stickers

There are specialist printers who will make address stickers for you very cheaply. These can be very useful as they personalise anything you care to stick a sticker onto. They can convey other messages than your address, and may be useful in campaigns. You could use a copier to copy messages onto address labels and use them as stickers. It is possible to get printers to print on to sticker material. Some can print stickers, and then cut them into different shapes. Speech bubble shapes enable the stickers to become the speech of all kinds of pictures in adverts. Stickers can cover up incorrect information, changing it neatly.

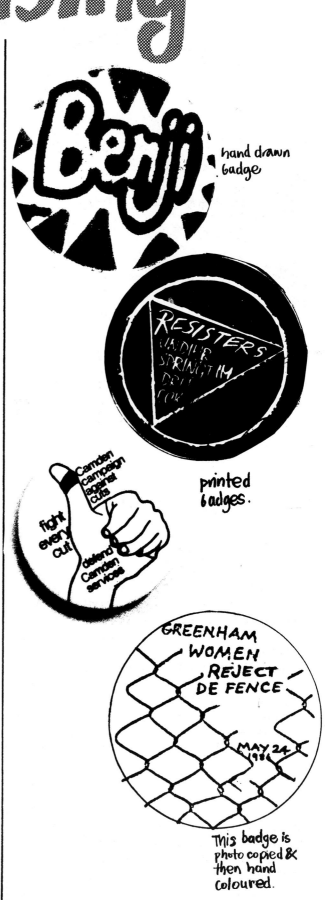

hand drawn badge

printed badges.

GREENHAM WOMEN REJECT DE FENCE

MAY 24 1986

This badge is photo copied & then hand coloured.

20

Fleet
Community
Education
Centre

Agincourt Road London NW3 2NY 01-485 9988
Fleet is an ILEA Community Education project.

a letterhead

Tee-shirts

Designing images that you are going to wear is harder than designing anything else. T-shirts can be screen printed easily and it is quite possible to print just a few copies. They can be printed from a simple paper stencil which is cut out of thin paper. A simple slogan or image can then be printed with a minimum of expense or difficulty. A more photographic quality image, will need a special stencil and a photographic positive. This expensive process will not be economic for just one or two copies; it will therefore involve you in decisions about producing lots of copies which a lot of people will want to wear.

Design the image and the slogan so that when the Tee - shirt is being worn, it can still be read. This means leaving a few inches from the edge of the shirt, which will be at the side of the wearer,before you start printing the image. Draw guide lines before you cut the stencil on the stencil paper, to show you where the image area can be.

Tee - shirt designs can come in all styles and messages; some comment on the wearer, others promote campaigns very sucessfully giving them an obvious support.

Headed notepaper

Designing your own letterhead, or business card, can make your letter far more authorative, yet it can be done by tracing lettering or photocopying, quite easily.

Your letterhead can include a symbol or logo, or it can be just lettering. You have to work out what sort of association you want people to have when they read your letter. It can say all kinds of things about you; some people have a variety of designs for different roles. Try designing yourself a letterhead as if you were an MP, a photographer, a plumber and yourself (if you aren't one of these).

As well as printing your own letterpaper, you can also use the same design as a card. An A6 card, (post card size) can be useful for short messages and to use as a visiting card. It can be cheaper to have four A6 cards printed at once, onto one A4 sheet and cut up the card once it's printed. Design three for friends and one for yourself, and print them together.

Designing a logo and letterhead for a group or organisation can suddenly make the existence of that organisation become a reality. Try and evolve a design that sums up the existence and aims of the group visually. But also, don't forget the practical functions of the letterhead. Typists don't like the letterhead to be too large, or on the left hand side! Experiment − there isn't a correct place or position for the name and address or even the post code.

21

print

Designing for print involves understanding the problems and limitations of the different processes. Careful design can avoid these problems and avoid extra costs. Most print methods now involve photographically copying-or printing, from an original which is known as the artwork. To make this artwork can be quite simple. It usually involves making images on paper, cutting them up, and pasting them onto a sheet of card.(see the techniques section on making images and paste up pages 31-58).

Copying

Simple printing techniques such as copying are getting better and better. Copiers can now reproduce colours, reduce, enlarge and even copy onto A2 as well as produce good quality solid images. With good copiers, anyone can become their own printer. Copiers aren't that good at fine detail in photos. It can also be difficult to get rid of paste-up edges but there are techniques that can help to overcome these problems.

Photo copying is so good and easy now, that design becomes all the more important. You can copy almost any image you want to, at the push of a button, so that the only limitation is your skill and imagination.

Stencil duplicating

This office method of 'printing' can produce better quality copies than most people imagine. Using stencils cut on an electronic scanner from artwork originals, the design can be almost as flexible as copying and it can be a lot cheaper. Duplicating can also be done in colour. Duplicators, however, can't run off big solid images such as heavy headlines or large photos and most can only do A4 size paper.

Offset litho printing

This method is the most commonly used in commercial and non- commercial printshops. It is useful for printing 500, 1000 or more copies, and can print colour, on most sizes and good quality images, including photos.

Screen printing

This method is used to print on fabric as well as paper. So you can print on to T-shirts, posters, glass, metal, or the 'point of display' work used in shops. You can do it yourself and use it to print large colourful prints though it will be difficult to print more than a few hundred.

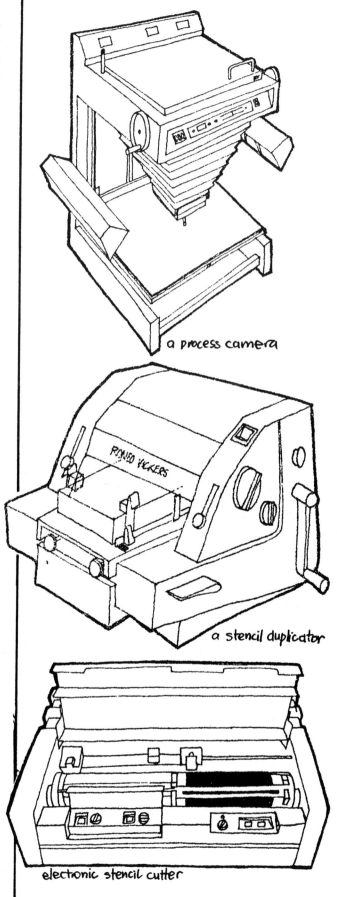

a process camera

a stencil duplicator

electronic stencil cutter

Costs

It is possible to design carefully to save costs in printing. The main way of saving on the print bill, and the best way to give yourself control over what is printed, is to do the design and paste up yourself. There can be quite a difference between the cheapest printers and the most expensive one. It can be better to go to the one that is most sympathetic to the job. Printers can quote a variety of different prices for the same job. Printers specialise to a certain extent and so it is important to go to the right sort of printer. Care is needed that cheaper quotes are not for less good quality materials or printing. Sympathetic printers can advise you on printing and keeping costs down so it well worth making a relationship with them. It costs far less to have offset printing done on coloured paper than printing a second colour.

Standard printing sizes such as SRA2, A3 & A4 can be printed on, and then cut up to become several different things. Design your print to fit the standard print sizes and plan your printing so that it uses all the sheet.

Photos can be the most difficult things to print well. Going to cheaper printers can mean that they are not so well printed or that they are expensive to print.

It is useful to have experience of the printing processes that you are designing for. Try to do your own printing at your local resource centre. If the publication is to be offset printed, visit the printers and see the whole process through. It will help you to make sense of their advice and to understand the costs involved. For more information about printing and establishing your own printshop, see the book 'Print: how you can do it yourself' in this series.

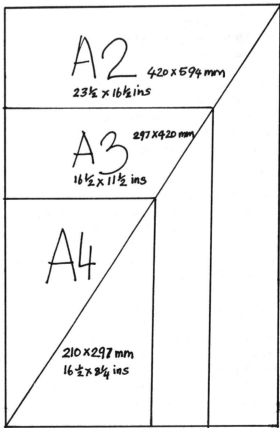

A2   420 x 594 mm   23½ x 16½ ins

A3   297 x 420 mm   16½ x 11½ ins

A4   210 x 297 mm   16½ x 8¼ ins

Standard International metric paper sizes.

23

audio visuals

There are all kinds of 'Audio- Visual' techniques that are easy and cheap to use. Designing credits or graphics for audio- visuals can use design approaches and techniques just as any other media. Audio – visual graphics, like graphs, diagrams, and other illustrations can be used to get over more complex information. They can be made interesting and visually appropriate to the subject they are dealing with.

Designing for audio-visual media has to take into account the linear and sequential use of images and information. You see one image after another, rather than seeing just one image by itself or a group of images together, as you do with an exhibition, or printed posters. You can interrelate sound and images to get your point over.

The way to plan this sequential series of images and sound is to produce a 'story board'. This is a 'rough' design or sketch of each scene of the story, with an indication of the sound track and the commentary that is to go with the images. The drawings on the story board, have to be clear enough for people to see what is going to happen in the finished 'programme'. This technique of planning both image and script together enables you to plan and design effectively, to get the most out of the audio-visual media. Linking the words and images vividly reinforces the message. Story boarding is done with animation and full TV credits, but it is a useful way of working for other simpler audio – visual media.

One of the simplest audio – visual 'programmes' is to just talk while showing slides. It is possible to copy colour slides on to paper with colour photo copiers, and write notes of your talk, like a story board under each copied image. In this way, you can really relate what you set to the image that all your listeners will be looking at. It can then be useful to look at the ideas in the talk, and see if you can make slides of any of the information that you may have given. It is quite easy to turn graphic diagrams or illustrations into slides, (see page 59). Your slide show can then become a programme, which can be thought of as if it were a TV programme.

This projector 'plays' tape slide programmes onto its own screen:

A carousel slide projector

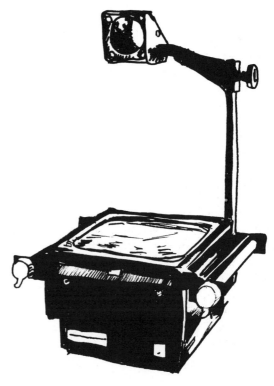

An overhead projector.

Tape slide

The next development is to think of recording your talk or making a sound track or tape, to go with the slides. You can then stay at home and the programme can still be seen by lots of people. This tape slide show can be projected using specially adapted projectors so that the slides change when a bleep goes on the tape. Some shows use two projectors which fade in and out giving quite a dramatic effect. Try and see how images work one after another. It may be possible to produce a series of slides that work a bit like animation, showing change and movement visually. It is possible to make slides from a computer screen. You can design and produce graphic presentations of the information that can be projected for a whole group to see.

Credits and other information for tape – slide shows can be shot on normal photos, keeping them in context with the subject. For example, a show on the housing conditions of an estate could have the credits shown as graffitti on a wall.

Slides should always be shot landscape (ie the longer side horizontal) and the information or main image should be placed well into the frame. Each slide should only have a small amount of information. Try to leave each one up on the screen for at least three seconds. If it has information on it, leave it up for as long as it takes you to read the information twice. It is a good idea to keep the information to about two lines or 10 to 15 words. Remember the proportions of a slide are 2 by 3. Artwork or the original, has to be that ratio too.

There are slide projectors for showing tape – slide shows, that are more like TV sets than projectors. Using them, you can design and produce slide - shows for just a few people to see at a time.

Overhead Projectors

You can also use overhead projectors for audio – visual programmes. These project light though a clear sheet of plastic or acetate on which you can hand draw notes or images. It is possible to make these positives on thermo copiers or photocopiers, and so use designed and good quality images. Colour acetates and transfer lettering, which is specially made, can also be used. Sheets of acetate, (cels) are made to fit on the projector screen which is usually around 10 x 10 inches. Card frames are made to mount the positives which give either a 9 x 9 inch image area or a 9 x 7 inch one. You can use strips of acetate or two sheets,one on top of the other,which can be moved creating many different effects. To produce images on these positives, you need to work out how the materials work with light projected through them. Special translucent materials in colour are available, such as pens, transfer lettering, lines and tones etc. Try and experiment with this form of visual presentation as it can be used to do all sorts of things. Again if you think through your presentation as if it were a programme, it will be possible to store it and use it again. It may even be possible to produce copies for other people to use when they are presenting the same information.

Overhead projectors can also be used to enlarge images for painting banners, murals etc (see scaling page 54)

Video/film

Film animation

Film animation is an expensive and time consuming process but it is one of the best ways of producing graphics for a film or TV programme. The drawings can move and so fit into the rest of the moving film or video. It is possible to do your own animation with any simple Super 8 film camera that has a single frame button. This means the camera can shoot one frame at a time which is how animation works. It is possible to animate all kinds of things as well as drawings. By filming chocolate smarties one frame at a time and moving them a little bit between each frame they can be made to dance, run or move in any way you want. The same is true with cuttings from newspapers, photos, or any other image.

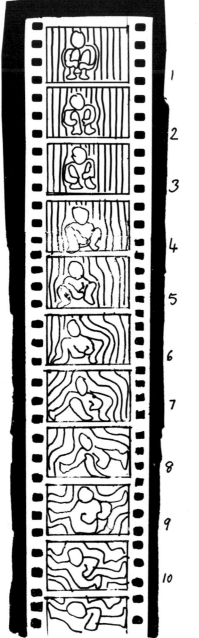

24 frames gives 1 second of action.

1½ sec

She points at the box number appearing in fast magic writing
we close in to the envelope as the woman walks off

2½ sec fade ups / Hold 5 secs

The three addresses fade on to the envelope at 1 second intervals. Each is a different colour All 3 are left on screen and held.

credits 20 sec

As the end of the credits roll up the woman is revealed pulling into view a large envelope

3½ sec

she pulls the envelope to the centre of the screen

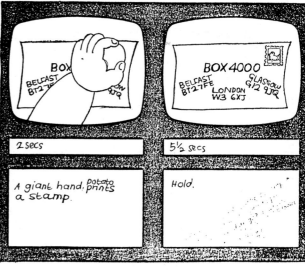

2 secs

A giant hand, potato prints a stamp.

5½ secs

Hold.

Leeds Animation workshop (a women's collective)

Video

If you can't use animation, it is still possible to give some movement to the credits or other graphic images with video. You can move the camera across the flat artwork, or close in on the detail. It is possible to put credits onto video with a typesetting system such as an Astern, which not only sets the type and puts it onto video but makes it move onto the screen in various ways, from the top down and from the sides etc. Credits can be hand-drawn on long sheets of paper and rolled under a rostrum camera which is the old way that most film credits were done. Today, with computer technology it is possible to film or record all kinds of graphic text and diagram from the computor screen. Sophisticated computer graphics for TV, can make all kinds of things happen. This is a very expensive technology to buy or use but it is possible to do quite a bit with smaller personal computers.

For very simply created video graphics try using images on paper. Use the techniques of pop-up books and pull out strips of paper to reveal information or images. It is possible to put information on acetate which can be filmed on top of a photo, creating an interesting design quite simply. A video camera can be mounted on a copy-stand if its strong enough. In this way simple animation can be done.

For all graphics for film or TV, it is important that the information can be read. Take care that the background image doesn't interfere with the text, and that there is enough contrast for the text to be read against the background. Very thin lettering can get broken up on TV, so use a fairly solid letter style which doesn't have very thin parts.

The design has to take into account the ratio of the TV format which is 3 x 4. It has also to be careful not to put too much information on to it at any one time. Read the text two or three times and leave it on the screen for that length of time.

If cuttings, quotations, or other images are used on video or film they must be the correct proportions to fill the screen. They can be picked out by shading all the cutting except the lines you want people to read. It may be best to reset the quotation in the proportions that will fit the TV screen rather than use the real thing, or it may be possible to cut out the lines you want and put them on a coloured background.

The equipment to make graphics for video or film may be obtained at resource centres or community-orientated film or video workshops. Colleges or Teachers' Centres may also have equipment that can be used cheaply. Commercial facilities and equipment can be hired, although their rates are very expensive. If you have everything worked out clearly beforehand, a few hours in a commercial studio to add the graphics may well be worth it.

Has this too much information for it to be read 2 or 3 times with out the audience getting bored with a screen full of words?

How long does it take to read this caption 2 or 3 times. Is it too long to leave up on the screen?

Has this too little?

27

Computers

A host system with BBC computer

modem

Communitel database can be edited to and updated

Computers are becoming both a useful medium as well as a very important design tool. In the design techniques section (see on page 43) we have covered some of the uses that computers can fill as design tools.

Computers, as a medium in their own right, can be used in different ways. They are uniquely adaptable to a small scale, participatory approach to media. You can interact, as well as just get access to information using computers. It is possible to produce your own 'data', as well as just read other people's. It has enormous potential, though at the present it is used for a mainly limited and mundane uses.

Computers can store and present information. Connected to the telephone system, they can communicate complex information easily and quickly. This gives them the potential of being an important medium rather than just a way of storing images or text.

Different computers have different graphic capabilities. This depends on the amount of memory they have, the programs available, and the monitor or printer to which they are connected to produce the image or text. With the smaller home computers you can see every little dot or 'pixel' that makes up the image. With greater memory capability it is possible to produce finer and finer definition images. The large machines are now so detailed that they·can be used for preparing four colour separations for printing or TV graphics.

Using so many different systems, programs and basic hardware, the full potential for communicating hits the problem of the incompatiblity of many systems. For example, many users may be able to get into a data base but only a few with the right machines could take programs from this data base to use on their own machines.

View-data

View-data programs enable you to arrange, design and present information so that people can see and read it. The computer with this sort of program gives the readers choices, so that they can go from one 'page' to the next depending on their choice or answer. It therefore works, not like a book, but as a tree where at each stage there are various next steps to choose from. On these sorts of programs, you can design the information to fit into this flow of choices. It is possible to use simple graphics or backgrounds and to help the reader find their way to the information they need.

You could use this system with an exhibition, or as a one-off. It is possible to lend the view-data program, with your information on it,to other users of the same equipment.

Data-bases

Data-bases hold information on computers centrally, and anyone can gain access using a computer connected to the phone. They would have to know the right phone number and access code, but once in, they could see around any section they wanted to. Programmes or information can be taken by recording onto another machine; there are even letter boxes and notice boards on which people can leave notes or information. There are national and commercial data-bases like Prestel or Micronet and there are 'private' ones set up by organisations and companies for their own purposes. There can also be smaller-scale, community- orientated ones as well.

The design of information is fairly limited in these sorts of systems, as each page is limited to a small number of lines of either text or images. However, it can be easy to change colour and so this media can be used to emphasis and differentiate information. The standard for the page size is laid down, following Prestel, having 920 characters per frame.

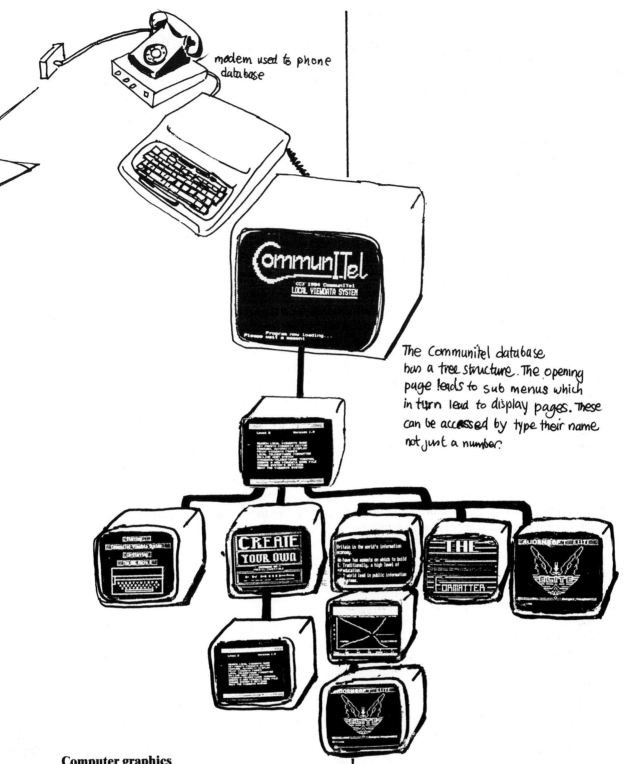

modem used to phone database

The Communitel database has a tree structure. The opening page leads to sub menus which in turn lead to display pages. These can be accessed by type their name not just a number.

Computer graphics

Computers are used to create graphic images for audio visuals, video, animation and print, using equipment such as the Quantrel Paint Box System. Images in these systems can be changed and modified, and work from images that have been digitised on special cameras. This expensive equipment is used for games, flight-simulation systems, architecture, other design and production jobs reflecting the priorities of society today. It can and will be developed for far wider uses in education research, and as a means of expression. Computer graphics artists in the USA have done wonderful things with this sort of equipment but it will take a long time, and great changes in technology and organisation, for it to be readily available to ordinary people.

Looking at the small personal computers available, there are all kinds of graphics software available that can be used to make images, move them around, paint pictures etc. The Macintosh computer comes with MacPaint and MacWrite programmes, and a Mouse device with which you can move the cursor around, so creating different images and tones as well as text. Other software and computer companies are following this course, so the smaller computers can now be used to produce quite interesting images, as well as processing text and playing games.

For further details on creating your own 'prestel' with BBC computer equipment contact CommuniTel 189 Freston Road London W10 6TH.

alternative media

The traditional media may not be the appropriate form for new sorts of messages or ideas. New ideas need new forms or ways to express them. Creating new forms or media may take you into many areas that aren't conventional media, or conventional design. Telephone trees, or paying key workers more,may be the most appropriate solutions to the design problems of improving an organisations image, or getting information out quickly. Creative thinking is needed.

Flags, scarves, bunting etc, can all have symbolic meanings or create feelings of unity and even carry messages. Designing these for an event may be a very good design solution. For example,dress can also get over the point of a demonstration for example more effectively than other media. If waiters had menues printed on their T shirts, would you get served quicker?

Sandwich boards and other costumes or make up, can all be used to get over a point.

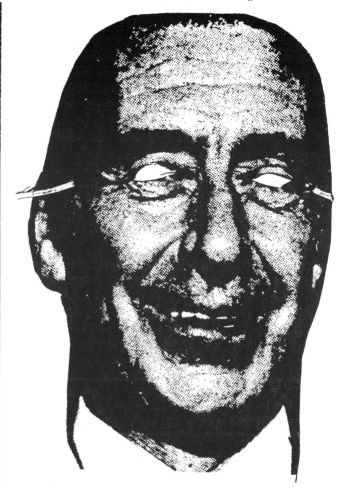

Masks can be made from printed photos – or drawings. Design a poster that can be cut out to make a mask and worn. A photo, printed, cut up and worn as a mask, can convert a whole crowd into the strangest group of Mrs Thatchers or Mr Reagans ever seen.

Murals can also present powerful images with a message that lots of people see. They can sum up and express the aspirations or commitments of a whole community. The image interrelates to the context it is in. Murals can usefully be considered as a media option.

Painted or sprayed slogans on walls, could also be thought of as a media. How could you design them better? Some groups use stencils to spray on walls. Others have used this graffitti to point out the incorrect nature and danger of cigarette adverts. Some graffitti has been so witty that it has been photographed and turned into postcards. If the graffitti artist had thought about this end use of their work, would they have designed it differently? Stencils and painting on the pavement or playground floor has also been used. The footprints lead to the door of the community centre need following,while the ghost images of dead people remind everyone of Hiroshima.

A post card by Terri Donavon.

The writing on the wall is graffitti in some places and to some people, while it is an important expression of identity and politics, to others. Media are changing all the time, and so the design of media should be pushing that change, and pushing society to change with it.

design techniques

An essential part of this handbook's message is to work out your design ideas before you get involved in the techniques of design practice. (See pages 6-12 on design approaches).

Familarity with the particular media you are to use is also important, so that you know the potential and problems of that media. (See pages 15-30 on media).

Once you have been through these stages you can start to work on the techniques to turn ideas into real images. This isn't too difficult, especially when you've had the experience of seeing your work through the whole process once. You start believing in it when you've seen the result. Once you know it's possible, you start to think about what you really want to do or say next.

You don't have to be an artist to produce, borrow, adapt or convert images. Design is about thinking visually and graphically, about communicating ideas.

When you do put images and words together, they tend to start telling stories; some of which may not be what you intended. Try cutting out photos from magazines and putting them together to tell a story. This simple exercise can be developed and all kinds of fantastic stories evolved. Stick cartoon bubbles on the pictures and you can make the 'characters' talk. By sticking captions and headings on your design you change the images' meaning again. A large 'Wanted' sign on top of any photo, makes the person in the photo an instant criminal. Two pictures together can become the before and after, or can be contrasted in all kinds of ways.

Try out these exercises and experiments so that when you do come to design your own page or story board etc., you will have had some feel for manipulating images.

For different design ideas and different media, there are different techniques to use. Here are some.

Add your own words to the bubbles and your own caption.

WANTED

FOR
CONSPIRACY

31

roughs

Thinking visually is helped by doodling pictures on paper (even if the end result is to be on film, or electronic media). Rough drawings or sketches can be very simple thumb-nail sketches for sorting out ideas (see page 6).

Same Size Roughs

Take the idea a stage on. It can be useful to produce a rough version of the design in the size you are going to produce it. This can be more 'finished' than the first rough ideas. It can show the position more clearly, but also the shape of the images to be used. Trace the headlines to work out if they will fit. Draw outlines or simple versions of the illustrations. It can be useful to colour them in, to give a visual impression of the page. A big black photo can be a strong image in the overall design; show how this will work in your rough. You can see how your ideas work, by looking at this rough and showing it to other people for their comments and reactions.

Some products you may be designing might gain a particular quality from their scale. Try and make the rough the right size, so you can see what that design looks like at full size.

Jigsaw Roughs

Once the material has been set or produced, you can use proofs to make a rough. You can cut them up and roughly glue them down to see if the text fits, and the design works.

With a poster you can move the headlines and illustrations around. Place these pieces on a piece of paper, under a sheet of glass. The glass will hold them down flat and will make them appear to be more like the finished, printed version. You could photocopy this pasted up rough in different arrangements to see which one works best. It can be a useful exercise to re-arrange the artwork, before you paste it up, to see that the design really does work well.

Dummies

It can be useful to produce a rough version of your book or magazine as a dummy. This can be sheets of paper folded together to make the correct number of pages that are to be in your publication. They don't have to be in the finished size but should be to scale. A4 paper can be easy to use folded to make A5 pages; this is quite adequate even if the finished product is to have A4 or A3 pages.

The dummy is used to work out what goes where, and which pages are to be printed next to each other. So mark out the numbers on the pages and then draw the articles and illustrations in pencil, estimating how much space should be given to each article. In this way you can see what elements go next to each other, and how this works as a whole. You can also work out the 'imposition' for a simple printed, folded and stapled magazine or booklet.

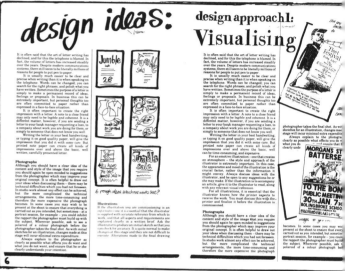

Collage roughs

You can cut up samples of type that **have** already been printed in other publications, with pictures etc, to give an impression of how the page is going to look. You could design an ideal page spread of two pages and the cover, to present to people and give them the idea and feel of the planned publication. Special text for this is sold as a dry transfer and is called 'body' text. Usually in latin, it is made in a variety of styles and sizes, so that it can be cut up and stuck down in the design you want.

Story-boards

For Audio-Visuals it is useful to break down the programme into scenes, and then into still images, for the planning and writing of the script. These can be used in a rough story-board that links rough drawings, with the sound and commentary. The images can be drawn in square or TV shapes according to the correct ratio, (3 x 4 for TV, 3 x 2 for slides, 3 x 3 for OHP). The sound and commentary are put in two boxes underneath. Using a story-board rough, you can assess how the story works, not only as a whole, but also in terms of how the sound and commentary will go with the images.

Roughs generally

However good the idea, or however familiar you are with a medium, it is advisable to produce a rough first. Even with some computer technology that allows you to change things, and so work things out on the screen, it can be advisable to produce a rough version first, and then correct and change it for the finished product.

grids

The technical limitations of the medium can form the foundation of your design. Drawing out a margin in which it should be produced, can be a useful aid to the actual design and production of the image. It is the first step in producing a 'grid' for your design. On a T-shirt the image has to start on the front of the wearer not under their arm. Likewise in printing you have to allow a margin at least on one edge for the press to grip and feed the paper. Each medium and sort of machine has a different technical constraint.

Once you have drawn this outer margin, you can start creating a consistent design for the text and the images. Usually headlines in a magazine take up the top 2 cm of the text area. This can be ruled in and left free of text, consistently throughout the magazine. It is better to design a page with columns, than to have the text right across the page. This is unreadeable on an A4 page so it is necessary to have at least 2 columns of text. Draw these in as you want them on the grid. This produces a standard page design or grid, which can be adapted and developed depending on the sort of publication or media being designed. Newspapers have seven or eight columns on far larger pages, and always use a grid so that the style and page layout is consistent.

You can buy pre-printed grids that have a variety of different layout possiblities on them and we have included one in this handbook (see page 66). Pre-printed grids are usually printed in blue. Light blue won't reproduce with offset printing so you can stick black designs or text onto this grid and use it as artwork. It is possible to rule your own grid in light blue pencil but this can be labourious if you have to prepare a great many pages.

The grid we have provided can be used by laying out your page on thinner layout paper, so that you can see the grid underneath as you paste up your page.

Pasting up or laying out onto a grid, can make your work far easier, more consistent and it is simpler to get everything straight and in place.

The grid can not only be a useful aid to designing pages, but also a design idea in its own right. You can design posters, tables of information etc., using the idea of the grid and dividing or interrelating information. To construct this sort of grid you can work out how much space the longest line of each sort of information will take, and set up your grid to take these lines. Once you've solved how to arrange the grid for these most difficult bits, you can arrange the rest of the information on the grid.

Rule out the grid in light blue (or in pencil which can be rubbed out before use). Align the information onto this grid. Where necessary rule in ink lines that will stay in the final design. These lines can be of varied thickness, depending on the information and how it needs dividing.

The grid can be a way of clarifying and arranging information; used in charts or graphs it will show complex inter relationships of numbers, times etc. To devise this type of grid requires a clear idea about how it will be used. Are people going to need to read across, or up and down? Are they looking for the times or the destinations? You can design the grid with thin or thick lines across; the information can be in colour, or arranged so that it is emphasised in different ways; holidays could be covered with tone for example. Sometimes people make the grid too apparent, boxing in the information so it is difficult to read across, or whatever you want or need it to do. Space between the information can be used to divide it as effectively as ruled lines.

Grids can be very useful in exhibitions and displays. They don't have to be drawn in, but can be used to design the panels or the different exhibits consistently. A set measurement from the ceiling to the begining of the exhibits, can establish a consistent line from which everything else can be planned.

The grid used to layout this book was:

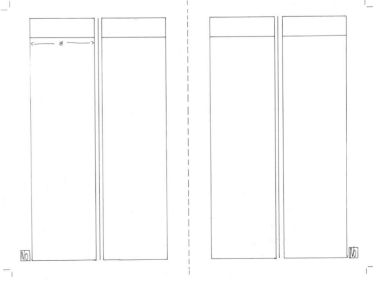

See page 66 for the grid you can use.

lettering

Lettering is an essential part of most design. Over the centuries it has been designed in many different contexts and for various demands, but it is read as standard symbols that everyone who can read has learnt to recognise. So drastic changes in design of lettering can't happen.

Lettering can be produced in many different ways, styles and sizes, depending on the design.

Basic lettering makes each letter a different width so that an 'i' is much thinner than an 'm'. Typewriters can't do this proportional spacing, which is why they have such strange designs for some letters and why they fit so few letters into a line.

Lettering is designed in lots of different styles but mostly they are either 'serif' or 'sans serif':

a serif typeface

a sans serif typeface.

Though there are many other styles or families of type faces:

Bodoni Bold

abcdefghijklmnopqrstuvwxyz&

In any one style of lettering there are useful variations so that you can have a thick version called a Bold, a medium known as a Roman and a thin version - a Light. It also can be used in a slanted version - *an Italic*.

Lettering can also be reversed out. That is, it can be produced white on a black or other coloured background. This can be done on a process camera, or you can do it yourself by lettering onto clear acetate and contact printing onto photographic paper.

spacing

To be clearly read as a word, lettering needs to have the letters spaced so that the spaces look even. With headlines or large lettering, this can be important. The space between two straight letters should be more than the space between the ends of two rounded letters.

Try to make sure that the headline doesn't become difficult to read because the words break up or join together. The space between words should roughly be the width of the letter 'i', but they can be slightly larger. Some spaces get so wide that it is less likely that people would read past the first word of a headline.

Lettering can be made by hand or using various mechanical methods. Whichever way it is made, great care with spacing and legibility is necessary.

ABCDEFGHIJKLMNOPQRSTUVWXYZ
£1234567890

Rockwell Bold

àbcdéfg hijklmñôpqrstüvwxyz
ABCDEFGHIJKLMNOPQRSTU
VWXYZ

34

hand drawn lettering

You can hand draw both headlines and text. If you can do clear and neat hand writing it can be very useful - it is so quick and cheap! It also gives your design a human quality. Hand drawn lettering can be very flexible in terms of design as you can so easily vary the length of line or the SIZE or the **thickness** or *style of* lettering.

Practice and tracing enable you to develop better hand lettering but you can draw out your lettering in pencil first and then go over it in ink. You could rule out guidelines in pencil to keep the lettering straight and even. The pencil can be rubbed out once the lettering is inked in.

Lettering can be hand drawn larger and reduced photographically when it is to be printed or used. Larger writing is easier to produce neatly than making it the size that it is to be used.

There are lots of other ways of producing lettering by hand that are not just hand writing. You can make out line lettering from hand drawn letters.

letter

This can be shaded in or made into white lettering on a black background.

tracing

Tracing is one of the most useful way of producing headlines, as it is so flexible. You can produce quite good headlines that look almost like type, but in the size and style you like. To do this you need to collect sample sets of the letter design from type books and photo copy them in various sizes. The quality doesn't have to be that good as the end result will be traced. Rule a pencil line on thin paper and trace the headline onto the line keeping the letters evenly spaced and straight. Trace the outline in thin pen and then fill in with a thicker, quicker pen. Tracing improves your free-hand letter writing as well as producing good results.

STENCIL

Joanna

Headlines and captions can be produced using stencils or plastic lettering guides. You need a ruling pen or a pen with a long thin knib to fit into the lettering guide and reach the paper. You can get these lettering guides with various sizes but only in a very few styles of lettering.

Stencils for headlines can be bought made of plastic, metal or special 'oil paper'. The lettering produced is rather crude but it can be appropriate for some designs.

It is possible to design your own stencil lettering — draw it onto 'oil paper' and cut it out with a sharp knife. You can then use this stencil over and over again creating your own style.

Photographic methods such as photocopying enable us to miss out all the recent stages of technological media and create a direct form of design that uses real writing and hand created letters and images. Instead of people seeing words coming from the 'industrial machine' they are obviously the creation of a person like themselves.

On the next page is a tracing of Eric Gill's original designs for a typeface called 'Joanna' from 1930. By tracing these you are really by-passing the technical intervention of the typesetting industry and going back to the drawings of a master designer.

ABCDEFGHIJKL
MNOPQRSTUV
WXYZ abcdefgh
ijklmnopqrstuvwxy
z
1234567890

'Joanna' designed by Eric Gill 1930

37

typing

Association

Typewriters and basic word-processing printers produce print of a standard design. These are widely accepted and easily understood by people. This text looks utilitarian and even if it comes out of very complex systems, people still associate it with the simple manual typewriter they have at home. Typing - because it is hand made and personal - is seen as a more direct method than the 'printed' text produced by typesetting.

m i

Fixed width letters

Most typing uses a one unit system, so that each letter is the same width. Making the 'i' and the 'm' the same width, involves designing these letters so that one is as wide as possible, and the other is narrow. This mechanical system affects the type design and makes it quite different to typesetting. It also means that you can fit far fewer characters on a line when typed than you could if they were typeset.

Design with a typewriter

Even with the mechanical limitations of type-writers you can use them to design and produce reasonable quality products. By playing within the technical limitations, you can produce all kinds of effects. However, design with such simple tools requires less of the normal typist's way of arranging text, and more of the design approach, working as if you were using printer's type.

As an exercise,
> **try using the tabulating**
> **mechanism of your**
> **typewriter**
>> **to align your**
>> **information**

so that it is clearer
>> **and**
>>> **better designed.**

Typewriters can be used to produce a variety of textures and other patterns. By moving the paper on which you are typing you can gently wave the lines. You can also type shapes or images. Poems have been typed in suitable shapes or patterns for their meaning. This concrete poetry shows what can be done with the humble typewriter:

```
words are images
words are images
words are images
words are images
words are imageswords are images
             words are images
             words are images
                          words are im
words words words w o r d s w o r d s w o
             o           o                sdrow are sdr
             r           d
             d           s
             s           w
             w         r o
              o    r  d
               r d  d
                  s
                 are
               images
```

Letter styles

Typing and word-processing print comes in several different styles - though usually in the standard fixed width. Typewriters usually have either 'elite' letters, which fit 12 letters to an inch, or 'pica' which is bigger and fits 10 letters to the inch.

Golfball and other electric typewriters, have different styles of letter. These can be changed by changing the golf ball or daisy wheel, or whatever actually produces the letters. In this way you can use typing to produce an interesting page, with different articles, in different typing styles. Also available are 'jumbo' typewriters which produce far larger typing and which can be far more in use in displays, sub headings etc.

```
3333333333333333333333333333333333333333333
3333333333333333333333333333333333333333333
```

Typing | Enlarged

Photocopiers can reduce typed text quite easily
- and some can enlarge as well. In this way,
a typed page can be designed with some typing
larger than other bits. You can reduce the less
important text, and enlarge the introductory
paragraphs, sub headings etc.

*This is the size
of the typing
direct from the
typewriter* →

*This is reduced
on a copier to
71%*

The whole design can be reduced 20% when printing
and still be easily read. But in this way you
can fit in 20% more text and it will still look
good. Notes and other detailed information, can
be reduced even more than 20%.

See page 54 for how to scale up or down. This
will help you to work out how long to type the
lines that are to be reduced. This way you can
make sure they will fit your column width or design.

ABCDEFGHIJKLMNOPQRSTUVWXYZ
abcdefghijklmnopqrstuvwxyz
1234567890
15 pitch

ABCDEFGHIJKLMNOPQRSTUVWXYZ
abcdefghijklmnopqrstuvwxyz
1234567890
12 pitch

BCDEFGHIJKLMNOPQRSTUVWXYZ
bcdefghijklmnopqrstuvwxyz
234567890
10 pitch

Typing a manuscript
If your text is to be typeset, it has to be typed
clearly for the typesetter to read and type from.
The quicker and easier it is to do this, the
cheaper it will be to have typeset.
- type the text in double spacing
- type on one side of the paper
- number the pages
- neatly and clearly indicate what is to be typed,
  as against instructions.

Some typewriters and computer printers can
produce proportionally spaced letters. The best
achieve a quality close to typesetting - good
enough for books or newsletters.

Word-processing has many advantages over typing,
as it has memory capabilities which enable you
to move text around, correct it and change it.
The text can be produced with both margins
'justified'. That is, with all the lines the
same length. They can even centre text, or make
some words bolder to stand out. These
capabilities all depend on the system you are
using and the quality of the printer used.

Reproducing
All typing needs to be evenly typed, with a
solid black print, if it is to reproduce well.
An electric machine with a carbon ribbon works
much better than a manual typewriter with a
fabric ribbon. The uneveness and grey typing
produced on a manual machine comes out badly,
especially with offest printing.

Typing for artwork
For typed text that is going to be directly
copied or printed, you can cut and paste it
up. Headlines, sub-headings, and pictures
can be included. Corrections can be made
by typing the line again correctly, and
simply pasting it on top of the incorrect
line. See page 57 for paste-up techniques.

39

typesetting

If you want your text to look as clear and presentable as possible, you will need to have it typeset. It will also fit more letters on a line. This can be worthwhile if space is limited or if you are paying a lot for the space or print. For example, if you are printing more than 1000 copies of a booklet, having the text typeset could save up to a third of your printing costs as there is less to be printed. This saving could cover the cost of typesetting, although this will depend on how much the printing costs will be.

There are various ways of going about getting your text typeset. The most common is to type your text clearly (see page 38) and take it to a typesetting company or co-operative. You will have to specify the sort of type, the size and the width of the columns (known as the measure), the space between lines and how you want paragraphs done. Community or co-operative typesetters are more likely to be helpful and to work with you on this than a commercial company. The charges are also likely to be very high at a commercial firm. Even getting a comprehensible quote can be difficult. Some firms quote in key strokes or 'ens', (which refers to the number of times they press a key) while others quote in words. There are likely to be 6 characters and spaces allowed for each word on average, so to compare the two prices, multiply or divide by 6.

There are various systems of typesetting available. The IBM composers are older machines that work by typing directly on paper, their results are quite good but tend to be uneven. They are also limited to setting between 8 and 11 point.

There are various versions of photo and computer typesetting systems. Some of these are limited to settings up to 36 point.

Typesetters can only stock a limited range of typefaces and styles of type. So before you choose one, it is a good idea to see the type catalogues or lists. Typesetters type the text on long strips of paper. This can then be cut up and pasted down on the artwork for printing or for any other use.

In typesetting systems where the text is recorded in the memory, any corrections or changes can be done to the setting, and a whole new copy produced. This can be rather expensive and it is always possible to have just a few lines reset, and then paste them on top of the incorrect line.

Using computers it is possible to typeset your own material, as described on page 43, or to have it done directly from your own computer's disk, see page 44.

Helvetica Light
Helvetica Medium
Helvetica Condensed
Helvetica Bold
Helvetica Bold Condensed
Helvetica Compressed
Helvetica Bold Outline
Helvetica Rounded Bold
Univers 45 (Light)
Univers 47 (Light Condensed)
Univers 55 (Medium)
Univers 57 (Medium Condensed)
Univers 65 (Bold)
Univers 67 (Bold Condensed)
Univers 75 (Extra Bold)
Gill Sans
Gill Sans Bold
Gill Sans Extra Bold
Futura Light
Futura Book
Futura Bold
Futura Extra Black
Futura Display
Times
Times Italic
Times Bold
Times Bold Italic
Rockwell Light
Rockwell Medium
Rockwell Bold
Rockwell Extra Bold
Avant Garde Medium
Avant Garde Bold
Eras Light
Eras Medium
Eras Bold
Eras Ultra
Raleigh
Raleigh Bold
Benguiat Book
Benguiat Book Italic
Benguiat Bold
Benguiat Gothic Book
Benguiat Gothic Heavy
Century Schoolbook
Century Schoolbook Italic
Century Schoolbook Bold
Plantin
Plantin Italic
Plantin Bold
Plantin Bold Italic

typesetting measurement

Whatever typesetting system is employed, people doing typesetting will probably think and refer to the type in terms of measuring systems established to deal with the metal letters used in letterpress printing. As each letter has a different width, the size of the typeface is taken as the height from the top of the highest letter, to the bottom of the lowest. This is measured in points and there are 72 points to the inch. The width of columns and the margins are measured in picas. There are 12 points to a pica and 6 picas to an inch. (ems are usually the same as picas).

The gap between lines (known as 'leading') is measured in points, but it is usually refered to as if it were part of the type size. For example if you wanted a 2 points gap on 11 point typesetting, you would ask for 11 on 13 and so on. If there is to be no gap between lines it is said to be 'set solid'. The gap between paragraphs can also be specified in points and can be varied as much as you want. The indents, if there are any, are also refered to in points.

x heights

The height of the main part of a lower-case letter, is called the x height. This can vary in size, depending on the design of the typeface. The size of the letter is measured by the overall height, and not the height of the x or any other letter of that sort. So it can be difficult to mix lettering of the same size but of different typefaces.

Typesetting specifications.

Once you have your text ready to be set, it has to be 'marked up' so that the typesetters know what you want them to do with it. This is done by putting your instructions at the start of the text, and marking in the margins wherever there is a change from the basic style. This is obviously best done in consultation with the typesetters who know the sorts of type they have in stock. It is a good idea to make sure they understand your marks.

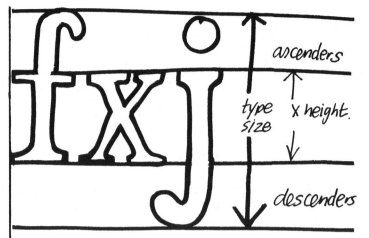

You have to specify:
● The size of the type to be used.
● The style of the typeface.
● If any text is to be in bold or italics.
● The space between lines.
● Whether the type is to be justified, centred, or ranged right.
● If paragraphs are to be indented or just indicated by a space.
● The column width or the measure.

As well as indicating the basic style you have to 'mark up' the text to show when the setting has to be changed. This is done by marking the text in question, and writing down in the margin what is to happen to it. If it is to be bold, it has to have a squiggly line under it and 'bold' written in the margin. You can use these standard symbols as proof-reading symbols, as well as marking up symbols:

margin notes	text marks.
caps	Set in Capitals.
lc	Set in lower case
ital/ ⌐⌐/	Set in italics
bold	Set in bold.
n.p	Make a new paragraph.
#/	Put in more/space
⌒	Close up
>	Add space between lines
less #	Less space between lines.
	Move to the right
	Move to the left
	Transpose
run on	Run on - no new paragraph.
⌐/	Delete characters or/words
new matter	Insert new text.

depth scale

As you can see from the type measurements and the casting off or copyfitting pages, it can be useful to have a special ruler to use when working with type. A 'depth scale' is one design that is good for measuring off the number of lines, in any basic size of type on a page. It can be used as a ruler in inches, millimetres and 8,9,10,11,12, and 14 points. So if you want to know how many 10 on 12 point lines there will be, you can use the 12 point scale to measure this out. You can also use this to measure out in picas, as they are 12 points too.

Use this 'illustration' to make yourself one. Cut it out and mount it on card. Use a sharp knife and a straight edge, being careful to cut straight and on the line. The inside shapes can be cut out too so that those scales can be used as well. This depth scale will then show you how many lines can be fitted in, in a variety of sizes.

Cover the depth scale you've made with clear, sticky acetate folding it over the edges and keeping the edges straight. This may not be as good as a proper plastic or metal one but it will serve most needs quite adequately.

Depth scale ruler with columns: 6 point | 8 point | 9 point | 10 point | 11 point | 12 point | inches | 13 point | cm | 14 point

effective publicity   design depth scale

42

typesetting with computers:
Desktop Publishing

There are now computers, software and printers that can be used to type, produce headlines or illustrations, and lay out pages. This capability will enable computer users to produce very good quality originals such as reports and newsletters which can be printed as well as being used as data in computer communications.

The software has been developed for different systems and with different capabilities. First of all it has the capacity to 'set' the text in type that is nearly as good as typesetting. Programs have also been produced to enable the user to move the text around and lay it out in whatever size is needed. There are also 'painting' programs that enable illustrations to be produced, with a number of different textures and paint or pencil lines. New software is being developed all the time, but at present it is most available for the 'business' type computer, such as the Apple Macintosh.

It is possible to buy a 'mouse' device which can be used as a pointer on the computer. This enables you to draw on the screen and control what happens. To draw or paint, the mouse is moved along a table. When its button is pressed, it activates whatever control it is pointing to. This makes it a very easy system to use, although it does take a bit of getting used to. It's rather like going back to playgroup for the first time and not being able to get paint on the paper! After a few attempts, however, it becomes quick and easy to use.

If a computer is used to set, draw pictures and lay out pages you will need to get the pages from the computer onto paper. To do it well, you need to have access to a Laser Printer. These are very expensive machines but can produce far higher quality prints than a normal dot matrix printer. It may be possible to share one of these machines between several users, as for most simple jobs a normal printer will do. A resource centre may well be a solution so that each user could come to a central place, and get their disk read by the Laser Printer so that it produces a page from the computer designed data. It could also be photocopied and run off at the same resource centre.

The technology is changing and being developed all the time. By the time this has been published, I hope that new systems will be available, making all these capabilities even cheaper.

At the moment the Apple Macintosh's Desktop publishing system seems the best. Not only does its typesetting capabilities enable it to set headlines as well as text, but it can also reduce and enlarge illustrations to fit, and in addition it has the MacPaint and MacWrite programs. This system is being distributed in Britain by Gestetner among others and it is possible to have a demonstration of what it can do. *

These systems can be used to create adequate illustrations or they can be used to lay out the page, leaving a gap for the photos or other illustrations. It is expensive to digitise existing images. You can, however, use the mouse device to trace them and use the computer to make them fit.

Here are some examples of type styles available with the Desktop Publishing System:

Times
abcdefghijklmnopqrstwvxyz

Helvetica
abcdefghijklmnopqrstwvxyz.

And some tones and affects available on this system using MacPaint:

This page was written and layed out on an Apple Macintosh using the Desk Top Publishing System and a Laser writer, with thanks to Gestetner for letting me use the equipment.

* For Details contact Gestetner Ltd.,
National Accounts Department,
210 Euston Road,
London, NW1. Tel: 01 387 7021
ext. 3205

43

typesetting with computers: from disk.

It is possible to record the text on computer disk, and have it read by a compatible typesetting machine which can then set the text directly. This avoids retyping the text with all the problems of proof-reading. Quite a few printers and typesetters offer this service.

Doing this requires a micro computer (such as the Amstrad PCW 256, Apricot, Apple II, IBM PC or compatibles) which usually uses a CP/M or a MS-DOS operating system. It requires a knowledge and understanding of typography. It also requires a typesetting company that will help you sort out the codes, and the other ways of presenting the text, so that the typesetting machine will understand the data and produce what you want. The coding and typing must be accurate as it can prove very expensive if the whole book comes out in 36 point headings, rather than the correct type. A variety of systems are available and some are easier to use than others.

It is possible to deliver the text on the disk, accurately typed and proof-read, and pay the typesetters to put on the codes and typographical instructions for their system. This will cost quite a bit and it could be better to pay them to teach you how to do it, so that the next time you could do this yourself. The expense of having the coding done for you, or of having it checked, will avoid the long process of proof-reading and it can be much quicker than having the whole thing re-typed. For simple text, uncoded text will work out cheaper to set in this way than if it were retyped from the manuscript.

If you are producing a fairly simple job without tables and display headings, adverts or charts, it is useful to do your own coding and have the disk read and typeset directly from it. This can work out at about a third of the cost of conventional typesetting methods. Conventional methods are usually cheaper if you are setting over 10,000 words, but doing your own computer typesetting means much quicker printing and it avoids having to proof read for mistakes that typesetters have made.

There are standard codes such as the Aspic codes. These are published by the British Printing Industries Federation (11, Bedford Row, London, WC1). Linotype, who make typesetting equipment, also produce their own code. Lithosphere Printing Co-operative have found that an edited version of Linotype's codes are the easiest to use and understand.

Here are some of them:

The codes have to tell the machine:
what size the type is to be:
›H10‹ that is, height 10 points
what the 'leading' is to be:
›L12‹ that is, 2 points between lines.
what the width of column or measure is to be:
›M14‹ that is 14 picas wide.
and what the fount is:
›F4‹ this refers to their list of typefaces. Number 4 is Times Bold Italic. They have a stock of 107 different typefaces and styles to choose from.
To indent the code is:
›i2R‹ if you want to indent 2 picas right.
To indent two to the left would be
›i2L‹
and to cancel the indent would be
›iC‹.
To advance 3 points (to give a bit of a space between paragraphs) would be ›A3‹.

With these commands the return has to be recoded, so every time the return is pressed and when a new paragraph is started, it is necessary to type in:
/QL for Quad Left to go back to the left hand margin.
To go to the right hand one, it is /QR
or to center it it is /QC.

This gives you some idea of what is involved and it is worth looking into the possiblity. First talk to printers and typesetters who offer this service. They will warn you of the expense that doing this yourself can involve if you make mistakes. They can also quote for doing the coding and for just setting your text direct from the coded disk.

This book you are reading has been set direct from the author's computer. The text that was coded by the author and read and printed out as typesetting at Lithosphere. (See the Directory for their address).

This option is important for the small publisher who is involved in computers, or who has access to one, and publishes enough to make it worthwhile. It becomes very attractive if authors, with the help of their publishers, can do this themselves. There are many small or medium sized publishers who could markedly improve their publications, by having them typeset using this technique. It will spread further and be developed as computers become more widely available, and as the hardware necessary to read the disks, improves and becomes cheaper.

copy fitting/ casting off

Before you have the text set, you should be able to calculate how much space it is to take up; or, vice versa, how much text can be fitted in a space with any sort of type.

The space in an advert, for example, will be small and precious – how many words can be crammed in, and still be read? Working this out is 'copyfitting.' A publisher may want to know how many pages a novel will have – working this out is 'casting off'. Both calculations are quite easy to do and they involve the same basic procedure. They can be done very accurately or less accurately. For casting off, it may not matter that you are wrong by a few lines or a bit more, so you can afford to calculate less accurately than with some copyfitting problems.

Both methods require a calculation of how long the text is. For less accurate calculations it need only be an estimation of the number of words. For more accurate calculations it may be necessary to count, or estimate, the number of spaces and characters in a line, or in the whole text.

For the less accurate method count the words in the first ten lines of the typed text and work out an average of words per line. You can then count the number of lines per page. This is usually quite standard but check the whole page just to make sure. Multiply the two together and you have a word count of the whole text. Say 10 words a line on average, 30 lines a page, and 10 pages in all. That makes 3000 words that are to be set.

The next step is to choose a sample of typesetting in the typeface you like, the right width of column, and with the right space between lines. You can then count the words in an inch of this type setting sample. By dividing this number into the number of words in the typed text you will have an approximation of the number of column inches of typeset text that will be produced. There are a number of variables including the space between lines, the size of typeface and the width of columns, all of which can be changed, if there is going to be too much typesetting for the space. Look for several samples to get different words per column inch.

example

① Count the number of words or characters in this text.

7 words a line X 18 lines = 126

────── 33 ────── X18 +35 -7

```
By knowing what space the typeset
text will take up before it has
been done, you will be able to
plan really accurately and design
your page or layout. Firstly, you
can vary the sort of typesetting so
that it will fit into a space; you
can sort out the remaining space to
be used for illustrations and head-
lines. These can be produced while the
the typesetting is being done, which
saves time. Although it can be
expensive if you get things wrong, it
can also be just as expensive if you
don't calculate the space necessary.
For example, you may produce typeset
text which is far too long and resetting
may prove very expensive.
```

② In a sample of typesetting there are 6 lines to an inch. & there are 9 words on average a line.
Therefore there is 54 words in a column inch of typesetting.

or in the copyfitting tables for 'times' there are 47 characters in an 18 pica line of 10 pt.

copy fitting/casting off continued.

For a more accurate method, you can count characters and spaces in the typing. To do this, rule a pencil line down the right hand side of the text marking the end of the shortest full line of typing. By counting the number of characters inside this line and muliplying by the number of lines, you get a figure for the characters on the page. It is then quite easy to count the remaining number of characters, on the other side of the pencil line, for the longer lines of typing. Added together they give an accurate character count for the page.

You can then look up typesetting copyfitting charts which tell you how many characters will fit any length of line with different typefaces of different sizes. These charts show how many characters of typesetting will fit in every pica of line length. So, for example, we may well have 18000 characters, from the character count. The chart tell us that there are 2.70 characters in a pica of 10 point typesetting. So if the line is to be 10 picas wide, we will have 27 characters in a line. Divide 27 into 18000 (=667) and you have the number of lines. Looking at the depth scale (see page 42) shows that there could be 55 lines of 12 point, to a column. (That is 10 point type with 2 point space).So work out what the sum is, and you have the number of pages and lines there will be.

You can buy typesetting charts for many typesetting systems; the typesetters may be able to provide you with some. Here are some charts for the commonest typefaces:

average number of characters per pica of line width.

	8pt	9pt	10pt	11pt	12pt.
times Roman	3.45	3.07	2.76	2.53	2.30
times italic	3.37	2.99	2.70	2.47	2.25
times semibold	3.21	2.85	2.57	2.35	2.14
times semi bold italic	3.19	2.84	2.55	2.34	2.13
times bold.	3.24	2.88	2.59	2.35	2.15

③ You can then divide the number of words in a column inch of type-setting into the number of words in the text: $\frac{126}{54} = 2.36$

or divide the number of characters in a line into the total number of characters in the text: $\frac{600}{47} = 12\frac{3}{4}$

④ Here is the typesetting done in 10pt Times Roman on 12pt. 18 picas wide.

By knowing what space the typeset text will take up before it has been done, you will be able to plan really accurately and design your page or layout. Firstly, you can vary the sort of typesetting so that it will fit into a space; and secondly, you can sort out the remaining space to be used for illustrations and headlines. These can be produced while the typesetting is being done, which saves time. Although it can be expensive if you get things wrong, it can also be just as expensive if you don't calculate the space necessary. For example, you may produce typeset text which is far too long and resetting may prove very expensive.

headlines

Headlines can have many different purposes. They can guide people through a complex text by titling, signposting, identifying it, and enabling people to find the part they are interested in. If this is the main use for them, then they can be designed as an index tool for people to find their way about easily. Some books have the chapter heading and the book title as a 'running head' on every page.

Newspaper headlines have their own design conventions. They tend to be more important visually than in other sorts of publications. However, even with formal publications, headlines need to be fairly large to grab the reader's attention. Prioritising is an important part of design, and the title or headline has to be one of the major features.

It may be necessary to write your own headlines, as well as designing them. Try to sum up the contents of the article, but make it simple and if possible witty. Headlines can help make sense of all kinds of material and group it together logically but also visually.

Subhead

There are a variety of headlines that can be used. The sub-head can be a summing up of a section of the article, or a way of breaking up a long stretch of text to help the reader keep going. This can be done by picking out a quote, or good line from the article, and setting it larger.

You can have a variety of levels of headline but care should be used to maintain the visual logic of the hierarchy. The chapter title should be larger and above the article or page headline; the sub headings should be clearly above the paragraph heading which in turn, should be clearly over the text itself. 4 levels is about the limit as any more become difficult to make sense of when reading.

Headlines can be made by hand drawing, or tracing (see back page 35), but they can also be made mechanically as well.

Transfer

The easiest way of doing this is to buy some transfer lettering such as Letraset. You can get it in a huge number of styles and sizes. It costs quite a bit for a sheet, but this sheet can be used for a number of headlines and so can work out quite cheaply per headline. However, you can run out of vital letters just before you've finished the job. Count the 'e's in the headline text to be set in the same size and style - make sure there are enough 'e's in the sheet of headline lettering. You can make some letters by cutting the remaining letters up on the matt side, and using bits of them to make the letter you need.

The lettering can be positioned on a light blue guide line, or on a line drawn in pencil on the back of a sheet of thin paper. It can be visually spaced so the gaps between the letters in a word will look even. Once the letter is chosen and positioned, it can be rubbed over with an old ball point making it turn grey. Make sure that it has been completely transferred before lifting the sheet. Press or burnish the letter to make sure it is firmly on the paper. Make sure that no cow gum gets on top of the lettering. If it does, it can pull the lettering off when you clean the gum off. Keep the backing sheet with the sheet of transfer lettering, to preserve it. When it gets old and dry the lettering tends to crack. Try and keep it in a box and in a cool place. If the letters do crack, you can fill in the cracks with a black pen, after the letters have been transferred to the paper.

Machine

Headlining machines can save a lot of time. They are however usually limited in the sizes and styles of lettering available.

One of the cheapest and easiest to use is the Kroy machine. This presses letters onto a tape, so making the headline. The tape is black on sticky plastic with a paper backing. The headline can then be pasted up normally, or unpeeled and stuck down on clear film positives.

This machine can vary the spacing between letters by a set amount. Smaller machines are limited to headlines of up to 36 points. If you want to do anything larger, you may gain by looking at the many photographic headlining machines available. These can do far more than the tape-pressing machines. It is possible visually to space letters and to reduce or enlarge to the size you need. With photographic headliners, it is sometimes possible to bend or wave the lettering as well.

If your text is to be typeset, it is often possible to have your headlines, or at least the sub headings, set at the same time. Many typesetters have systems that go up to 36 points or 72 points and so they can set the headlines as they do the text.

Pictures

Pictures can be used to illustrate ideas or information, and to give the design a style and feel, to which people respond. People generally understand and relate to pictures, and often get more from them than words. It can therefore be worthwhile to spend time and creative energy, getting the right picture for your product. This can often involve 'picture research', rather than having to make one yourself. Pictures include many sorts of images from diagrams, graphs, plans and maps to cartoons, drawings, collages and photographs.

Investigating the range of images that can be used is a good exercise. Too often people use the sort of image that everyone else uses, rather than the most appropriate sort for their particular information.

The idea of pictures illustrating an idea or message is very important. Pictures show what you are really trying to say very clearly and vividly. But pictures should convey a message, not just break up the text, or decorate a product. Images should be thought out, and produced or found for definate uses. It is therefore important to choose images carefully if the whole design is to be successful. Also, images with meaning need to be carefully thought though, as they can promote stereotypes about people or give other 'hidden' messages.

Walter Crane.

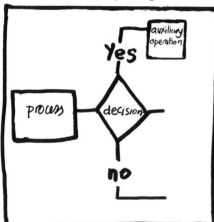

flow chart

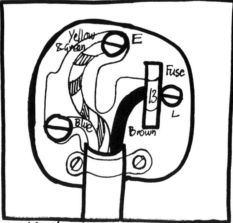

wiring diagram

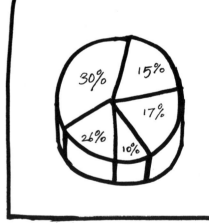

pie chart

Diagrams

Converting information into a visual form, can help people to understand it far more easily. Various diagram formats have been developed to do different jobs. Computer graphics, particularly, have developed many different ways of presenting numerical and other information in diagrams, charts, graphs, flow diagrams or maps. All of these are worth exploring and using for different purposes. It is important to be clear exactly what information you are trying communicate with a diagram. You should then consider what sort of diagram is the most appropriate.

Once you are clear about how the information is to be read, it is possible to use colour, lines or tone, to help differentiate the information. People can then read what they need to know. It should be designed so that comparisons are clearly made and the information can be read in the way you intend, both easily and quickly.

Clearly a flow diagram is a useful way of showing a progression of stages, while a map shows directions or relationships, and a graph compares quanties. Work out the sort of diagram that is most useful for your information!

Drawings

There are many styles of drawings that can be used. However, a conventional pencil drawing may be difficult to reproduce without loosing the subtle variation in tones. When printed, it has to be treated like a photo and must be made into a half tone (see page 52). With photocopying, pencil drawings can be reproduced slightly better, though some of the fine details may be lost.

Where possible, it is often better to produce drawings in black ink, with simple lines and cross hatching to give the impression of tones. These can be reproduced far more easily than drawings done in pencil.

Styles of drawing can dictate how images are received. Cartoon style drawings can give a light, fun approach to information. On the other hand the serious style of some artists, can present a very different mood. Even quite simple drawings can be very effective elements in a design. Used boldly, they can make a whole page work effectively.

It is possible to make effective drawings even if you are not good at drawing. For example you can trace pictures from photos and use several to make one drawing. It is simple to put people together, or change a stern face into a happy one. Traced drawings are easier to reproduce than photos, in some media. You can use other drawings or illustrations, as source material to trace or copy from. Try keeping a cuttings album and collecting material before you need it, rather than having to search for suitable pictures just before a deadline.

You can reduce or enlarge drawings to fit your design, but as it isn't so easy to change the ratio of the height and width, be careful to produce drawings which fit the design. Often drawings are easier to produce larger and then have reduced, to fit the final design.

There are all kinds of special drawing pens available that will give an even black line for use in design. Simple black felt tips can be used just as well, although some don't give an even black, especially when used over white correcting fluid. Ball point pens don't give an even line and tend to produce blotches.

PREVENT STREET CRIME

Cath Tate

Collage

Another way of producing images is to put photos or drawings together in a collage. The visual power that this gives you can be fantastic. Just try sticking the head of your favourite politician onto a suitable body!

Collect magazines that can be cut up and use them to make collages of suitable images. For direct displays you can use any coloured or black and white image. For printing, it can be better to use just black and white images. Those that have already been printed can then be used directly, while photos that have not been printed need to be screened into dots, to make a half-tone (see page 52). Screening in this way is best done after you have assembled your collage. Use cow gum to stick the images onto the collage as this will stick most paper flat. Try to avoid shadows or white edges so that you can create the impression of a whole image in the collage. To make sure that the collage is effective, it may be necessary to use a pen to touch up the image, once it has been assembled.

For even better effects, it is possible to re-photograph the entire collage, and then use the print of this, as the photo that is to be screened. With care you will be able to make collages in which it is difficult to see the joins.

other graphic forms

There are all sorts of other symbols and images, that can give point and power to your designs. Standard symbols such as ? & !, can be used in the text or as central elements in the design. Numbers, borders and other decorative features can also be used boldly and imaginatively. They can be photographically enlarged, or just drawn in. Be careful when drawing straight on the artwork with pieces of bumpy paper pasted up. It may be better to draw your lines or symbols on separate pieces of paper, and stick them on, or draw them on the grid sheet before you paste up the rest of the material. For thick lines, draw or rule the outline first and then fill it in, making sure that it is an even black image.

Cartoon conventions, such as bubbles for thought and speech, can be used even if there are no other cartoon images. You can even make a full stop talk!

There are typographical elements such as 'bullets' or large spots that can be useful for showing the different parts of a list. They emphasise the listing, but without the prioritising that numbering gives.

To create borders, draw simple lines round the edge of the page or around an article. This can be a way of separating and drawing attention to one part. But borders can also be more decorative or meaningful. A ship-shaped border can hold information about ships, for example. You could design a logo with a border that goes round a poster. This can then be printed, and the particular information hand-drawn in the middle.

You can buy borders and other images as transfers, or stickers. The same companies that produce transfer lettering, sell transfer borders, images for architects to use and other pictograms. The border designs are particularly striking.

Stickers are sold with many nice images and can be useful for all kinds of design uses. Silver or gold stars and these flowers:

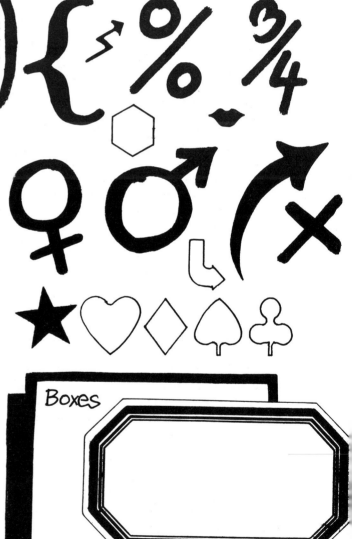

Boxes

can all be used in a variety of ways, but although the silver stars come out black in a copier, they will be lost in offset printing.

If you can't afford stickers or transfers, you can always cut out borders and images from other printed sources. Keep a cuttings book until you find a use for them.

photographs

Photographs can be specially taken, or they can be obtained from existing stock. Picture libraries, organisations, and all sorts of other publications, can provide photos. So part of the design work may be picture research. If you do need to take a photo, it can be useful to work out beforehand what the design requirements of the image are. Try to sketch out how the photo should look and work. Will it be used as a portrait, or a landscape picture? You need to be clear about this if you are having the photograph taken for you, as it can help the photographer take exactly the right picture for the design use. It is therefore a quite different sort of photography from the type that most amateur photographers are used to.

If you have to work with photos that are not quite right, you can still do quite a bit with them. It is possible to crop them (ie.cut them down) and so change their ratio and proportions to make the photo look better, but also make the point you want. Whole characters can be removed from the picture by cropping so that it will tell quite a different story to the one in the original photo. This sort of technique can be useful for the less drastic purpose of making a visual point, alongside every other picture. Good images can be used in a variety of ways. Try cropping a print in different ways to see which is the best. To do this, make yourself two L-shaped pieces of white card. Use them on top of the photo to give an impression of different crops. Photocopy the results, and compare the effect of the cropping on the picture.

Contexting
Photos will be put with headlines and other images when used with text. They will all affect how the image is read. Think about this in laying out your design. The most obvious example of hampering the design's meaning is when, in colour supplements, a glamorous and affluent image appears next to an image of the starving third world. Suddenly both images take on a whole different meaning altogether.

People in photos can be a powerful element in the page design. If they are looking into the page or at you the reader, it can bring the page together. If on the other hand, they are looking out, or to the next page, it can take the readers attention away from the page and off, flicking through the publication.

Using photos
Photos being used for print processes need to be glossy. They can be larger than the size required for your artwork as in the screening of the half-tone, they can be reduced to fit. They do however need to be the right ratio, (see scaling page 54). For cheaper print processes, they need to have slightly

whole picture.

cropped photo.

cropped photo.

less contrast than normal, with all the mid tones and the greys that make up most of the picture well pronounced. Print the photo on a soft grade of paper. In the printing process the contrast will also be lessened, so the original photo needs to be quite good to start with. Vital detail in the shadow area may not work well when printed in a newspaper for example.

For TV and film you need to use a matt print. This should also be quite large, at least 8x10 inches and larger if the camera is going to move across it or zoom into it. The photo should be in the right ratio for the TV (3x4) and mounted on card to keep it flat.

Line

Photos can be used in 'line', which is when they are printed without any greys and in very contrasty black and white. This can be done by re-photographing the photo onto line film or onto bromide or PMT paper. A process camera can be used for this, and can produce these prints quite quickly and cheaply. A photocopy of a photograph will tend to have the same effect, especially if the original print has been made on hard paper to start with.

Obviously some pictures will just not work when printed in line, as all the vital detail will get lost. Others will become far stronger and have a greater impact. Some details and patterns come out much stronger in line – they can either make the picture, or ruin it. A line photo which works well, can be far more use in a poster or other design, which requires impact. Line prints can be printed in different colours or tones. They can be used as symbols, and for other graphic techniques that cannot use a real photo.

Line prints can be directly pasted onto artwork, and then printed. Make sure you know how a print will look before you use it, as if you are not careful it may end up as a black square. Line prints can also be screen printed far more easily than photos

a line print used on the cover of 'Waterlines'

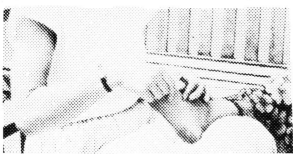

Half-tone photos

To print the greys in photos requires them to be converted into a pattern of dots – the half-tone or screening. These dots are of different sizes to give the impression of the various tones in the photo. To convert a photo requires it to be screened or photographed through a half-tone screen, on a process camera. At this stage, its size can be changed to fit the design, though not the ratio of its sides.

Half-tone screens may differ in quality. For printing on good quality paper the screen can be 120 dots to the inch, where the dots are very small. For a newspaper, they may need a 60 or 80 dot screen, where the dots are more obvious. Fine screen dots on less good paper and with lower quality printing, can get lost or fill in, creating the grey and blotchy photos of many small publications.

a photogram used to illustrate an article on 'where to buy a needle & thread!'

Other sorts of screen are made so that instead of dots, the photo can be made of lines or circles. This can fit into a design idea, and be quite effective. Specialist process camera operators often offer this service.

You can put half-tone screen images on photographic paper (called bromide paper) or onto film. Film is used by cutting and taping the screened half-tone negative into the main negative with the headlines and text. Half-tones on paper can be cut out, and stuck on the artwork, and printed along with all the other line images. You can therefore ensure that the correct image goes in the right place. With a screened print you can cut out any unwanted part of the photo, so that unnecessary backgrounds can be removed.

Photograms

Photographs made without a camera are called photograms. They are made by exposing photographic paper to white light with objects on the top, to create the image. Anything that stops light getting to the paper, will produce a white image on a black background. In this way, quite dramatic images of simple objects can be made easily. With access to a photographic darkroom, photographic paper and chemicals, photograms are technically very simple to produce. The important thing is to sort out which objects work and which don't. Flowers and feathers produce very striking results, whereas rounded and uninteresting shapes can be impossible to identify. It is necessary to experiment to produce the results you are after. This technique can enable you to produce images directly from the object you are trying to illustrate.

Some small flat objects such as leaves and lace can be and enlarged or reduced, just like a photonegative in the enlarger. Prisms and other objects, can produce very interesting photograms directly on the paper. Moving the object during the exposure can also create interesting effects, though again this requires experimentation to get right.

Using the photogram technique, you can create designs or design images. You can also use it to make lettering and drawings become white on a black background. Put your lettering on clear plastic instead of paper, and make sure it is opaque. It can then be contact printed by simply pressing it flat, with a sheet of glass against a sheet of photographic paper, and exposing it to light. This can be done with any lettering or drawing, provided it is solid enough to stop the light getting to the paper.

A image from a NUPE Ad.

This process of producing white images on a black background can be done by a printer in a similar way. It is known as 'reversing out', and can be done by the printer so that lettering for example can be reversed out of images as well as flat colour. To do this, produce the lettering or image that is to be reversed out on a tracing paper overlay. Position it in the correct place on the background. Obviously it will be cheaper if you do this yourself, but the results may be of better quality if the printer does it for you.

Published pictures

Photos that have been printed in other publications can be used, especially if they've been printed on good quality paper. Photos from newspaper usually have a poor half-tone dot, and so will block if they are reprinted. It is then best to start from an orginal continuous tone print and have it screened again. If you have to use a printed picture with a poor half-tone you can have it photographed slightly out of focus and then have it screened again, especially if it is to be reduced. If it is to be enlarged, the original dots can be used and should give quite a good effect.

53

scaling up or down

Images can be reduced or enlarged to fit a design. The photgraphic flexibility this can give, enables you to design exactly how you want. It is a freedom that needs exploiting and a power that can influence your design thinking. How would this small image be,very large for example?What would ten of these look like as a border, when they have been reduced?

When changing the size of an image, the ratio of the sides stays the same, however small or large it becomes. To work out the size it will be when reduced or enlarged without changing the ratio, simply draw a diagonal line on the back of the image, from one corner to the other. Using this line you can measure the width or height that you have decided and draw a line across to the diagonal; then measure off the other side from the point on the diagonal line, to the edge of the image. This will give you the new size, but with the same ratio of the dimensions.

Several photographic and non photographic processes can be used to change the size of any image.

By hand

You can use a grid of pencil lines over the image (on tracing paper if necessary). These small squares can be used to analyse the image, and a series of larger squares drawn on another sheet of paper. It is then much easier to enlarge the image by drawing what is in each small square, into each of the larger squares.

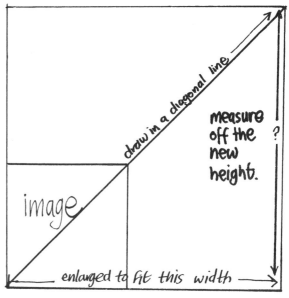

Photocopiers

These can now reduce and enlarge images. The size of an enlargement is often limited, but it is possible to copy copies. With simple images, the re-copying will not be too much of a problem. Some copiers tend to lose so much in quality, that re-copying copies several times over,can make the image break up and change in appearance. Photos especially will loose their details, and the quality and range of greys that they normally have, will get lost.

Process cameras

Special large process cameras are used in printing to copy images and artwork, including text. These cameras make negatives to print from in the size that the image is to appear. They can produce prints on bromide or PMT paper, and can reduce or enlarge. They usually give far better quality than photo copies, and can be used on the artwork to be printed, without losing quality. Photos can be screened and used direct on the artwork in the same way.

OHP

For very large enlargements, especially those to be painted on banners, walls or stage back drops, you can project images using overhead projectors. The image can be drawn or copied onto clear plastic and put on the projector. It can then be used to project onto the wall or banner, or just onto paper, and the image can be drawn in and painted. You can also use this method to draw large writing for displays. Copy the lettering typeface onto plastic, and project it onto a wall. Using a large piece of paper, draw off the letters by moving the paper across the wall to the correct letter. To get the letters straight you should use a base line. The image can be made smaller or larger by moving the projector nearer or further away.

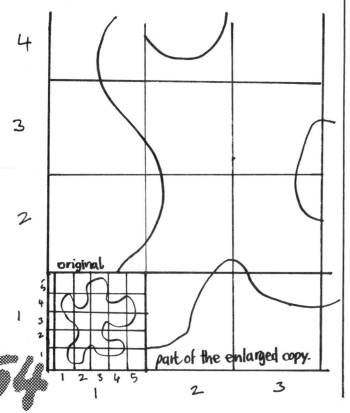

tone

You can give areas of your image, or the whole page or design, a tone; this is a grey or light shade of the colour printed. It can be done by using a pattern of dots or lines. They are quite small and therefore appear to be a flat area of tone.

This can done by asking the printer to put the tone on a given area of the design when it is printed. This is indicated by marking the tone area on an overlay sheet on top of the artwork.

It can be added by using a sheet of sticky tone that is produced in the same sort of way as transfer lettering. This can be cut and stuck down in place on the artwork. Be careful to make sure the sticky side doesn't get dirty, and don't stick it on top of the artwork if there are glue or paste up edges, as they will show up under the tone.

The tone is available from the printer or as a transfer, in a variety of 'darknesses' expressed in percentages (100% being black). It is also available in different sized dots and lines, etc., depending on the sort of effect you want to produce. It is even available in a progression from black to white.

Tone can be used to produce different colours when over-printing and using two or more colours. With a simple two-colour printing job, a third colour can be produced by over-printing one tone on top of another. This can be varied by choosing different percentages of tone. Be careful to make sure that the colour looks good when doing this, and also that the angle the tones are placed in relation to each other, doesn't produce moire patterns.

By sticking sheets of tone on a clear acetate sheet you can use tones with the photocopier. You can put a white dot screen in front of a photo or some lettering, and produce a copy with the image in a sort of tone. This can then be cut out and used in artwork. Hand-lettering can also be screened in this way to make quite interesting effects.

examples of transfer tone.

white dot screened lettering

spraying

Sprays can be useful in creating images and effects for all kinds of media. They can give a tone effect, with is useful for both illustrations and displays. Spray tones can merge and fade away if skilfully used. By using paper and masking tape, you can create a stencil to cover the areas of the image that you don't want to be sprayed. Some parts of the image are sprayed, while others remain clear, and this can create quite interesting effects. A whole stencil can be made of plastic or card which, if it is in one piece, can be used to spray a simple image on notices, displays, placards or even walls. The spray design can be photocopied or printed in a design, and it will give the effect of a tone, without having to be screened like a photo.

You can use an old toothbrush to splatter ink on paper, but a diffuser is better and aerosol cans can also be quite good. Air brushes are very expensive but good for fine work. They are used for touching up photos, and giving even colour to illustrations.

Here are some examples of different sprays and spray effects. See if this technique can be a help to any of your design problems.

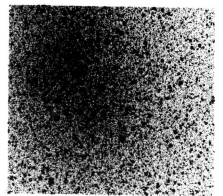

a spray from a diffuser

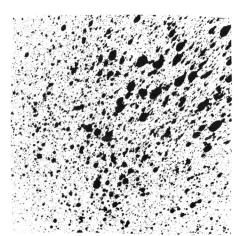

a spray from a tooth brush.

Simon O'Grady & Fuse.

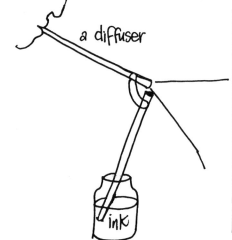

a diffuser

ink

56

paste up

Once all the elements of the design have been produced, they need assembling to become the finished product. For printed and other photographic media, it usually has to be pasted up to become a complete original usually known as 'the artwork'. This is exactly how the finished page will look and is then photographically copied and printed.

The paste up is the process finally used to put the design into practice. To check that everything fits and looks right, cut all the elements out and assemble them in place. Don't cut too near to the image and leave roughly a quarter or an eighth of an inch of paper around the edge. Scissors can be used for this, but sharp knives or scalpels can be useful for fine work.

If the elements are all there, and fit together to look well, you can start pasting down. It needs to be as flat and as clean as possible, so don't use a water-based glue as this will buckle the paper. There are various glues available that are suitable; Cow gum, for example, and waxers and sprays. Cow gum is better than most, as even after the paper has been stuck down, you can still move it around to position it exactly, before the glue dries. However, it does tend to smell and make a mess. Waxers are good if you are doing a lot of paste up and though they are quite expensive initially, they are cheaper to run. Waxers can lightly stick an image, so that it can be peeled off easily, if it is not in the right place. Sprays will stick things flat, as you spray an even coating to the paper. However, you will need to spray over scrap paper to avoid covering other surfaces in glue, and once in place, it is less easy to move or peel off. Cow gum can be disolved in cigarette lighter fuel. So if you have to pull it off, once it is dry, disolve the glue and it will come off easily. Dried pieces of cow gum can also be rolled into Cow gum rubbers. These can be used to clean up the artwork, as any unwanted pieces of glue around the edges of the paper will be taken up by the ball of cow gum.

Pasting up should be started at the top of the page, and carefully continued down the page, from the top to the bottom. Make sure that you don't get glue on the images, and that you don't accidently move the pieces, once they have been positioned.

Cow gum or other glues, may take the ink off some images, such as a printed newspaper headline or a photo, so the glue must not get on the image itself. Use scrap paper to glue onto and have plenty available. Glue should be spread thinly on the corners of the back of the image, and quickly stuck down onto the artwork. For about 30 seconds it can be moved around so you can check that it is square with a set square, and then press it down to dry.

If you are pasting heavy papers, such as photos for an exhibition, it is best to use Cow gum or sprays. Cow gum can be used to cover both surfaces with a thin coating, and left to dry for a minute or so. Then when the photo is pressed into place, it will stick instantly and quite firmly.

If the paste up edges show, or the artwork is very messy and has lots of corrections, you can photocopy it, and paint out the shadows. This copy can then be used as the original. You can have a bromide or PMT print made which will also remove some of the shadows and can also be scratched or painted with white paint to remove unwanted images. This will be quite expensive compared with a photocopy but of much better quality and 'blackness'.

Once the artwork is made it can be photographically copied for whatever media it is intended. It is necessary to make sure that artwork is well protected, so it can be a good idea to mount it on card. This will ensure that it won't get bent, and if you cover it with tracing paper, it will keep clean. Tracing paper can also be used to instruct the printers or photographers who the artwork belongs to, what is to happen to it, and in what colour it is to be printed. It is a good idea to include a phone number in case they have some questions when doing the job.

It can also be an advantage to paste up your artwork on a larger sheet of card than the actual image. You will then have a margin in which to put names and instructions about crop marks, fold marks and registration marks.

Crop marks are positioned at the corners and mark where the page is to be trimmed to. The printers will print on a sheet that is slightly larger than the finished paper so they will cut or trim the sheet once it has been printed and will use the crop marks as a guide.

Fold lines are also drawn in the margin and show where the sheet is to be folded. This needn't be done, unless you are going to a large printer who is to do the folding for you.

Colour for printing

In printing, colour is produced by the ink put on the press, and not by the colour of the original. The artwork therefore, is usually produced in black. Each colour to be printed, involves producing a separate sheet of artwork. They will usually be made on sheets of tracing paper or acetate, and these are stuck onto the main artwork which should be mounted on card.

Registration marks are used if you are doing two or more colours. They are put on each layer of artwork and register so that when printed, each cross will fit on top of the others and the colours will then be in the correct place. You need to be accurate when drawing these lines in, as otherwise the colours will not be printed in the right place, and gaps will be left or the colours will overlap.

To print 'full colour' you need to print 4 'process colours', one on top of the other. Printing colour photos, for example, is very expensive as it requires the breaking the photos down into the 4 colour printing plates, and then into dots to be printed. This is done on complex scanning devices and large process cameras.

It is cheaper to use 2 or 3 colours printed from your own handmade artwork, than 4 colour separations, for which the photographic work alone will be very expensive.

Colour for other media

You can use colour in other media far more easily than with printing. It can therefore become a useful design feature that needs to be used. Colours tend to react with each other. When complementary colours are put together it causes the eye to see them as 'conflicting'.

Red and green for example, react when put together. Colours can be arranged around a circle in the order they appear in the rainbow. Those that are opposite each other in this circle are complementary, and so should not be used together.

Colours also have associations for people. These may be conscious, such as the political associations with red and blue, and can also be unconscious as for example, associating green with bad food. Be careful with your choice of colour as it can be quite powerful. How many times have you forgotten the name or publishers of the book you are looking for, and have just gone through the shelves in a library, looking for the right colour?

Colour can be used to pick out particular aspects of the information given. Subheads or instructions can be a different colour to the main text. If you do too much, however, it will confuse the reader. If everything is different it is difficult to assess what is normal.

To have colour, you can use paints, felt tips or coloured paper. Coloured paper can be very easy to use and be cut to the required shape quite easily. Mounting images on coloured paper can be a useful device for grouping information, as well as making it more attractive. Be careful however, that the bright mounting colour doesn't influence the colour of the image itself. Experiment by putting a small square of grey on a blue background, and then on a red one. Look carefully at the grey square and it will appear to be different shades on each background. There are many other effects that can be achieved with pure colour, and they are worth investigating if you are doing more of this sort of design.

Process colours:

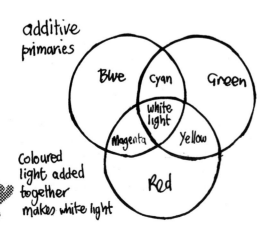

additive primaries

Coloured light added together makes white light

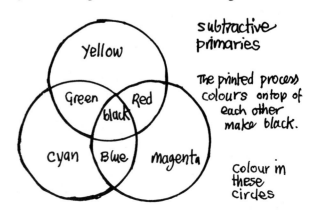

subtractive primaries

The printed process colours ontop of each other make black.

Colour in these circles

making slides

Making slides can be done in
various ways:

You can photograph artwork onto film with a
camera. This can be done outside, but you need
to make sure that the camera is held parallel with
the artwork and that the light is even across it.

It is better to use a copystand which will hold the
camera and illuminate the artwork. The camera
should be held firmly, and this is especially
important if the copystand is to be used for a large
video camera. The stand will hold the camera at a
right angle to the base board. Its lights can be set
at 45% to the image so that the four lights give a
good even light. Photo floodlights give a good,
constant light source. Use a sheet of
non‑reflecting glass to hold down the artwork
when shooting. A macro‑lens fitted onto the
camera will enable you to shoot very small images
or details, as well as the whole of the artwork.

If the lights are tungsten lights you must make
sure that colour film is also indoor tungsten film.
It is possible to put a filter on the camera if you
have to use outdoor daylight film indoors. The
exposure can be judged from the reading given by
a mid‑tone grey sheet, reflecting 18 light. It is
advisable, however, to try different exposures to
get each slide perfect.

It is possible to make your own copy stand by
converting an enlarger stand. Take off the enlarger head, and fix the camera on instead, then fix
up the lighting so that it is even.

It is also possible to buy special copystands which
are useful if you need to do a great deal of this
work. When using copystands you should use the
slowest possible film and a delayed action setting
to eliminate camera shake. Also,be careful not to
get between the image and the lights when
shooting,as it will alter the exposure.

Black and White Slides.
You can make slides on black and white film. For
simple text or other line artwork, you can use line
film such as Kodalith. You can get this in a long
roll of 35mm film which is loaded into standard
cassettes. It requires a special developer, and is a
very slow film − about 6 ASA. So you will need
to experiment to find the correct exposure. What
Kodalith does give, is a clear black and white
negative which, when used as a slide, gives bright
white lettering or other images on a black
background. The clear lettering can be coloured
by felt tip or coloured acetate, if you wish.

Other black and white film such as Plus X or High
Contrast Film can also be used. These may be
easier to use and develop, but they won't give as
good a result as Kodalith.

It is also possible to reverse develop black and
white film to make positives which can be used as
slides. Kits of the chemicals needed to do this can
be bought.

Polaroid instant slide film
Polaroid now make instant slide films. These are
either in colour, black and white, or in line,
known as 'graphic high contrast'. They are
processed in a special developing unit, which
produces them almost instantly. The exposed film
can then be mounted and used as slides. It is an
expensive process, but worthwhile if you need
quick results.

Rostrum Cameras
Rostrum cameras are copystands which are especially set up for photographing flat images for
slides or video, or for film animation. They have a
light source, as well as a flat base board, so that
they can also be used to copy transparencies, as
well as artwork. The light source can be of
different colours so that you can make coloured
slides from simple artwork. They can be used to
make several exposures on one slide, using
different images.

A pin bar system is used to register the images
and is vital for multiple exposures or animation.

Computer graphics
It is possible to shoot slides directly from a
computer screen. Special camera set‑ups exist to
do this. By using slides in this way, computer
graphics can be valuable for large public presentations. Complex data and graphs, for example, can
be shown in a clear and comprehensible way. (See
page 28.)

Hand−made slides
You can make slides by hand without a camera.
All kinds of materials can be used. It is more
convenient to use old bits of film that are the right
size for slide mounts and projectors. You can get
old film that has been exposed and is black; this
can be scratched on to make images. Alternative-
ly you can take clear film, on which you can draw
with ink or felt tips. Paper cut to fit, and coloured
acetate can also be used. The coloured acetate
will project a colourful image, or you could colour
the scratched film with felt‑tip pens.

Slides can be made from printed images using
sticky Transpaseal. Stick the Transpaseal over the
image, rub it on well and then wash off the paper.
The image should stay on the clear plastic, which
can then be cut and mounted as a slide, or as an
overhead projector positive.

mounting

Mounting single images

It can be useful to mount single images such as photos and artwork. This can be done by using a dry mounting press which heats a sheet of glue onto the back of the image and presses it onto card. A special press is necessary which may be available at photographers' resource centres or colleges. It is the best way of mounting photographs securely. You can, however, also use Cow gum, (See paste up, page 57) spray mount or double sided tape to do the same job.

Mounting exhibitions

It is very useful to mount exhibitions and displays on larger sheets of card. In this way the pictures, captions and headings can all be put together in the correct way. The exhibition can be hung on the wall quickly and easily just by putting up the boards in the right order. This is best done by glueing the images onto card which is then covered to protect it (See page 61). If it is protected, you can then simply tape the images on or even use Blu–Tak to hold them in place. Laminating is another way to fasten the images onto the board; in this case you will only need to glue them lightly to keep them in place until they are laminated.

Window mounts

You can cut a window mount of the same size as the image. This makes the image look valued and picks it out so that it is framed by the surrounding mounting. Try this for special images, or portfolios of work. To make a window mount cut out the window from the first sheet of card with the knife at an angle of 45 degrees to the surface. Use a sharp knife but be careful to use a strong metal edge to cut along and avoid going too far beyond the next line when you reach a corner. When the window is cut, mount the image on another sheet of card that is the same size as the first, and glue the window card on top of it.

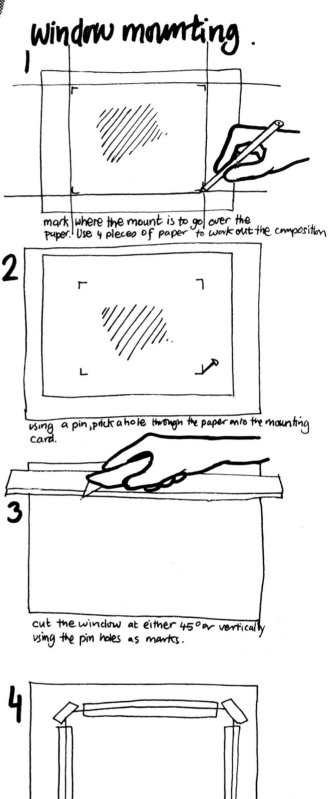

window mounting.

1. mark where the mount is to go over the paper. Use 4 pieces of paper to work out the composition

2. using a pin, prick a hole through the paper onto the mounting card.

3. cut the window at either 45° or vertically using the pin holes as marks.

4.

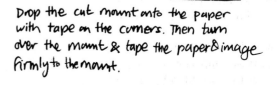

Drop the cut mount onto the paper with tape on the corners. Then turn over the mount & tape the paper & image firmly to the mount.

laminating

The easiest way of protecting your display or exhibition is to slip it into a clear portfolio wallet. These can be bought in many sizes and can be used to hold displays or give them protection. This has the same visual impact as lamination, but can be used again and again with different contents. You can cover the exhibition with sticky clear film such as Transpaseal which must be put on carefully to avoid the formation of air bubbles. Use a long ruler to spread the roll as it comes off the backing sheet. Once covered in this way it must be remembered that you can't change it or add to the exhibition.

Commercial laminating can either cover over the surface of an exhibit, or it can sandwich the board in layers of plastic. With both methods it is necessary to have gaps around the images so that the plastic can stick to the backing board. With front lamination, you can laminate most thicker boards, but sandwich lamination needs quite a thin card. Sandwich lamination leaves a margin of plastic around the board. This protects its edge and can be used to insert rings, through which the exhibition may be fastened onto the wall.

The sandwich process has been used to laminate menues in restaurants   and other frequently used items. Once you have laminated it, however, you can't change the prices!

The covers of records and books are often laminated. To do this a very thin plastic coating is put over the cover so that it will stay shiny and clean even though it gets a great deal of use and handling. Larger printers can do this when they print your job, although it will cost quite a bit extra.

Before deciding which method of protection to use, consider how useful each one is for your particular purpose.

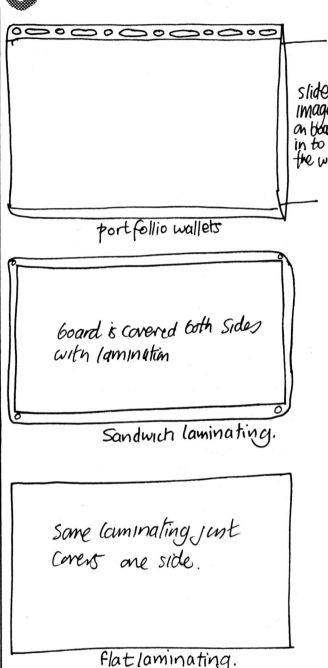

slide image on board in to the wallet.

portfollio wallets

board is covered both sides with lamination

Sandwich laminating.

Some laminating just covers one side.

flat laminating.

finishing

Design has to take into account how the final product is to be used. Any product can to be thought of as a 3-dimensional object, as well as a flat one. How will people use it? How will it be handled? and so on. It may be used by lots of people, or sold in shops. A book, for example, may be displayed in bookshops with shelves of limited size and which show just the spines. It may have to copied from. All these possible uses need to be taken into account when considering a design.

Finishing is the term used for trimming, folding and binding print. However, the 'packaging' concept is useful for any communications project. Design can take into account the finishing and so save money as well as help the product to be used more. It is,however, an expensive part of the production process.

Trimming
Printed sheets are sometimes a little bit bigger than the standard size as this allows for a margin to be trimmed off after printing. In this way the image can be printed right up to the edge of the paper. Books and magazines are usually trimmed once they have been bound. Because of this, the binders must know the order and position of the pages and how they have been printed onto the paper to come out correctly (the imposition). The printed sheets have to be imposed properly if the book is to be collated, bound and trimmed as you intended on the finisher's machines.

Cutting
You can have printed sheets cut up to any size you want. It is therefore possible to get several different jobs printed at the same time, and onto one sheet of standard paper. This can work out much cheaper although all the separate designs need to be printed in the same colour and to the same quantity.

Folding
There are lots of different ways of folding paper. Try using them in the design. A fold can divide information, or cover it. It can make an interesting object out of less interesting information. Small jobs and complex folding can be done by hand, although machines can do quite a few different folds for you:

Binding
Books and booklets can be bound in lots of ways, depending on how long they are to last, whether they need to be opened flat or have a spine and or how much money is being spent.

The cheapest form of binding is stapling. You can staple through between 50 and 100 sheets, and it is stronger if it is stapled through the fold.

Binding books with a spine involves glueing and this is known as perfect binding: paperback books are perfect bound. Books can also be sewn and bound in 'hard-back' format. Both are expensive, though obviously hard-backs are the most expensive to produce. Some printers and finishers, however, do have a book production line and so can give a cheaper price for the printing and finishing of books in a standard size.

There are several plastic grip and ring systems to consider. Ring systems allow books to be opened out flat and this can be very useful if you need to copy from them, or use them on a table whilst your hands are full.

Boxes
You can design your package so that it can be printed and cut out in one process. The outline for a flattened box would be something like this:

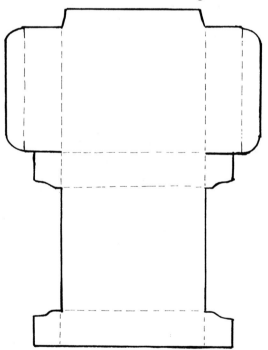

Consult the printers or finishers on the shape they recommend and can print and cut cheaply.

Packaging
It can be far cheaper to choose a standard package for your product. A label or cover can be printed and slipped into the package, or glued on the outside. Complex shapes may well be expensive to cut and so, for small numbers, it is best to do it yourself by hand.

images

people & things

These images can be copied or cut out and used in your own designs. They are not here to discourage you from producing your own, more appropriate images, but are to help you overcome some common problems quickly. When using any of the images here, please credit this handbook as the source, or where indicated, the artists themselves. If you have a suitable image for addition to this section please send it in to us and we will try to include it in future editions.

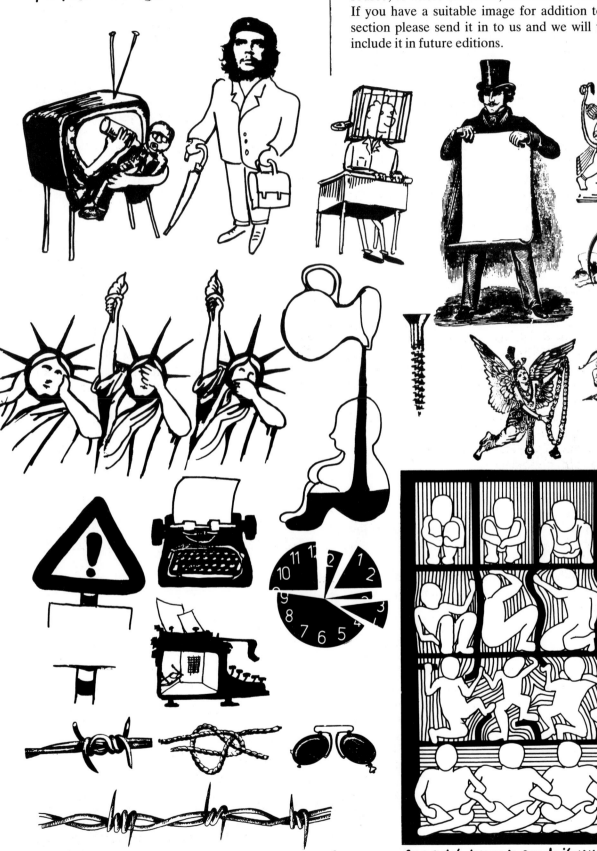

from print: how you can do it yourself

Maps are useful for showing relations between countries

Troops out of Ireland
Symbol

or different views of the world

Peters projection

Mercator Projection

Bill Sanderson
New Internationalist

new internationalist

hands are useful symbols for:

for land lords

oppression

unity

having a tea & chat.

Magic for Socialism!

Paul Colbeck.

drawing hands can draw itself.

65

grids

These grids are for you to use in your design work.

The page grid is to be traced or used through layout paper. Pin it to the work top and put sheets of thin layout paper over the top so that you can still see the grid through the paper. When finished, the artwork on the layout paper should be glued to card to protect it.

The badge grid is to photocopy and use in making artwork for printing 55mm badges.

A4 page

A5 page

67

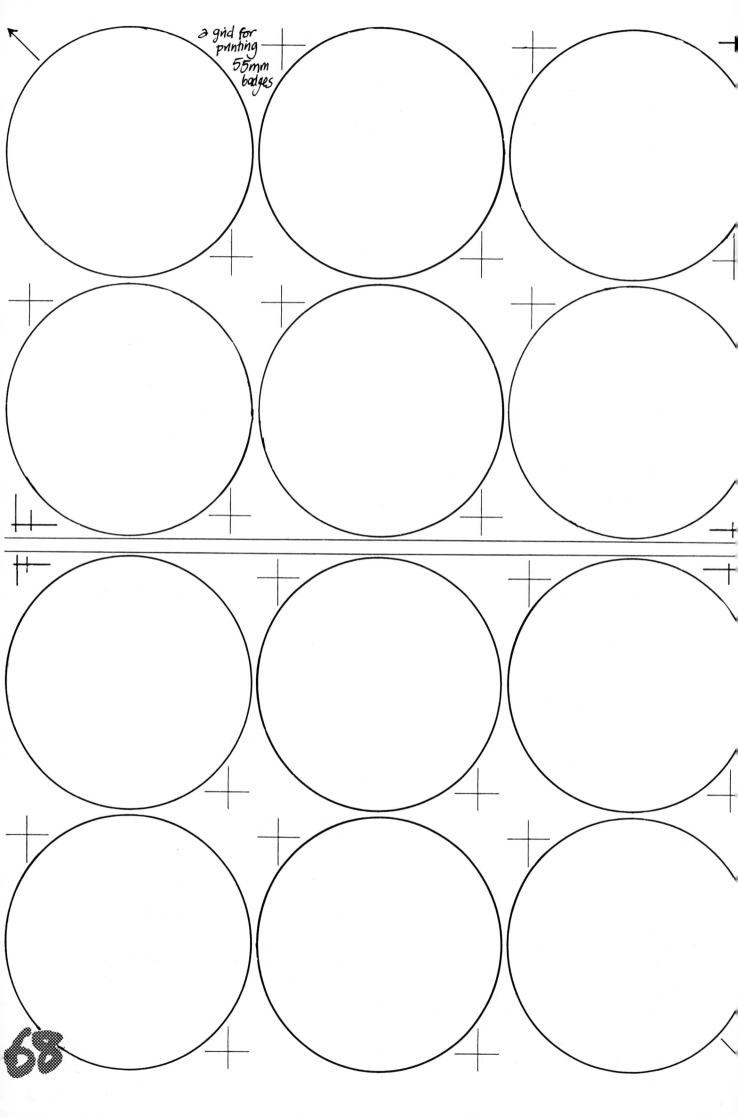

a grid for
printing
55mm
badges

68

book list

Inspiration

Design for the real world
by VJ Papanek, Granada, London 1974

Pioneers of modern typography
by Herbert Spencer, Lund Humphries, London 1982

The Word as image
by Berjouhi Bowler, Studio Vista

New graphic design in Revolutionary Russia
by Szymon Bojko, Lund Humphries, London 1972

The dictionary of visual language
by Philip Thompson and Peter Davenport, Penguin Books, London 1982

Constituents of a theory of the media
by Hans Magnus Enzberger, in: The Sociology of Mass Communications, Edward Arnold, London 1977

Graphics

Illustrated graphics glossary
by Ken Garland, Barrie and Jenkins, London 1980

The complete guide to illustration and design techniques and materials, edited by Terence Dalley, Phaidan, Oxford 1980

Do−it−yourself graphic design
edited by John Laing, Ebury Press, London 1984

Graphic idea notebook
by Jan V White, Watson−Guptill Publications, New York 1980

Graphics Handbook, an introduction to design and printing for the non−specialist by Richard McCann, Health Education Council, London 1985

Printing

Printing it
by Clifford Burke, Wingbow Press, Berkeley 1972

Production for the graphic designer
by James Craig, Pitman Publishing, London 1974

Graphic Communications
by Richard J Broekhuizen, McKnight, USA 1979

Studio tips for artists and designers
by Bill Gray, Van Nostrand Reinhold, New York 1976

Print it
by Colin Cohen, Kaye and Ward, Tadworth, Surrey 1981

Alternative Printing Handbook
by Chris Treweek and Jonathan Zeitlyn with the Islington Bus Co, Penguin Books, London 1983

Print: How you can do it yourself
by Jonathan Zeitlyn, InterChange Books, London 1986

How to Screen Print: a set of 4 Wall Charts
by Chris Treweek, Macmillian

Audio Visuals

The over head projector
by Judith Wilkinson, British Council, London 1979

Street Video
by Graham Wade, Blackthorn press, Leicester 1980

Audio−Visual Guide for community groups
by Joan Munro and Deborah Leob, CPF, London 1985

Photography

Committing Photography
by Su Braden, Pluto Press, London 1983

Information Technology

The World Wired Up, Unscrambling the new communication puzzle
by Brian Murphy, Comedia, London 1983

Changing the Word, the printing industry in transition
by Alan Marshall, Comedia, London 1983

Typesetting for micro users, a beginner's guide to improved text presentation, by Belinda Naylor−Stables, Quorum Technical Services, Cheltenham 1986

words

A

A sizes: see Paper sizes

Air brush: a spray gun used for very fine adjustable spraying of ink or paint. Good for graded tones and touching up photos.

Alignment: lining up lettering on a margin — SeeRanged.

Ampersand: &

Animation: making drawings or other images move on film by shooting the images one at a time and changing them between each frame.

Artwork: the original that is to be copied and printed. Also referred to as camera-ready artwork, the mechanical (in the USA) and the paste up.

Ascenders: top of the letters above the x height, on letters such as bhdklt etc.

B

Bleed: to have printing done right to the edge of the paper requires the image to be printed 1/4 inch over the edge which is then trimmed off.

Bold: a thicker letter style

Bromide: a photographic print often used to refer to prints made with photomechanical, or chemical transfer methods. These make a copy on a process camera, without using a film negative. They are often called by their trade name, eg. a PMT or a copyproof.

C

Camera ready artwork: artwork that is ready for the camera and to be printed. It implies that everything is layed out as it is to be printed.

Casting off: estimating how much space a text is going to take up, once it has been typeset. See Copyfitting.

Cel: a clear plastic sheet used to paint on for animation. It is punched with holes so that it can be registered in the right place when it is to be shot.

Copy: (1) in newspapers the text is known as 'copy'.

(2) To reproduce by photo copier.

Copyfitting: to work out how much typesetting can fit in a given space. See   Casting off.

Crop: to cut off part of a photo.

D

Delete: to remove letters or other images. The proof reading symbol is: **𝓎/**

Descender: part of the letter below the x height base line: qpyjg.

Didot point: the European type measurement size which is slightly different from the Anglo American point.The Didot point is .0148ins or 0.375mm.

Digital: computer systems break down information into binary digits, and can then process and transform them so reproducing them exactly as needed.

E

Em: a square of the size of type in use. Usually taken as a 12pt em or a pica.

En: half an em. Also used as an average letter width.

Electrostatic: method is used in photocopiers to make copies.

F

Face: the style of lettering, a typeface.

Fax/facsimile: a copy that is trasmitted electronically via the telephone. High quality ones are used so that newspapers can be produced at several printing plants at the same time.

Finish: to bind, trim or fold print.

Flow chart: a diagram to show the flow of an activity or process using lines and boxes.

Flushed left or right:type aligned either on the right or left. See Ranged.

Fount: a type alphabet in a particular style or face.

Full point: a printer's term for a full stop.

G

Galley: a long strip of typesetting.

Gutter: space between columns of text or pages.

Golf Ball: a type head for typesetting or typing from, as used by IBM and other machines.

G/m2 or Gsm: unit for measuring the thickness or weight of paper.

Grid: the 'bones' of a design, marking the margins and columns.Particularly useful in magazine page design.

Graphic: anything that is visual as in 'graphic design'. Also used for something very striking and vivid. Used sometimes to describe illustrations or images that are not type, which is confusing.

H

Halftone: a way of printing continuous tones of photos and drawings by a pattern of dots.

I

Impose: to arrange the pages on a printed sheet so that when it is folded, bound and trimmed, the pages will be in the right order.

Information technology: the overall term for electronic media, especially computers and telecommunications. See page 28.

J

Justify: to make each edge of a column of type, straight.
See Ranged or Flushed Unjustified is when only the left hand margin is straight.

L

Line: an image that is only black and white, as opposed to a tone or a half - tone image.

M

Mark up: to write the instructions for the typesetter alongside the text.
Master: term used for spirit duplicator originals, from which copies are taken. Also used for stencils and the plates in other printing methods.
Measure: the width of a column of typesetting.
Moire: an interference pattern caused when two screens, for making half - tones, are put on top of each other. This can happen when re - screening images that have already been screened.

O

Offset: short for offset litho printing. The image is offset onto a rubber roller, the blanket from the plate. This inked image is then pressed onto the paper.
Overlay: images to be printed in a second colour are pasted up on a sheet of tracing paper or plastic over the first piece of artwork.

P

Panning: moving a film or TV camera across a scene or a flat image. Can be used to give life and movement to a still image.
Paper sizes: the main ones in use today are the Standard International Metric sizes, the 'A' sizes. A1 is 594 x 841, A2 is 420 x 594, A3 is 297 x 420 and A4 is 210 x 297 mm.
Perfect binding: a glue binding for paperback books.
PMT: Photo Mechanical Transfer, a trade name for a chemical transfer method of producing photo prints on a process camera without having to produce a fim negative.
Pica: a 12 point em used as a typographic measurement for column widths etc. Also the name for a standard large typewriter style which has 10 letters in an inch.
Pixel: in computer graphics an image is made up of small dots of light, pixels, the smaller they are the higher definition of the image.
Pictogram: a n image that can be read, instead of a word.
Process camera: a camera that can produce prints and negatives the same size as they are to be printed. Used to reduce, enlarge, reverse out and screen halftones.
Program: the computer software that tells it what to do.

Proof: an initial copy of typesetting and any printing, so that it can be checked for mistakes.

R

Ranged left/right: setting text either with a straight edge on the left or right. See Flushed or Unjustified.
Ream:500 sheets of paper.
Register: two or more colours that are being printed on the same paper, need to register exactly, so that they are in the right place in relation to each other when printed.
Reverse out: to make an image white out of black instead of black on white. Can be done on special bromide paper.
Reprographics: term to define the smaller office copying and small - scale printing that wasn't really 'printing'.
Rostrum camera: a set up for filming or photographing animation, or slides from flat artwork.
Run: the number of copies printed

S

Serif: the bits on the end of some letter designs. Sans - serif means letters without them.
Scanner: a machine that electronically scans colour transparencies and makes colour separations. It is very expensive. Also a cheap machine an electronic stencil cutter that cuts an image into stencils for stencil duplicating.
Screen printing: silk - screen printing or screen - process printing, using a stencil and a mesh to print with.
Separations: to print in colour involves having different originals or negatives, plates and printing inks, for each colour involved. Colour separations are the originals or negatives for each colour needed.
Stitch: to staple.

T

Transparency: a photographic slide or positive colour film.
Trim: to cut the finished printing. to the required size
Typeface: the style or design of typesetting or printed lettering.
Type scale: a ruler for measuring type marked out in different type sizes.

W

Web: a roll of paper which large printing presses can print on for producing 1000s of copies.
Wild Track: the sound recording taken for film or video without any images being shot.

71

acknowledgements

I would like to thank the many people who have helped, supported and encouraged the production of this handbook.

There are too many to name them all. But I would like to thank: my editors Alison Clixby & Francis Gladstone, and Victor Nollen & Andrew James for help in typesetting.

Graham Betts for his work making the bromides & the cover.

I would also like to thank Sushila Zeitlyn for help in writing & editing the book as well as supporting me through the whole process of producing this book.

Martyn Partridge, Peter Philips Tim Carruthers, Ruth Mertens Suzy John, and the staff & members of the Fleet Community Education Centre have helped & encouraged my work on publicity & for this book.

Jonathan Zeitlyn

72

directory

- printers
- Art material suppliers

Free listings:
resource centres
co-op & community
printers.
Arts associations & centres
educational institutions

The following listings have been put in free. They are not to be taken as a guaranteed endorsement of suppliers or resources but are hopefully useful. If I receive reports of any unhelpfulness, I will remove the offenders from this section. Also, if you have a service or product you would like to be listed in future editions, please send details.

The display ads have been paid for and likewise are not to be taken as an endorsement of the product. If we receive complaints about products and services included, we will remove them from the next edition. Please let us know your views.

ART MATERIALS

LISTINGS

Resource Centres

London

Actionspace
16 Chenies Street
London WC1
01 631 4468

Activision
242/244 Pentonville Road
London N1
01 837 7842

Albany Video
The New Albany
Douglas Way
London SE8
01 692 0231

Anarres
10a Bradbury Street
London N16
01 249 9212

Asian Film Collective
2 Alkerden Road
London W4 2HP
01 995 1841

Basement Project
St. George's Old Town Hall
Cable Street
London E1
01 790 4020

Berwick Film Collective
7–9 Earlham Street
London WC2
01 240 2350

Black Audio Film Collective
89 Ridley Road
London E8
01 254 9536

Ceddo Film & Video Workshop
Seven Sisters School
Seaford Road
London N15
01 802 9034

Chats Palace
42–44 Brooksby's Walk
London E9
01 986 6714

Cinema Action
27 Winchester Road
London NW3
01 586 2762

Claimants Educational Trust
296 Bethnal Green Road
London E2 0AG

CLIO Co–op
91c Mildmay Road
London N1
01 249 2551

Converse Pictures
Bon Marche Building
444 Brixton Road
London SW9 8EJ
01 274 4000 ext 200

Cultural Partnerships
90 De Beauvoir Road
London N1 4EN
01 254 8217/7541

Fantasy Factory
42 Theobold's Road
London WC1
01 405 6862

Film Work Group
78/79 Lots Road
London SW10
01 352 0538

Four Corner Films
113 Roman Road
London E2
01 981 6111

Greenwich Mural Workshop
The Albany
Douglas Way
London SE8
01692 0231

Greenwich Resource Centre
MacBean Centre
MacBean Street
Woolwich
London SE18
01 859 9092

Hackney Youth Communications Project
18 Stoke Newington Road
London N16
01 254 1193

Hammersmith & Fulham Video Project
16 Askew Crescent
London W12
01 740 7271

Haringey Media Unit
30 Philip Lane
London N15
01 801 7699

Interchange Studios
15 Wilkin Street
London NW5 5NG
01 267 9421

Irish Video Project
c/o 118 Talbot Road
London W11
01 459 1036

Ivy Community Video
5 Washbrook House
Tulse Hill London SW2
01 674 8901

Junction Resource Centre
248/250 Lavender Hill
London SW11
01 228 1163

Lambeth Video
254a Coldharbour Works
London SW9
01 274 7700

London Film Makers' Co–op
42 Gloucester Avenue
London NW1
01 586 4806

Loughborough Community Centre Ground Floor
Woolley House
Loughborough Road
London SW9
01 737 0157

Media Resources Centre Shoreditch District Library
Pitfield Street
London N1 6EX
01 739 3877

Mediumwave
3/4 Oval Mansions
London SE11
01 582 3779

North Paddington Community Darkroom
510 Harrow Road
London W9
01 969 7437

Oxford House
Derbyshire Street
London E2 6HG
01 739 9093

Paddington Printshop
1 Elgin Avenue
London W9
01 286 1123

Poster Collective
20 Lithos Road
London NW3
01 431 1550

The Print Place
Bede House
351 Southwark Park Road
London SE16 2JN
01 237 3881

Retake
25 Bayham Street
London NW1
01 388 9031/2

Sankofa
Unit 5
Cockpit Yard
Northington Street
London WC1
01 831 0024

Star Video
100 Powerscroft Road
London E1
01 986 4470

Theatro Technic
26 Crowndale Road
London NW1
01 387 6617

Tom Allen Centre
Grove Crescent Road
London E15
01 555 7289

Union Place Resource Centre
122 Vassall Road
London SW9
01 735 6123

West London Media Workshop
118 Talbot Road
London W11
01 221 1859

Women In Sync
Unit 5/6 Wharfedale Project
47-51 Wharfedale Road
London N1
01 278 2215

Women's Media Resource Group
90 De Beauvoir Road
London N1 4EN
01 254 6536

South Of England

Barefoot Video
50 Brunswick Street
West Hove
Sussex
0273 773206

Beaford Centre Community Project
34/36 High Street
Barnstaple
North Devon
EX31 1RJ
0392 75285

Brighton Film & Video Workshop
Learning Resources
Brighton Polytechnic
Walts Building
Moulsecoombe
Brighton
East Sussex
BN2 4GJ
0273 693655 ext 2145

Brighton & Hove Community Resource Centre
Prior House
Tilbury Place
Brighton BN2 2GY
0273 606160

Bristol Film Makers Co-op
37-39 Jamaica Street
Bristol BS2 8JP
0272 426199

Bristol Media Workshop
c/o University Settlement
43 Ducie Road
Barton Hill
Bristol

Exeter Film Workshop
Spacex Gallery
45 Preston Street
Exeter EX1 1AZ
0392 31786

F Stop Photography Workshop
2 Longacre
London Road
Bath
Avon
0225 316922

Fair Exchange
76 Victoria Street
Exeter EX4 6JG
0392 32617

33 Film and Video Group
33 Guildford Street
Luton
Bedfordshire
0582 419584

Hastings Unemployed & Claimants Advice Centre
Upper Central Hall
Bank Building
Hastings
East Sussex
0424 428375

The Minories
74 High Street
Colchester
Essex CO1 1UE
0206 577067

Mostly Photographic Gallery and Workshop
10/11 Market Place
off Alexandra Street
Southend-on-Sea
0702 352784

Mount Pleasant Photography
Mount Pleasant Middle School
Mount Pleasant Road
Southampton
Hampshire
SO9 3TQ

The Neighbourhood Centre
11/13 Curriers Lane
Ipswich
Suffolk
0473 212165

Oxford Artists' Group
116 Abingdon Road
Oxford
OX1 4PX
0865 725128

Oxford Photography Ltd
14 Farringdon Road
Oxford
OX2 6RT
0865 50384

Pelican Resource Centre
Link Road
Newbury
Berkshire
RG14 7LU
0635 47277

Reading Centre for the Unemployed
4-6 East Street
Reading
Berkshire
0734 596639

UB40
62 Howell Road
Exeter
0392 73597

Watershed Media Centre
1 Canons Road
Bristol
BS1 5TX
0272 276444

Women In Moving Pictures
50 St Andrews Road
Montpelier
Bristol

Workshop Films
20 Henrietta Street
Bath
BA2 6LP
0225 63590

Midlands

118 Workshop
118 Mansfield Road
Nottingham NG1 3HL
0602 582369

Bath Place Community Venture
Bath Place
Leamington Spa
Warks
0926 38421

Birmingham Film Workshop
The Triangle
University of Aston Arts Centre
Gosta Green
Birmingham B4 7ET
021 359 4192

Birmingham Trade Union Resource Centre
7 Frederick Street
Birmingham B1 3HE
021 236 8323

Cambridge Darkroom
Dales Brewery
Gwydir Street
Cambridge
0223 350725

Cinema City
St Andrews Street
Norwich NR2 3AD
0603 22047

Clifford House Video Project
c/o 2 Manor Farm Cottages
Trysull
Wolverhampton WV5 7JF

Community Assoc of West Smethwick
5 Sandpiper Court
Woodland Drive
Smethwick
West Midlands

Coventry Resource & Information Service
Unit 15
The Arches Industrial Estate
Spon End
Coventry
0203 77719

Derby Community Photography
St Kits Community Centre
Stepping Lane
Derby
0332 32941

East Anglian Film Makers
22-24 Colegate
Norwich
Norfolk
0603 22313

Leicester Independant Film & Video Unit
The Workspace
Newarke Street
Leicester
0533 559711 ext 294

National Playing Fields Assoc. Playtrain
Resource Centre
Ward End Park
Washwood Heath Road
Birmingham B8 2HB
021 338 5557

New Cinema Workshop
24-32 Carlton Street
Nottingham NG1 1NN
0602 584891

Norwich Video Workshop
Yare Valley Adult Education Centre
Bishop's Close
Thorpe St Andrew
Norwich NR7 0EH

Nottingham Video Project
The Workshop, ICC
61b Mansfield Road
Nottingham
0602 470356

Queen's Walk Community Centre
Queen's Drive
Robinhood's Way
The Meadow
Nottingham
0602 864183

Sutton Video
28 Lucknow Drive
Sutton-in-Ashfield
Notts

St Paul's Project
120 St Paul's Road
Balsall Heath
Birmingham B12
021 440 4376

Triangle Photography
Aston University
Gosta Green
Birmingham
021 359 3979 ext 4526

Video Cambridge
Burwell House
North Street
Burwell
Cambridge CR5 0BA

WELD
New Trinity
Wilson Road
Handsworth
Birmingham 19
021 554 5068

Wide Angle
BCA
Jenkins Street
Small Heath
Birmingham
021 772 6041

Worcester Arts Workshop
c/o The Old Quilt Factory
Angel Place
Worcester
0905 21095/20565

Women's Film Consortium
c/o Highgate Baptist Church
Conybere Church
Conybere Street
Highgate
Birmingham 12
021 440 5230

North of England

Active Image Ltd
Croft Cottage
Snail Hill
Moorgate
Rotherham S60 2B7
0709 67676

Amber/Side Workshop
9 Side
Newcastle-upon-Tyne
NE1 3JE
0632 32200

Artivan
8 Bankfield Terrace
Armitage Bridge
Huddersfield
W Yorks
0484 665410

Aware
4 Sefton Grove
Lark Lane
Liverpool 17
051 727 7421

Banner Film & Television
11 Swaledale Road
Sheffield S7 2B7
0742 556875

Bannerworks
9 Spink Field Road
Birkby
Huddersfield
W Yorks HD2 2AY
0484 513772

Blackburn Action Factory
New Mill Community Centre
New Chapel Street
Lancs
0254 661292

The Blackie
Great George's Street
Liverpool L1
051 709 5109

Bradford Film Group
c/o Bradford Film Theatre
Chapel Street
Bradford
0274 720329

Bradford Mobile Workshop
3 Hallfield Road
Bradford BD1 3RP
0274 722425

Byker Photography Workshop
Adjacent 26 Raby Way
Byker
Newcastle-upon-Tyne
0632 2650649

Carnegie Photography Workshop
Carnegie Unemployment Centre
Finkle Street
Workington
Cumbria
0900 61874

Commonground
87 The Wicker
Sheffield S3 8HT
0742 738572

Counter Image
19 Whitworth Street West
Manchester M1 5WG
061 228 3551

Film Co-op
Albreda House
Lydgate Lane
Sheffield S10 5FH
0742 668857

Hendon Photography Group
c/o 4 St Ignatius Close
Hendon
Sunderland
Tyne and Wear
0783 654948

Humberside Video
c/o Posterugate Gallery
6 Posterugate
Hull HU1 2JN
0482 20450

Junction 28
New Street Centre
New Street
South Normanton
Derbyshire
0773 813343

Leeds Animation Workshop
45 Bayswater Road
Leeds 8
0532 484997

Leeds Video Unit
Belle Vue Centre
201 Belle Vue Road
Leeds 3
0532 440015

MARC Copy Shop
61 Bloom Street
Manchester M13 LY1
061 236 0350

Midnag
Leisure & Publicity Dept
Town Hall
Station Road
Ashington
Northumberland
0670 814444

Merseyside Black Media Workshop
90–92 Whitechapel
Liverpool L1 6EN
051 709 9460

Newcastle Media Workshop
5 Saville Place
Newcastle–upon–Tyne
0632 322410

North East Films Group
Hollinbush
Dale Head
Rosedale
N Yorks

North Ormesby Photography Group
c/o Pavilion Community Arts
The Pavilion
Esk Street
North Ormesby
Middlesborough
Cleveland TS3 6JF
0642 225290

Open Eye
90–92 Whitechapel
Liverpool L1 6EN
051 709 9460

Photography Workshop
Maryport Unemployment Centre
John Street
Maryport
Cumbria
0900 4283

Powerhouse Video Collective
8 Aireville Drive
Shipley
Bradford DB18 3AD

Sheffield Independant Film
173–175 Howard Road
Walkley
Sheffield
0742 336429

Swingbridge Video
10a Bridge Street
Gateshead
Tyne & Wear NE8 2BH
0632 776680

Trade Films
36 Bottle Bank
Gateshead
Tyne & Wear
NE8 2AR
0632 775532

Tyne & Wear Resource Centre
2 Jesmond Road
Newcastle−Upon−Tyne
0632 811911

Walker Photography Project
Back 495a Welbeck Road
Walker
Newcastle−Upon−Tyne 6
091 2652729

Wanbeck Community Initiatives Centre
Station Villa
Kennilworth Road
Ashington
Northumberland
0670 853619

Washington Photography Project
Biddick Farm
Fatfield, Washington
Tyne and Wear
091 416 6440

West End Resource Centre
87 Adelaide Terrace
Benwell
Newcastle 4
0632 731210

Workers Film Association
9 Lucy Street
Manchester M15 4BX
061 848 9785

York Film Workshop
8 The Crescent
Blossom Street
York YO2 2AW
0904 641394

York Women's Film Group
Sprockettes
25 Belle View Street
York
0904 25145

Scotland

Commedia
11 Douglas Terrace
Haymarket
Edinburgh EH11 2BJ
031 337 4922

Community Communications
c/o TPAS
266 Clyde Street
Glasgow G1
041 221 8021

Dumfries Action Centre
Holywood Building
2 Assembley Street
Dumfries DG1 2PM
0387 69161

East End Community Resources Centre
St Mungo's Academy
Crown Point Road
Glasgow G40 2RA
041 556 5891

The Environment Centre
Drummond High School
Cochran Terrace
Edinburgh EH7 4QP
031 557 2135

Film Workshop Trust
17 Great King Street
Edinburgh EH3 6QW
031 556 2078

Hamilton Resource Centre
St Cuthberts
Reid Street
Burnbank Hamilton
Blantyre
0698 821518

Inveralmond CHS
Willowbank Ladywell
Livingston
West Lothian
West Lothian 38093

Optical Tracks
22 Royal Circus
Edinburgh EH3 9SS
031'225 2105

Second City Workshop
17 Kennedar Drive
Glasgow G51
041 440 1285

Video In Pilton
Craig Royston High School
Pennywell Road
Edinburgh
031 332 7801

Wales

Aberystwyth Media Group
Barn Centre
Alexander Road
Aberystwyth
Dyfed
0970 615968

Bwrdd Ifimiau Cynraeg
The Old Normal College
College Road
Bangor
Gwynedd
0248 364687

Caernarfon Community Association
12 Palace Street
Gwynedd
LL55 1AG
0286 5055

Chapter Video Workshop
Market Street
Canton
Cardiff
0222 396061

Deeside Documentary Workshop
118 The Highway
Hawardell
Clwyd.

Deeside High School Resource Centre
Queensferry
Deeside
Clwyd CH5 1SE
0244 821656

Ely Photographic Workshop
6 Jackrow Square
Ely
Cardiff
0222 593440

Flint Photography Workshop
43 Prince of Wales Avenue
Flint
Clwyd

Powys Video
Theatre Powys Drama Centre
Tremont Road
Llandrindod Wells
Powys
0597 4444

Swansea Video & film Co−op
37 Beaufort Avenue
Langland
Swansea
0792 69783

Valley & Vale Community Arts
The Old Junior School
Maesteg Road
Tondu
Mid Glamorgan
0656 724799

Wrexham Community Video
Church House
Rhossdu Road
Wrexham
Clwyd
0978 264051

Wrexham Documentary Photography Workshop
115 Coed Aben
Wrexham LL13 9NG

Northern Ireland

Arts and Reasearch Exchange
22 Lombard Street
Belfast 1
0232 224429

Belfast Film Workshop
30 Joy Street
Belfast
0232 233874

Belfast Media Workshop
22 Lombard Street
Belfast 1
0232 240123

Camerawork Darkrooms
36 William Street
Londonderry
0504 265923

Derry Video Workshop
36 William Street
Londonderry
0504 268048

Upper Springfield Resource Centre
195 Whiterock Road
Belfast BT12 7ID
0232 228928

Co-operative & Community Printers

London

Asian Community Action Group's Multi-Lingual Printshop
5a Westminster Bridge Road
London SE1
01 928 9208

Bread 'n' Roses
2 St Pauls Road
London N1
01 354 0557

Calvert's Press
31/39 Redchurch Street
London E2 7DJ
01 739 1474

Community Copyart
9 Kingsford Street
London NW3
01 267 7342

Community Press
29 St Pauls Road
London N1
01 226 0580

Fly Press &Badger Ltd
52 Acre Lane
London SW2
01 274 5181

Islington Bus Company
Palmer Place
London N7
01 609 0226

Lasso Women's Co-op
86/100 St Pancras Way
London NW1
01 267 1284

Leveller Graphics
52 Acre Lane
London SW2
01 274 2288

Lithosphere Printing Co-op
203-205 Pentonville Road
London N1 9NF
01 833 2526

Oval Printshop
54 Kennington Oval
London SE11
01 582 4750

Paupertype
122 Michael Cliffe House
Skinner Street
London EC1
01 278 3816

Redesign
9 London Lane
London E8 3PR
01 533 2631

See Red Women's Workshop
90a Camberwell Road
London SE5 0EG
01 703 0070

Trojan Press
10a Bradbury Street
London N6 8JN
01 249 5771

Ultra Violet Enterprises
25 Horsell Road
London N5
01 607 4463

Women In Print
90a Camberwell Road
London SE17
01 701 8314

Words Illustrated
1 Thorpe Close
London W10
01 968 6344

South of England

Access Photography
c/o Bristol Settlement
43 Ducie Street
Barton Hill
Bristol
0272 556971

Stowmarket Youth Centre
Childer Road
Stowmarket
0449 612252

Thamesdown Community Press
Jolliffe Studio
Wyvern Theatre
Theatre Square
Swindon
Wilts SN1 1QT
0793 26161 ext 3139

Midlands

Daily Information
10 Kingston Road
Oxford
0865 5337

Saltley Action Centre
2 Alum Rock Road
Saltley
Birmingham B8 1JB
021 328 2307

Saltley Neighbourhood Printing Co-op
7-11 Washwood Heath Road
Saltley
Birmingham 8
021 328 1954

Sawtry Print Workshop
Homecraft Centre
Green End Road
Sawtry
Cambridgeshire
PE17 5UY
0487 832105

Triangle Press
The Triangle Arts & Media Centre
Holt Street
Birmingham B4 7ET
021 359 7682

Voice
Unit 51
260 Wincolmlee
Hull HV2 0QA

North of England

Amazon Press
75 Back Piccadilly
Manchester 2
061 228 2351

Bradford Printshop
127 Thorton Road
Bradford 8
0274 45720

CAPS Annexe
Fordfield Road
Sunderland
Tyne and Wear
0783 79095

Handprint Community Workshop
Old Stewards House
Northgate Huddersfield
HD1 1RL
0484 516804

Impact Foundation
3 Temple Court
Liverpool
L2 6PY
051 236 6662

Open Road Printing Co-op
57 Mickelgate
York
0904 37806

RAP
The Old Co-op
Spotland Road
Rochdale
Lancs
0706 44981

Sheffield Women's Printing Co-op
87 The Wicker
Sheffield S3 8HT

Tyneside Free Press
5 Charlotte Square
Newcastle Upon Tyne
0632 320403

Vixon Print
2-4 Roscoe Street
Liverpool 1
051 709 2709

Whitechapel Press
3 Temple Court
Liverpool L2 6PY
051 236 6662

Scotland

DASS Information
Castlehill House
1 High Street
Dundee DD1 1TD
0382 26492

Easterhouse Festival Society
10 Trondra Place
Glasgow G34 9AX

Edinburgh Council of Social Service
Ainslie House
11 St Colms Street
Edinburgh EH3 6AG
031 225 4606

Garnock Valley Community Project
37 Main Street
Kilbirnie
Ayreshire
050 582 3198

Glasgow Print Studio
128 Ingram Street
Glasgow
G1 1EJ
041 552 0704

Laurieston Information Centre
80 Sterlingfold Place
Gorbals
Glasgow G5
041 429 3154/3254

Printmakers Workshop
29 Market Street
Edinburgh EH1 1DF
031 225 1098

SPP Limited
Unit One
Cunningham Road
Spring Kerse Industrial Estate
Stirling
0786 64797

Wales

Argraffwyr Eryri Printers
Hen Efail Bethal
Caenarfon
Gwynedd
0248 671196

Cross Print
The Cross Centre
1 High Street
Pontardawe
0792 863955

Cwmbran Community Press
13 Victoria Street
Cwmbran
Gwent
06333 62940/65717

Cymric Federation Printers
Neville Street
Cardiff CF1 8LP
0222 21951

Everyday Printers & Designers Ltd
10 Four Elms Road
Adamsdown
Cardiff CS2 1LE
0222 482742

Fingerprints
Ty Penderyn
Pen-y-wain Lane
Roath
Cardiff
0222 482582

Set Left
Royal Stuart Workshop
Adelaide Place
Buttown
Cardiff
0222 488133

U-Print
Chapter
Market Road
Canton
Cardiff CF5 1QE
0222 396061

Northern Ireland

Crescent Co-operative Printshop
2-4 Univesity Road
Belfast 4
0232 247388

Great West Belfast Community Assoc.
234 Grosvenor Road
Belfast 12
0232 228295

Queens University Students Union
University Road
Belfast BT7 1PE
0232 224803

Arts Associations and Centres

London

Acton Community Arts Workshop
Acton Hill Church
1a Gunnersbury Lane
London W3
01 993 2665

Barnet Arts Workshop
Avenue House
Finchley Road
London NW3
01 346 7120

Greater London Arts
9 White Lion Street
London N1 9PD
01 837 8808

Community & Recreational Arts in Barnet
East End Road
Finchley
London N3 3QE
01 346 9789

Lenthall Road Workshop
81 Lenthall Road
London
01 254 3982

Moonshine Community Arts Workshop
Victor Road
London NW10
01 969 7959

Tower Hamlets Arts Project
178 Whitechapel Road
London E1
01 247 0216

Walworth & Aylesbury Community Arts Trust Printshop
Shop 8 Taplow
East Street
London SE17
01 708 1280

South of England

Artspace Portsmouth Ltd
Aspex Gallery
27 Brougham Road
Southsea
Portsmouth
0750 812121

Blooming Arts
East Oxford Community Centre
Princess Street
Oxford
0865 245735

Brighton Community Arts Project
Kempton Pier
110 St George's Road
Brighton
0273 697493

Hubert House Community Arts Project
Vincents
Little Brook Manor Way
Temple Hill
Dartford
Kent
0322 24500

Jolliffe Community Arts Studio
Wyvern Theatre
Theatre Square
Swindon
Wilts SN1 1QT
0793 26161 ext 3149

Luton Community Arts Trust
33 Guilford Street
Luton
0584 419584

Media Arts Lab
Town Hall Studios
Regent Circus
Swindon
Wilts SN1 1QF
0793 26161 ext 3133

Mobile Arts Co-op
Salisbury Arts Centre
Bedwin Street
Salisbury
Wlts SP1 3UT
0722 21744

New Metropole Arts Centre
The Leas
Folkstone
Kent
0303 55070

Plymouth Arts Centre
38 Looe Street
Plymouth
0752 660060

South East Arts
9-10 Crescent Road
Tunbridge Wells
Kent TN1 2LU
0892 41666

South Hill Park Arts Centre
Bracknell
Berks RG12 4PA
0344 427272

South West Arts
Bradninch Place
Gandy Street
Exeter EX4 3LS
0392 128188

Southern Arts Association
19 Southgate Street
Winchester
Hampshire SO23 9DQ
0962 55099

St Edmunds Arts Centre
Bedwin Street
Salisbury
Wilts
0722 20379

Midlands

Blackfriars Arts Centre
Spain Lane
Boston
Lincs
0205 63108

Corby Community Arts
Lincoln Square
Corby
Northamptonshire
0536 743731

East Midlands Arts
Mountfields House
Forest Road
Loughborough
Liecester LE11 3HU
0509 218292

Eastern Arts Association
8-9 Bridge Road
Cambridge
0223 357596

Hawtonville Arts Project
The Community Centre
St Mary's Gardens
Newark
Nottinghamshire
0636 706982

Jubilee Community Arts
Whitehall Road
Greets Green
West Bromwich
West Midlands
021 557 1569

Lady Lodge Arts Centre
Orton Goldhay
Peterborough
0733 237073

Lincoln & Humberside Arts
St Hughs
Newport
Lincoln LN1 3DN
0522 33555

Lowestoft Arts Centre
Regent Road
Lowestoft
Suffolk
0502 65397

New Perspective Arts Workshop
13 Curriers Lane
Ipswich
0473 212165

Northampton Arts Development
Trinity Methodist Church Rooms
Wellingborough Road
Northampton
0604 27158

Norwich Arts Centre
Reeves Yard
St Benedict's Street
Norwich NR2 4PG
0603 660352

Nottingham Community Arts & Crafts Centre
41 Gregory Boulevard
Hyson Green
Nottingham NG7 6BE
0602 782463

Roseberry Community Arts Project
Queen's Drive
Robinwoods Way
The Meadow
Nottingham
0602 864183

Telford Community Arts
10 High Street
Madely
Telford Shropshire
0952 58557

Trinity Arts Ltd
516 Coventry Road
Small Heath
Birmingham 10
021 773 7510

University of Aston Arts Centre
Gosta Green
Birmingham B4 7ET
021 359 4192

West Midlands Arts
Brunwich Terrace
Stafford ST16 1BZ
0785 59231

North of England

Bootle Arts in Action
482 Stanley Road
Bootle
Merseyside L20
051 933 5168

Bradford Community Arts Centre
The Old Quaker School
17-21 Chapel Street
Leeds Road
Bradford BD1 5DT
0274 582528

Brewery Arts Centre
Highgate
Kendal
Cumbria LA9 4HE
0539 25133

Buddle Arts Centre
258b Station Road
Wallsend
Tyne & Wear
0632 624276

Castle Chore Community Arts Centre
Castle Chore
Durham City DH1 4AR
0385 46251

Darlington Arts Centre
Vane Terrace
Darlington
County Durham
0325 483271

Fleet Arts Project
The Old School
The Fleet
Belper
Derbyshire DE5 1NM
0773 820484

Great George's Project
Great George Street
Liverpool 1
051 709 5109

Hulme Community Arts Project
The Old Bank
Hulme Community Activities Centre
1 Clapton Walk
Hulme
Manchester 15
061 226 9815

Junction 28 Community Arts Project
New Street Centre
New Street
South Normanton
Derbyshire
0773 813343

Junction 37 Community Arts Workshop
156 Sheffield Road
Barnsley
S Yorkshire
0226 298955

Merseyside Arts
Bluecoat Chambers
School Lane
Liverpool L1 3BX
051 709 0671

North West Arts
12 Harter Street
Manchester M1 6HY
061 228 3062

Northern Arts
10 Osborne Terrace
Newcastle upon Tyne
NE2 1NZ
0632 816334

Northumberland Community Arts
34 Green Batt
Alnwick
Northumberland
NE66 1TU
0665 603069

Outreach Community Arts
The Community Arts Centre
Northumberland Avenue
Hull HV2 0LN
0482 226420

Pavilion Community Arts
The Pavilion
Esk Street
N. Ormesby
Middlesborough
Cleveland
0642 242533

Shape-up North
Community Arts Centre
191 Belle Vue Road
Leeds LS3 1HQ
0532 431005

Them Wifies
109 Pilgrims Street
Newcastle-Upon-Tyne
0632 326717

Village Arts
North Skelton Village Hall
North Skelton
Saltburn-by-the-Sea
Cleveland
0287 52392

Yorkshire Arts Association
Glyde House
Bradford
W Yorkshire BD5 0BQ
0274 723051

Scotland

Cranhill Arts Project
33 Lamlash Crescent
Cranhill
Glasgow
041 774 8595

Dunhope Arts Centre
St Mary's Place
Dundee DD1 5RD
0382 26331

Scottish Arts Association
19 Charlotte Square
Edinburgh EH2 4DF
031 226 6051

Wales

Chapter Arts Workshop
Market Road
Canton
Cardiff CF5 1QE
0222 396061

North Wales Association for The Arts
10 Wellfield House
Bangor
Gwynedd LL57 1ER
0248 353248

South East Wales Arts Association
Victoria Street
Cwbran
Gwent NP4 3JP
06333 67530

Valley and Vale Community Arts
The Old Junior School
Maesteg Road
Tondy
Mid Glamorgan
0656 724799

Welsh Arts Council
Holst House
Museum Place
Cardiff CF1 3NX
0222 394711

West Wales Association for The Arts
Dark Gate
Carmarthen
Dyfed
0267 234248

Northern Ireland

Arts & Reasearch Exchange
22 Lombard Street
Belfast BT1 1RD
0232 224499

Crescent Arts Centre
2-4 University Road
Belfast 4
0232 242338

Educational Institutions

London

Barking College of Technology
Charlecote Road
Dagenham
Essex RM8 3LD
01 592 2217

Camden Training Centre
Pratt Street
London NW1
01 482 2103/4

Chequer Learning Resource Centre
Chequer Centre
The Central Institute of Adult Education
Chequer Street
London EC1
01 388 6048/7106 ext 49

Community Education Dept
London College of Printing
Elephant and Castle
London SE1 6SB
01 735 8484

Kingsway Princeton College
Grays Inn Road
London WC1
01 278 0541

Richmond Upon Thames College
Egerton Road
Twickenham TW2 7SJ
01 892 6656

South of England

Berkshire College of Art & Design
Marlow Road
Maidenhead
Berkshire SL6 6DS
0628 24302

Brunel Technical College
Ashley Down
Bristol BS7 9BU
0272 41241

Exeter College of Art & Design
The Mint
Exeter EX4 3BL
0392 55282

Guilford College of Technology
Stoke Park
Guilford GU1 1EZ
0483 31251

Maidstone College of Art
Oakwood Park
Oakwood Road
Maidstone
Kent ME16 8AG
0622 57286

Oxford Polytechnic
Gipsy Lane
Headington
Oxford
OX3 0BP
0865 64777

Plymouth College of Art & Design
Tavistock Place
Plymouth PL4 8AT
0752 27633

Portsmouth College of Art, Design and Further Education
Winston Churchill Avenue
Portsmouth
0705 826435

South Fields College
Aylestone Road
Leicester LE2 7LW
0533 541818

Southampton College of Higher Education
East Park Terrace
Southampton SO9 4WU
0703 28182

Ware College
Walton Road
Ware
Hertfordshire SG12 9JF
0920 5441

Watford College
Hempstead Road
Hertfordshire WD1 3EZ
0923 41211

Midlands

Isle of Ely College
Ramnoth Road
Wisbech
Cambridgeshire
PE13 2JE
0945 2561

Lincoln College of Art
Lindum Road
Lincoln LN2 1LY
0522 23268

Lonsdale College of Higher Education
Kedleston Road
Derby DE3 1GB
0332 47181

Matthew Boulton Technical College
Aston Road
Birmingham B6 4BP
021 359 6721

Nene College
Saint George's Avenue
Northampton NN2 6JD
0604 714101

Norwich City College
Ipswich Road
Norwich NR2 2LJ
0603 60011

West Bridgeford College of Further Education
Greythorn Drive
West Bridgeford NG2 7GA
0602 812125

North of England

Blackburn College of Technology and Design
Fielden Street
Blackburn
Lancashire BB2 1LH
0254 64321

Central Liverpool College of Further Education
Hope Street
Liverpool L1 9EB
051 708 0423

Granville College of Further Education
Granville Road
Sheffield S2 2RL
0742 760271

Kitson College of Technology
Calverly Street
Leeds LS1 3HE
0532 462978

Manchester Polytechnic
Cavendish Street
All Saints
Manchester M15 6BR
061 228 6171

Teesside College of Art
Green Lane
Linthorpe
Middlesborough
Teesside TS5 7RJ
0642 821441

York College of Art & Technology
Exhibition Square
York YO1 2EW
0904 704141

Scotland

Duncan of Jordanstone College of Art
Perth Road
Dundee DD1 4HT
0382 23261

Glasgow College of Building & Printing
60 North Hanover Street
Glasgow G1 2BP
041 332 9969

Napier College of Commerce & Technology
Colinton Road
Edinburgh EH10 5DT
031 447 7070

Scottish Community Education Council
Atholl House
2 Canning Street
Edinburgh EH3 8EG
031 229 2433

Northern Ireland

Belfast School of Visual Communication
Art & Design Centre
York Street
Belfast BT15 1ED
0232 28515

Republic of Ireland

Dublin College of Technology
Bolton Street
Dublin 1
Dublin 749913

InterChange

Based in Kentish Town, North London, InterChange is a community centre in the widest sense; providing a comprehensive range of projects, services and facilities, it exists to stimulate greater community involvement and activity.

From the InterChange Centre, we run community arts and education projects including a Weekend Arts College, an alternative school and a city farm. The multi-media resource centre gives low cost access to expensive audio-visual, printing and computing technology. InterChange's organisation development team provide advice, training and consultancy on all aspects of running community organisations.

InterChange Books are aimed at helping groups and individuals organise themselves effectively and achieve their own objectives. Drawing on InterChange's wide experience of community action, InterChange Books are practical and clearly written handbooks, which de-mystify professional topics such as the law, publishing and printing, and which help people cope with bureaucracy.

This book was first produced in 1987. A lot has changed since then! The world it seems, has caught up with the notion that people want to design and produce their own media. Suddenly there is a 'market' in it. Technology is being hastily lashed together, labelled and improved. 'Desk Top Publishing' has been created. We can come up from below the desk and discover that there is a personal computer there waiting for us to play with!

The initiative for change is coming from the personal computer industry rather than from printing and design. They are producing cheaper and easier to use software-programmes, such as the Desk Top Publishing programmes. Computer printers and other hardware are now available making the printouts and images produced by small computers better. Laser printers can produce letters of almost type quality, with a resolution of 300 dots to the inch. Whole pages can be designed and laid out with the computer using the Desk Top Publishing programmes. You can forget about paste up if you get access to this sort of technology.

Connections are being made so that the user of personal computers and Desk Top Publishing can get their 'data' printed out on typesetting quality printers. These now understand 'PostScript', the page description language that the computers and most Desk Top Publishing programmes use. All these changes mean that more people need to think about design. Now it is so easy to put a box around text, or design it in any other way, you need to think how you want or need your publication to look. Generally it can be useful to try out several designs and see what they look like on paper. Give things space, restrain yourself from boxing all your information — you can't emphasise everything — so you have to be careful in your choices.

Style Sheets

Desk Top Publishing packages design for you. One way this is done is using 'style sheets'. These turn your information into standard designs. They are built into the programme and automatically turn your words into a book page, newsletter, magazine or even letterhead. These styles can be modified to fit your needs. They do however, enable you to develop consistent design or headlines, sub heads, introductory paragraphs, the standard text, notes, running heads and page numbers. Some programmes enable a grid to be designed before the text is assembled. Style sheets are electronic 'user-friendly' grids or designs.

Programmes

It is difficult to pick out the differences between all these Desk Top Publishing programmes. They are being developed and changed so fast this book would need updating every year.

Word processing programmes are also being changed and developed. Some top end programmes can now perform some of the basic lay-out tasks such as the columning of text that Desk Top Publishing programmes do. Look at the latest release of 'Word Perfect' or 'Word'.

'Timeworks Desk Top Publishing' is a new programme on the lower end of the market. It is for IBM compatible computers and Atari STs. It has almost all of the features of 'Ventura', one of the best Desk Top Publishing programmes, but is 1/6th of the price!

OCR

Optical Character Recognition (OCR) machines scan text that has been typed or printed on a dot matrix printer. This converts it into digital information that computer typesetting systems can handle. This is just one more way of avoiding the labour of retyping the text for typesetting or Desk Top Publishing. OCR scanners cannot 'understand' hand written text or corrections. But these changes can be added once the text is in the computer. This Update text was handled ths way by Lithosphere Printing Co-operative.

Printers

Once the text has been processed it usually needs to be saved on disk and then printed out using a printer. Many printers find it difficult to understand the word processing codes used. It can be easier to save the text as letters only — ASCII characters. This can then be imported into a Desk Top Publishing programme and laid out as columns, headlines etc. These programmes then use PostScript or another language to send the data to the printer's memory. This then is printed out in a good quality print or copy which can be used as an original for printing.

PostScript is also used for typesetting quality printers that produce bromide print or film. These give a fine resolution with more than 1000 dots per inch (dpi) compared to the laser printer's 300 dpi. However the differences are quite difficult to see. You can also produce a large design and reduce it in printing or copying to get a finer resolution. The Linotronic 300, 200 and 100P use PostScript to typeset and print out the whole page designed on a computer. Some designers, printers or specialist bureaux now offer a print out service, printing from your disk a high quality copy.

Liquid crystal technology is being developed to be used in cheaper printers. This will mean that the cost of laser printers will come down. However printers are quite expensive to run. Their drums need replacing after a comparatively few copies. They may be equipment that could be shared by several user's organisations.

Scanners

Scanners are machines that convert images into digital information. In this way computers can handle pictures and incorporate them into the page. Scanners now are cheaper and simpler. Some are hand-held and cost just a few hundred pounds. Once the images are in digital form in the computer's memory it can be moved around, stretched (see Update logo), traced, screened and laid out with the text. Cheaper scanners however, only produce images with 200 dots per inch. More expensive ones using cameras can scan with greater resolution, well enough to screen photos into half tone dots.

Resources

New design technology is ideal, not just for individuals or businesses, but for sharing. Scanners, laser printers, Fax etc., are useful for resource centres where people or organisations collaborate and use the equipment when they need it. Community, voluntary and campaigning groups need access to it as much as other enterprises.

Learning to use it is best done with a bit of guidance and a lot of time playing. Neal's Yard Desk Top Publishing Studio may be a good place to start. They have introductory courses on Saturdays and offer individual tuition, but only charge £5 an hour for using their equipment. (DTP Studio, 2 Neal's Yard, London, WC2. Tel. 01 379 5113.)

Electronic Presentations

As well as printing out on paper it is possible to develop information and design it for displaying or presenting on a TV or computer screen. New computer programmes have been developed to do this on personal computers. Text and graphics are designed using various programmes on the computer. They organise information, graphs, pictures, etc, as frames or 'slides'. These 'screen-fulls' of information are then arranged in order. They can be animated or made to fade or wipe from slide to slide. Some of these programmes have 'interactive' possibilities. The viewer can choose which information to see next.

These presentations can be recorded on video and edited in with live video action. They can then be shown on video play back machines on TVs. If there is to be a large audience these presentations can be 'captured' on slides or OHP transparencies. Computer graphics are very good at turning statistics into graphs. Specialist computer graphics services offer slide or transparency making. They charge £5 per slide or transparency.

The information on computer screens can be shown on an overhead projector. This is done by using a liquid crystal machine such as Kodak's 'Data Show'. This fits on a projector. The light goes through the Data Show 'screen' and projects, in monotone, the information on the computer screen onto the OHP screen or the wall.

Fax

Another digital development that has taken off in the last two years is Fax. These machines, like scanners, digitise images usually only with 200 dots per inch. It is possible to send any image or copy to another Fax user. Bureaux also handle Fax but charge as much as £1 per Ad sheet. Having your own can reduce the cost per copy sent, to less than the amount it would cost in postage. Maybe when designing the distribution of information you could consider using Fax instead of designing a newsletter. Fax can be very useful in receiving and sending proofs. The printers, designers or typesetters can send you proofs to be checked quickly.

Photo Copied Sheets

New photo copiers and laser printers can copy onto clear film. Most of these machines use heat to fix the copy onto paper so when using film it is best to use a special film made to withstand heat. It is sold for use in copiers to make OHP transparencies but this film can also be used to make cheap and quick slides.

A slide show needs to be drawn, written or pasted up onto a grid of slide mount shapes. It is easier to work on an A3 grid which is reduced to A4 in copying. On A3 each image will need to fit into a square like this:

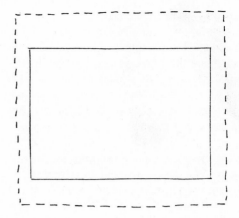

Draw out 24 of these on an A3 sheet. The image goes in the middle box. The dotted lines are for cutting up the slides when it is copied.

Try pasting up images, drawing or even using a laser printer to set type to fit a slide. Simple outline images work best.

Cut out the dotted lines and mount the film on normal slide mounts. Hopefully the solid lines should not show. Once mounted the slides can be coloured in with OHP translucent ink pens. The slides enlarge the images onto a big screen. They therefore don't look perfect when projected. They look copied, but they are quick and easy to do. Use them to experiment with slides. Combine them with conventional slides or play around with the ideas of sequence.

Image Banks

Good illustrations and images can be more useful than anything else in communication. An 'Image Bank' can be useful as it could help you collect and share images. One approach using a competition has produced a useful collection of copyright-free sporting images. This has been published as the book, Sporting Image, by InterChange Books, to help people publicise sports.

Another one has been published and given away in Bangladesh to any organisation involved in Rural Development. In exchange for this first edition the recipients give their images in exchange. This will be published in a 2nd edition. It will therefore represent a collaboration between many artists, designers and organisations. Contact TMPS, BRDB, Kawran Bazaar, Dhaka, Bangladesh.

Try collecting images that you think will be useful for you in a ring file. You can copy them and lend them to others. Maybe we should work on scanned and digitised Image Basnks for use with computers and Desk Top Publishing.

Recycled Paper

Recycled Paper is now so good it can be used to print with full colour. It used to be second rate but now it has a quality all of its own. It is remade from waste paper, as opposed to 'virgin' paper made from wood pulp, and ultimately from trees. Waste paper merchants recognise 38 different grades, although in practice they sort into 10. In general the better quality waste paper used, the better quality recycled paper you get from the paper mill.

The range of coatings, colours, thicknesses is growing and has improved dramatically in the 1980's. Investment in new machinery by paper mills, research by Paperback, and the development of new products have all played their part. The range of papers now includes watermarked and laid paper with matching envelopes for business letterheads; matt coated papers to take process colour and screened pictures; papers made to copier specifications and precision cut; a laser printer paper; a smooth 'Bond' printing paper suitable for publishing; computer listing paper, good quality card for folders and business cards. In addition, papers traditionally made from lower grade waste are now being promoted as recycled, and their properties used to enhance the design required.

This Update is printed on recycled 100gsm Sylvancoat paper from Paperback Ltd, Bow Triangle, Business Centre, Unit 2, Eleanor Street, Bow, London E3 4NP. The Association of Recycled Paper Suppliers (ARPS) partially covers the country, contact Paperback for a list — otherwise, try purchasing through your local paper merchant, specifying an ARPS member as a source. Send off for some samples and ask printers to use this sort of recycled paper. Try this not only for the trees and the planet, but also for the quality of your design.

Addresses

Lasso Co-operative have moved to 20 Sussex Way, London N7 6RS. Tel: 01 272 9141/2 for design, artwork and typesetting.

Mobile Arts have moved to Netherhampton Road, Harnham, Salisbury, Wilts SP2 8HE. Tel: 0722 25919. They have just updated their set of DIY plans for portable screen printing equipment. £10 individuals. £15 organisations + 50p for postage and packing.

Neal's Yard Desk Top Publishing Studio. 2 Neal's Yard, London, WC2. Tel: 01 379 5113. For training and access to Desk Top Publishing technology.

Paperback Ltd. Bow Triangle, Business Centre, Unit 2, Eleanor Street, Bow, London E3 4NP. Recycled paper suppliers, they will also provide a list of other recycled paper suppliers. Sales: 980 2233, Fax: 980 2399.

Books

Sporting Image: Do-it-yourself design for sports publicity. Copyright-free graphic images and much more. InterChange Books. £8.95. 1987.

Editing, Design and Book Production: A guide for independent publishers. Charles Foster. InterChange Books, 1989.

Visual Messages: An Introduction to Graphics. C. J. Breckon, L. J. Jones, C. E. Morhousde. David and Charles plc. 1987.

BluePrint Publishing Ltd. Publishers of books on printing and design for the professional. 40 Bowling Green Lane, London EC1R ONE. Tel: 01 278 0333.

Graphic Books International. PO Box 349, Guernsey, Channel Islands. Tel: 0481 53125. For professional books on graphics, photography.

Design for Desktop Publishing. John Miles, Gordon Fraser, 1987.

Audio Visual Handbook. A complete guide to the world of audio-visual techniques. Alan McPherson and Howard Timms, Pelham Books. £9.95.

Further Information Wanted!

We hope to continue updating this handbook. Please send us any further information you feel would be of interest to other readers. If you would like to receive further Updates please send a SAE to InterChange Books, 15 Wilkin Street, London, NW5 3NG.